Rationality Gone Awry?

Rationality Gone Awry?

Decision Making Inconsistent with Economic and Financial Theory

HUGH SCHWARTZ

Foreword by Shlomo Maital

Westport, Connecticut
London

Library of Congress Cataloging-in-Publication Data

Schwartz, Hugh H.
    Rationality gone awry? :   decision making inconsistent with
economic and financial theory / Hugh Schwartz ; foreword by Shlomo
Maital.
        p.   cm.
    Includes bibliographical references and index.
    ISBN 0–275–96014–5 (alk. paper)—ISBN 0–275–97104–X (pbk.: alk. paper)
    1. Economics—Psychological aspects.   2. Decision making.   I.
Title.
HB74.P8S365   1998
330—dc21   97–43957

British Library Cataloguing in Publication Data is available.

Library of Congress Catalog Card Number: 97–43957
ISBN: 0–275–97104–X (pbk.)

First published in 1998

Praeger Publishers, 88 Post Road West, Westport, CT 06881
An imprint of Greenwood Publishing Group, Inc.
www.praeger.com

Printed in the United States of America

The paper used in this book complies with the
Permanent Paper Standard issued by the National
Information Standards Organization (Z39.48–1984).

10 9 8 7 6 5 4 3 2 1

To my mother,
Beatrice Schwartz,
and in memory of my father,
Sidney Schwartz

Contents

Foreword

You cannot solve a problem with the same level of thinking that created it.
—Albert Einstein

Theories are like declarations of eternal love—neither are ever completely true. Both theory and protestations of love raise the question: How *nearly true* are they?

In the social sciences, economics reigns supreme—at least, its adherents *think* it does—because it *has* a theory. As Richard Thaler notes,

Most economists believe that their subject is the strongest of the social sciences because it has a theoretical foundation, making it closer to the acknowledged king of sciences, physics. The theory, they believe, is a tool which gives them an inherent advantage in explaining human behavior compared with their weaker social science cousins.[1]

Modern economic theory is largely derived from Leon Walras' classic *Elements of Pure Economics* (1874). Walras posited free, open markets with perfect symmetric information and utility-maximizing or profit-maximizing agents, modelled convergence of prices to equilibrium using the device of an auctioneer, analyzed dynamics using the "tatonnement" process, and built the foundations of multimarket general equilibrium.

I once expressed regret that, in Milton Friedman's phrase, "we curtsy to Marshall, but we walk with Walras," and suggested that the economics profession would today have theories that hold water if it had espoused Marshall's *Principles of Economics* (1871) instead of wholeheartedly embracing Walras' *Elements*.[2] I based this view on Marshall's appealing behavioral definition of economics: "the study of men, as they live and move and think in the ordinary business of life."

But I now think this view is wrong. By walking with Walras, economic theory went very far, farther probably than would have been the case had theorists been limited by Marshall's partial equilibrium analysis. However, like most paradigms, Walras' auctioneer has outlived her validity and usefulness. The Walrasian paradigm is no longer true *enough*. As Thaler observes, "when economists restrict their investigations to those explanations consistent with the paradigm, to the exclusion of simpler and more reasonable hypotheses," then "the tool becomes a handicap." This is scientific myopia.

As Thomas Kuhn has shown, established paradigms do not commit suicide. They bandage their wounds repeatedly, until they are put to death by an inexorable challenger. The "perfect symmetric information" assumption has been largely relaxed within the realm of the existing paradigm. But the assumption of maximization (rationality) has not. Yet as Leibenstein observed nearly two decades ago in a famous essay, "it is rare to find anyone arguing that maximization is a universal description of behavior. . . . it is an assumption that is most frequently stated rather than supported."[3]

In the two decades since Leibenstein's article, a mountain of empirical evidence has accumulated that refutes the maximization assumption.[4] The result: the Herrnstein paradox:

> [T]he economic theory of rational choice . . . accounts only poorly for actual behavior, yet it comes close to serving as the fundamental principle of the behavioral sciences. No other well-articulated theory of behavior commands so large a following in so wide a range of disciplines.[5]

The maximizing paradigm is alive and well, because building a sufficiently general alternate paradigm has proved to be exceptionally difficult. We still lack what both Richard Thaler and Hugh Schwartz call a "theory of systematic error"—a theory equal in generality and aesthetic beauty to that of utility maximization. A theory of error that involves non-maximizing behavior, George Stigler once observed, is "a mighty methodological leap into the unknown."[6] Robert Barro and Stanley Fischer go farther, calling "a theory of systematic mistakes" internally contradictory.[7]

Rationality Gone Awry? seeks to lay the foundations for a theory of error, one that can replace Walras and his auctioneer. Hugh Schwartz understands that this is no small task. He tackles the job systematically, first by lucidly and insightfully surveying behavioral studies of non-maximizing anomalies relevant to economics and finance, and second by identifying "which of those anomalies contribute to a genuinely behavioral theory of decision making." He takes a reasonable, moderate position on conventional economic theory, suggesting that maximization serve as a preliminary stage, to be modified by the orderly deviations from maximization commonly known as "rules of thumb." Schwartz seeks a powerful descriptive theory of decision making as a complement to the present normative economic theories that rest on the premise of optimization.

Science often progresses by combining disciplines that previously seemed ill matched. The genome project merged genetics with computer science; neither discipline alone could have done the job. Mechanics merged with electronics. The semiconductor industry emerged when physics (electronics) joined with chemistry (photolithography). Computer science merged with neurophysiology to produce neural networks.

Hugh Schwartz sees economics and finance progressing by merging with psychology. But I believe there is a problem with interdisciplinary research in general. The term "interdisciplinary" serves as a rubric for two types of research:

- Brilliant integrative research by those who at great effort have succeeded in fully understanding both contributing paradigms, and

- Third-rate research done by those who mask their incompetence by hiding under "interdisciplinary" camouflage nets.

The atmosphere of revolution and innovation that characterizes interdisciplinary research makes it difficult at times to distinguish between the two, and hampers progress.

As founders of the Society for Advancement of Behavioral Economics (SABE), I and my colleagues, John Tomer and Ben Gilad, purposely wrote SABE's terms of reference for potential members in a way that singlemindedly avoided Type I errors (rejecting oddball behavioral theories that might have a germ of truth) at the cost of incurring numerous Type II errors (accepting behavioral theories that were unfounded). We believed that behavioral economics was like modern atonal music—hard to tell good from bad, but absolutely vital to play it all and play it often, so that enough listeners could have the opportunity to put it to the test. Ultimately good theory, and good music, emerge from free competition between fraud and felicity.

Rationality Gone Awry? comes just in the nick of time. By ranging widely over the behavioral economics and finance literature, and creatively summarizing and organizing it, Hugh Schwartz helps prepare the foundations for the next leap forward—a general theory of "non-rationality." His book sharply lowers the entry barriers for scholars interested in behavioral issues by bringing outsiders up to speed in a little over 200 pages, a third of which comprises a cleverly annotated bibliography. He writes with authority. His interesting case study of Uruguay, which illuminates the rules of thumb employed by Uruguayan businessmen, recalls Goethe's maxim: "Thinking is better than knowing, but *looking* is best of all." Like Leibenstein, a behavioral prophet who was above all a skilled observer with the sharpest pair of eyes in the business, Schwartz knows firsthand how people make economic decisions, because he has spent many years in the field observing them. And, he believes, they do not in general maximize.

The aspect of the maximization postulate that most angers me is its "Catch-22" clause. In Joseph Heller's memorable novel, the protagonist could not get out of the army on a psychiatric clause because the very fact he wanted to leave the army proved his basic sanity. The *Merriam-Webster Dictionary* defines Catch-22 as "a problematic situation for which the only solution is denied by a circumstance inherent in the problem."

Leibenstein noted the Catch 22–like nature of the maximizing postulate in a 1985 essay:

[S]uppose the options are A and B, and the economic agent selects A; and an observer argues that this is a sub-optimal choice since the profits under A are less than under B. . . . [an] Unidentified and Unmeasured [*sic*] Factor F . . . "fudge factor" . . . is stuck in, . . . [so that the] utility of A . . . plus F is greater or equal to the utility of B. . . . there is no information whether the "fudge factor" really exists . . . such [factors] almost always come to mind.[8]

So, when Schwartz begins *Rationality Gone Awry?* by observing common non-rational behaviors—obesity, smoking, lack of exercise, drinking, drug addiction—that do us harm, utility maximization always pops up with a rational explanation. For instance: those who take drugs get greater utility from the narcotic than the disutility inherent in the damage to their health and lives:

Note further that if heroin were used even though the subsequent adverse consequences were accurately anticipated, the utility of the user would be greater than if he were prevented from using heroin.[9]

Einstein was right. You cannot solve the problem of the maximization postulate with the same level of economic thinking that gave rise to it. A closed paradigm can never be refuted by remaining within its own boundaries. Milton Friedman's statement that unrealistic assumptions are acceptable provided theories predict reality is no help, because maximization no longer adequately predicts reality.

A new level of thinking is needed. I hope and believe *Rationality Gone Awry?* will help lift us to that new level.

Why do people write books? In his essay "Why I Write," George Orwell gave four reasons: sheer egoism, esthetic enthusiasm, historical impulse (desire to see things as they are), and political purpose (desire to push the world in a certain direction).[10] In Hugh's case, Orwell scores only three out of four.

After *Rationality Gone Awry?* has had some time to percolate into the consciousness of scholars around the world, I look forward to calling, with Hugh, an informal gathering of interested persons, to examine what shape the new systematic theory of error is taking. Perhaps we will hang over our conference room a large banner with Richard Herrnstein's postulate: "suppose people fundamentally and individually misbehave, as the evidence indicates they do."[11]

Suppose people "misbehave." Suppose they do not maximize. How, then, do they invest their money, choose their jobs, buy their cars, choose their mates, and pick their brand of beer? A new frontier of exciting ideas awaits those who walk through the door opened by *Rationality Gone Awry?* It's enough to make Hugh and me wish we were a generation younger.

Shlomo Maital

Davidson Faculty of Industrial Engineering and Management,

Technion-Israel Institute of Technology, Haifa, Israel, and

Visiting Professor, MIT-CAES and MIT School of Management

NOTES

1. Richard Thaler, *Quasi Rational Economics* (New York: Russell Sage Foundation, 1991), p. 162

2. Shlomo Maital, *Minds, Markets and Money* (New York: Basic Books, 1982), pp. 14–15.

3. Harvery Leibenstein, "A Branch of Economics Is Missing: Micro-Micro Theory," *Journal of Economic Literature* 17 (1979), p. 494.

4. See for example, Richard Herrnstein, *The Matching Law: Papers in Psychology and Economics*, ed. Howard Rachlin and David Laibson (Cambridge, MA: Harvard University Press, 1997).

5. Richard Herrnstein, "Rational Choice Theory: Necessary But Not Sufficient," *American Psychologist* 45 (1990), p. 356.

6. George Stigler, "The Xistence of X-Efficiency," *American Economic Review* 66 (1976), pp. 213–216.

7. Robert Barro and Stanley Fischer, "Recent Developments in Monetary Theory," *Journal of Monetary Economics* 2 (1976), pp. 133–167.

8. Harvey Leibenstein, "On Relaxing the Maximization Postulate," *Journal of Behavioral Economics* 14 (1985), p. 14.

9. George Stigler and Gary Becker, "De Gustibus Non Est Disputandum," *American Economic Review* 67 (1997), pp. 76–90.

10. George Orwell, *A Collection of Essays* (Garden City, NY: Doubleday, 1954), pp. 315–316.

11. Herrnstein, *The Matching Law*, p. 250.

Preface

Rationality Gone Awry? Decision Making Inconsistent with Economic and Financial Theory is aimed primarily at intermediate-level students of economics, business administration and other applied programs, along with former students of such courses who are currently active in business or public service. Professionals in these fields who seek a solid introduction to behavioral economics and behavioral finance also may find it useful, as much for the annotated bibliography as for the text itself.

The book deals primarily with recent empirical findings concerning the way in which people actually make decisions about financial and economic matters. An increasing number of deviations from the rationality of traditional decision theory have been documented—enough to undermine the case for always treating the normative, prescriptive theory of even the most sophisticated academic models as an adequate predictor of what transpires in natural economic settings. Yet that traditional, perfectly rational mode of decision making probably will continue as the starting point for predictions as well as for guidance until a comprehensive behavioral theory of decision making becomes available. In the meantime, supplementary courses of action can be taken to improve our understanding of decision-making behavior and our ability to predict real economic outcomes.

I was first introduced to a behavioral approach to decision theory through an article by Ward Edwards, as part of an economic theory course taught by James Tobin many years ago. Later, at Case Western Reserve University, I gave an initial presentation in this area, at that time also citing work in operant conditioning, but B. F. Skinner was kind enough to explain to me that the concerns I expressed related almost exclusively to cognitive psychology rather than to the behavioralism of psychology with which his name has been so intimately linked. In 1976–1977 I was granted a year leave of absence from the Inter-American Development Bank (IDB) to undertake a study of decision making in the metal-working industries of Argentina, Mexico and the United States. In the process I obtained many helpful suggestions from Ward Edwards and Paul Slovic. Presented at a conference of the IDB, the Economic Commission for Latin America and the United Nations Development Program in Buenos Aires in 1978, that study was published in a revised form in the *Journal of Economic Behavior and Organization* in December 1987. Some of what I was learning was incorporated into a mission report prepared for the IDB in 1988, but it was not until after leaving the Bank that I could devote substantial time to the area. This took the form of occasional conferences while I was a Fulbright Lecturer in Uruguay, a course on Behavioral Economics and Behavioral Finance at the Technological Institute of Monterrey in Mexico and a set of lectures on the same topics at the Federal University of Paraná in Brazil where, as in Uruguay, I taught first as a Fulbright Lecturer. For these opportunities I am most grateful to Professor Ruben Tansini, chairman of the Department of Economics of the School of Social Sciences of the University of the Republic, Professors Fábio Dória Scatolin and Seuly Simòes Alves Pinto, directors of the Department of Economics at the Federal University of Paraná, and Professor Aníbal Rivera, chairman of the Finance Department at the Technological Institute of Monterrey (who first suggested that I prepare this book and who has arranged for a Spanish translation), as well as to many members of all three departments.

I am deeply grateful to Herbert A. Simon, Joan Nix, Catherine Elliott and Mordecai Kurz for extensive comments on an earlier version of this manuscript. In the last case, I sent the manuscript so late that it was not possible to incorporate as many changes as I would have liked, though even time would not have led me to incorporate as many changes as Kurz, who characterizes himself as "entirely unsympathetic" to behavioral economics and behavioral finance, would have wished. I also want to express my very considerable gratitude to Donald Hester for detailed comments on several chapters of an early draft. Recommendations for further readings or more selected comments on some of the ideas presented here were offered by Hugo Boff, Loretta Breuning, David George, Ramón García Fernández, Alvaro Forteza, Howard Kunreuther, Donald Lamberton, José Gabriel Porcile Meirelles, T. Y. Shen, Paul Slovic, John Tomer, Karl-Erik Wärneryd and Peter Zoll. In addition, Alan Blinder, Franco Modigliani, Shoshana Grossbard-Shechtman and Lawrence Summers each answered a specific inquiry. I have attempted to take many but not all of the suggestions into account. Let me add my appreciation to my wife, Maria Rosa G. Schwartz, for her help on many matters in preparing the manuscript, to the Library of Congress, where much of the research was undertaken, and to the staff at Greenwood as well as to Betty Pessagno and John Donohue for editorial assistance. Finally, I am indebted to the numerous authors cited in the bibliographical sections, especially to Herbert A. Simon and Richard H. Thaler. I am pleased to acknowledge Professor Thaler's willingness to include, in Chapter 5, substantial material from his study, "The Psychology of Choice and the Assumptions of Economics." Excerpts from and adaption of the chapter of that name appeared as pp. 99–130 of Alvin E. Roth, ed., 1987, *Laboratory Experimentation in Economics: Six Points of View,* published by the Press Syndicate of the University of Cambridge, The Pitt Building, Trumpington Street, Cambridge CB2 1RP; 32 East 57th Street, New York, NY, 10022; 10 Stamford Road, Oakleigh, Melbourne 3166, Australia. Copyright © Cambridge University Press 1987. First published in the United States of America. Reprinted with the permission of Cambridge University Press.

I also would like to acknowledge material quoted in Section D of the Bibliography and Reader's Guide from *An Evolutionary Theory of Economic Change* by Richard R. Nelson and Sidney G. Winter (Cambridge, MA: Harvard University Press, 1982). Copyright © 1982 by the President and Fellows of Harvard College. Reprinted by permission of Harvard University Press.

I would be most grateful to readers for comments and suggestions.

Hugh Schwartz
1627 Great Falls Street
McLean, VA 22101-5059, USA

Introduction

Some of us eat excessively, exercise too little, smoke cigarettes and drink or take drugs, all of which can seriously undermine our health (as we are well aware) and may even affect our ability to hold down a job that pays for those tendencies (as we should recognize). Even beyond such transgressions, most of us never come close to realizing our full potential. So it is too with organizations and nations. Indeed, the gap between what is feasible and what is actually accomplished may have widened in recent decades. Nonetheless, most economic analysis continues to focus on optimization and on what movement toward that goal entails. This is true on the microeconomic side of the ledger, but macroeconomics too emphasizes what it takes to achieve maximum national income in the short run, subject to objectives (inflation, growth and the rate of employment)—two and perhaps all three of which are seen primarily as factors that can contribute to a more nearly optimal national income in the long term.

Moves toward optimality are seldom easy and are sometimes virtually impossible to implement. Moreover, while everyone seeks to do *relatively* well, it is doubtful that a goal as demanding as economic and financial optimality is the objective of many consumers, or even of some of the most successful enterprises in all circumstances. It would seem to make sense, then, to complement our understanding of what is involved in optimization—which is of course essential to economics as an analytical discipline—with a better comprehension of the seemingly less-than-maximizing approaches to problem solving that are often employed in the marketplace. Many approaches are orderly and predictable, and involve what seem to be at least a quasi-rationality. Efforts to understand decision making and adapt analytical approaches accordingly are being undertaken in an ad hoc manner by some economists and financial analysts—and by many of the most successful businesspeople and investors. Perhaps it is time to go about this task more systematically. That is what recent efforts in behavioral economics and behavioral finance are all about, and the intent here is to set forth the basic notions of these developments.[1]

The essential validity and considerable usefulness of the reasoning developed by modern economic and financial analysis are clear. Consumers, producers, investors and governments gain by taking advantage of the general insights and the detailed logic of what has been worked out in economics and finance. It is not only that those who fail to exert themselves are not among the economically and financially most successful, and that the forces of Supply and Demand explain much that we observe around us, but also the Principles of Modern Economics and Finance now provide us with a much better understanding of such day-to-day matters as why the introduction of safety regulations does not always lead to better safety, why employees do not always perform as well as their employers hoped for when they hired them, and even of decision-making processes within the largely social bounds of the family. The last mentioned, a decidedly socioeconomic phenomenon, reveals the applicability—or, rather, the fact that there is *some* applicability—of the reasoning of economic analysis to problems long regarded as lying outside its domain, and this extension of the reach of economic reasoning has been spearheaded by economists from an intellectual tradition that had long insisted on the limited confines of their discipline.

Nonetheless, the techniques of economics and finance leave a number of questions about important matters unanswered. Simple market forces of Supply and Demand do not always explain the prevailing prices of individual goods and services, nor the level of larger market phenomena such as the Stock Market. Moreover, contrary to the new understandings just referred to, some employees exceed the achievements expected by their employers (many employees, in some enterprises), and some safety precautions justify the costs involved to an even greater extent than ever anticipated. There are many other qualifications as well. The general framework economists and financial analysts have offered and that they continue to employ—made more precise each day—leaves some matters unexplained and does not always predict well. There certainly has not been an improvement in the predictive power of economics even remotely commensurate with the additional efforts that have been made for that purpose. The basic paradigm of economics does not appear to adequately capture some actions of those who are among the most successful survivors in the economy. And what explains why it is that we sometimes seem to learn so slowly and unevenly from experience, even with all the improvements in decision-making techniques, this despite the costs of such shortcomings to ourselves and to society at large?

Consider a number of important aspects of how decisions are made.

- Most consumer decisions are characterized by rough-and-ready comparisons, even though the benefits of some additional inquiry and calculation often would justify the added cost that those entail. Emotional and other psychological factors and the implications of an action for one's relative position influence decisions about many purchases. In addition, few consumers fail to survive because they did not make the best buys possible. Indeed, many appear to live more happily than acquaintances who uncover means (generally time-consuming and sometimes not entirely agreeable) of negotiating purchases at prices better than those paid by their neighbors.

• In deciding on courses of action, businesspeople and investors as well as consumers frequently weigh almost as seriously costs incurred in the past—the sunk costs that they can no longer do anything about—as new costs that have not yet been incurred and are really the only ones relevant.

• Most people tend to treat the same value of money differently according to whether it has been placed in a checking account, a savings account, or what is meant to be a long-term investment—this, even though the reasoning of economics and finance would indicate that a dollar from one account is worth neither more nor less than a dollar from another.

• Some decisions between consumption now and consumption later suggest preferences over time that are inconsistent with one another.

• Most of us are inclined to make some choices that we know are not in our long-term interest. Or rather, we are inclined to make such selections unless we tie our hands in advance—which would seem to contradict the high value that we place on freedom of choice and access to a full range of opportunities (or that we claim to place on such values, on first and often quite sincere reflex).[2]

Nor do markets always iron out all of the errors, inconsistencies and irrationalities of individuals within what most would regard as a reasonable period of time. There is increasing documentation of the imperfection of many markets, even financial markets with their large and continuing flow of transactions and the relatively easy opportunities for feedback and adjustment. At the macroeconomic level, it is not always clear what choice really involves and whether there is a unique best approach to many problems (even if the likely conflicts of individual values did not impede optimization), or what explains the implicit tradeoffs. There does not even appear to be an unequivocal "best way" of achieving rapid economic growth, for example. Rapid economic growth has been obtained in circumstances of virtually unfettered markets (Hong Kong), in situations characterized by strong intervention in the context of an export-emphasized market orientation (Korea, Taiwan and Chile), and in circumstances marked by strong intervention with an emerging, but still quite circumscribed, market orientation (China). A possibly comparable tradeoff, moderately high growth combined with a strikingly improved quality of life, has been achieved in the context of major government intervention for socioeconomic infrastructure within an otherwise market-oriented economy (Curitiba, Brazil). Most disturbingly, moreover, many well-trained and highly capable economists have elicited contradictory lessons from these experiences, though in the last few years the tendency has been to back away from some of the more extreme positions. What has been emerging has been a recognition that some differences in the analyses and in the policy recommendations may be required for different situations.

It is the position of this short volume that a growing body of evidence from the behavioral social sciences helps explain individual deviations from what economists and financial analysts consider rational behavior, as well as part of the ability of overall communities to achieve comparably high rates of economic growth with very different sets of economic policies. The emphasis here is overwhelmingly on the micro side of the ledger, and indeed on decision making at the level of the individual, but economists such as Axel Leijonhufvud have called for the application of this type of reasoning to macroeconomics as well, and some efforts along those lines are underway.

This book has two goals. The first is to outline the wide array of behavioral considerations that appear to be relevant to financial and economic decision making. At the same time, an effort is made to distinguish between those about which the other social sciences (and biology) are in agreement, or for which there is at least no obvious disagreement, and those for which the signals are mixed or unresolved. Attention will be given primarily to those factors in the first group for which anomalies with traditional economic theory have been documented.

The second goal is to indicate which of those anomalies contribute to a genuinely behavioral theory of decision making, and what can be done to take account of the other anomalies and less completely resolved considerations that do not yet achieve such an objective. The book does not imply that the existing theory of rational decision making should be abandoned, either as a normative theory[3] or even as a starting point for predicting actual behavior. However, it is an argument for extending greater recognition to the rules of thumb used by decision makers and for devoting more effort to identifying and quantifying the biases that those useful simplifications reflect. What is advocated, then, is that predictions about actual decision making involve two steps. The preliminary indications would be those of traditional financial and economic analysis, but these would not be put forward as the probable results, as is now generally done. Rather, they would be systematically modified to take account of the deviations from traditional rationality that empirical evidence leads us to expect from the use of rules of thumb. That should greatly improve our ability to cope with the challenge of anticipating the results of actual decision making in natural economic settings—whether or not it facilitates the eventual construction of a satisfactory descriptive theory of decision making to accompany the existing normative theory.

Part I introduces and summarizes the behavioral approach to financial and economic decision making. Part II deals with the same themes but elaborates them somewhat further. Economists, financial analysts and those with at least intermediate-level preparation in the analysis of decision making might want to proceed directly from this Introduction to Part II, though if they are willing to bear with a measure of repetition, something will be gained by beginning with

Part I. Part III contains two appendixes, one of which is a case study. Part IV provides an annotated bibliography of many of the leading contributions relevant to behavioral finance and behavioral economics.

NOTES

1. Some economists believe that nonmaximizing behavior is infrequent, but others maintain that even much of this behavior only *seems* to be nonmaximizing while, in reality, it is not. Thus, in their view, there is no need to develop a behavioral approach to economics and finance. A few comments on this position will be offered later in the text.

2. This phenomenon, that of Ulysses in *The Odyssey*, was first pointed out in the literature of economics by Robert Strotz in the 1950s and has been elaborated on by Elster 1984. That book, along with Elster 1983, provides tremendously stimulating expositions of rationality and irrationality, drawing extensively on the broad body of Western learning and literature.

3. To do that, it is not enough to show the existence of anomalies. Following Kuhn, "once it has achieved the status of a paradigm, a scientific theory is declared invalid only if an alternative candidate is available to take its place" (Kuhn 1970, 77).

Part I

The Basic Argument

Chapter 1

Overview

HOW ECONOMISTS AND FINANCIAL ANALYSTS HAVE EXPLAINED THE WAY PEOPLE MAKE ECONOMIC AND FINANCIAL DECISIONS

A generation or so ago, people used to joke that economic forecasts were much like those that dealt with the weather—hardly very reliable. Since that time, weather forecasts, which deal with strictly physical phenomena, have improved a great deal. It would not seem that the same can be said for economic forecasts, perhaps because many economic forecasters have proceeded as if behavioral idiosyncrasies and institutional differences were not important considerations, or perhaps because they attempted to incorporate into the analysis behavioral factors which, while they may have seemed plausible, did not always reflect the findings of psychology and the other behavioral social sciences. Since economics developed relatively rigorous foundations and began to devote serious attention to empirical studies before the other social sciences, it may not be surprising that the field has tended to turn up with its own assumptions about the way in which individuals and enterprises behave. Such assumptions are usually consistent with the way it has defined rational behavior (though for contrary examples, see the comments of Arrow and Plott in note 12 to this chapter). Thus, economists have tended to develop their own psychology of consumer behavior and their own sociology of markets, in implicit if not always explicit terms.

In the late 19th century some economists did turn to psychology or they attempted their own psychological explanations, and for a number of years many drew on Benthamite hedonistic formulations to support theories of marginal utility, but the early psychological work only reinforced what they had been assuming. Then, as psychology began to criticize such views, mainstream economics divorced itself from the behavioral findings of the social sciences. Leading economists began to look to the physical sciences, particularly physics, as a model. The increasing concern with quantification and use of mathematics, and particularly the preoccupation with the analysis of states of equilibria, altered the nature of economic inquiry. It lessened the concern of mainstream economics for patterns of behavior that did not reflect an attempt to maximize, and it reduced what had been an emerging interest in the processes of *reaching* equilibria. For a number of decades, most prominent mainstream economists concerned themselves with a much narrower and more technical set of issues than had Adam Smith, John Stuart Mill and Alfred Marshall.

These behavioral concerns infiltrated more of what was taught in schools of business administration and what was recommended by management consultants. Of course, some individuals in economics and finance took the disciplines of psychology, sociology and anthropology more seriously. Prominent among these in the late 19th Century and first half of the 20th Century were those who called themselves institutional economists. Some of these individuals, as well as a number of others who attempted to take the other social sciences into account, branched off into subfields such as labor, agricultural and transportation economics, and later, into marketing, consumer economics and industrial organization. There were those, such as Thomas Schelling, who, concerned with problems of international conflict, utilized and contributed to the analyses of political science. In addition, there was Albert Hirschman, who turned his attention to an extraordinarily wide range of considerations from preference formation to broad political and socioeconomic problems and borrowed from wherever he could in an effort to analyze the manifold problems with broader-than-economic dimensions.

Schelling, Hirschman and their followers were exceptions. During the 20th Century, and particularly after the Second World War, more and more economists ignored the work of the social sciences. While a number of leading economists endeavored to show the behavioral social sciences how the analyses of those fields could be strengthened by applying the approach of economics, they made little effort to see if anything in those other areas might benefit economics in return. When a few economists, most notably Herbert Simon (also a professor of psychology and computer science, as well as an expert on organization and administration), insisted that it was a mistake to assume that businesspeople sought, and were capable of maximizing profits, this dissenting group was largely ignored for many years—even when they researched efforts to achieve what they termed bounded rationality and created formal techniques to help advance that end. Business administration specialists and business consultants began to pay increasing attention, however, and more of the behaviorally oriented economists became associated with schools of business and public administration.

Only in the last few years has the attitude of economists as a whole begun to change. This has been due especially to two developments. First, an initially small group of cognitive psychologists interested in decision theory conducted experiments, the results of which contradicted several fundamental propositions of economics, and they began to communicate their results in the professional journals of economics as well as psychology. This led to verification efforts by economists with a similar specialty, experimental economics. The result was the discovery of an increasing number of economic anomalies, economic behavior that did not conform to the rationality that is critical to mainstream economic theory.[1] Perhaps the most striking of the experiments were those that demonstrated that with only the slightest alteration in the wording of propositions, and with the meaning obviously still the same, many people changed the choices they made, virtually from one moment to the next. This reversal of preferences seemed to contradict one of the most fundamental axioms of economic analysis, what economists call transitivity.

Coinciding with this development were the efforts of a few economists, perhaps most notably George Akerlof, to analyze decision-making processes that had been relatively ignored by other colleagues. Akerlof's revealing explanation of the used car market ("the market for lemons") was the first of these analyses. Later, he incorporated findings from cognitive psychology into a maximizing framework in evaluating alternative work environments (discussed briefly in Part II). Then he broadened his questioning of traditional economic theory. In "Loyalty Filters," he stated:

In addition, persons, by having a choice over their experiences, can exercise some choice over their values; or perhaps, more typically, persons may choose for their children experiences that will lead them to have desired social values. Insofar as this occurs, values are not fixed, as in standard economics, but are a matter of choice. Economic theory, which is largely a theory of choice, then becomes a useful tool in analyzing how these values are chosen. . . .

. . . as persons go through different experiences, their loyalties change. . . . Loyalty filters . . . have implications concerning the goals that individuals attempt to attain. The modeling of each of these aspects of reality constitutes a departure of importance from standard economic models, capable of explaining such phenomena as cooperative behavior, class loyalties, and much institutional behavior. . . .[2]

Several years later, in dealing with the relatively neglected problem of anomalies over time, Akerlof wrote:

Although each choice may be close to maximizing and therefore result in only small losses, the cumulative effect of a series of repeated errors may be quite large. . . . In each case individuals choose a series of actions without fully appreciating how those actions will affect future perceptions and behavior. The standard assumption of rational, forward-looking, utility maximization is violated. The nonindependence of errors in decision making in the series of decisions can be explained with the concept from cognitive psychology of undue salience or vividness. . . .

A clear moral of the procrastination model is that time-inconsistent behavior is especially apt to occur when there is some fixed cost (perhaps not very great) to beginning a task, the "periods" are short, and the per period cost of delay is low. . . .

Once people have made decisions, they avoid information that does not support that decision because it is psychologically painful. . . .

A . . . modern view of behavior, based on twentieth-century anthropology, psychology, and sociology is that individuals have utilities that do change and, in addition, they fail to foresee those changes or even recognize that they have occurred. . . . [3]

Meanwhile, studies of financial market data, some of which dealt with extensive periods of time, were discovering many cases that seemed to contradict the conclusion of leading financial economists and financial analysts that markets tend to be highly efficient, and this was especially true of financial markets. Among the findings of the new work in behavioral finance was a strong challenge to the conclusion that the prevailing prices of equities on stock exchanges reflected all relevant contemporary data but provided no indication of what prices might be in the future. Economists studying labor markets, marriage and the family, cooperation in business organizations and economic development also were uncovering apparent anomalies, but it was the replicable studies of experimental economics and the stunning findings of financial economics that caught the attention of many economists. These studies transformed behavioral economics and behavioral finance into a growing, albeit still highly controversial field, particularly among those teaching in Schools of Business Administration and other applied programs and, more recently, among some investment companies.

THE OBJECTIVES OF FINANCIAL AND ECONOMIC ACTIVITY: THE GOALS OF INDIVIDUALS AND ENTERPRISES

Psychological, Sociological, Cultural and Political Considerations

No sooner had a prominent social scientist written persuasively on the role of Protestantism and economic progress, when another documented the early rise of capitalism in Catholic countries. Years later, in the early 1950s, an expert on Korean culture wrote that economists who expected that country to respond to incentives in a manner similar to the Europeans and the Americans only revealed their failure to understand the importance of cultural factors. When, indeed, an even more rapid economic advance was manifested than in the West, some observers contended that it was due to the role of certain strains of Confucianism. Doubtless there will be further revisions following the financial, economic and moral crises of the 1990s, especially as a consequence of the events of late 1997.

Cultural and economic anthropology can likely improve our understanding of financial and economic affairs, but except at the level of rural projects, we do not yet seem to have much of a handle on how to go about it. The possibilities for generalizing from sociology also seem to have been limited to date, although economists dealing with marketing and labor have benefited from findings in this area and social psychology. Moreover, both sociology and social psychology should prove relevant to the work of mainstream economists on a topic that has been gaining increasing attention, that of coordination within enterprises.[4] Political science should be able to help in a number of ways and has been receiving attention through the World Bank's effort to understand the "governance" factors that might explain why similar economic stabilization programs function much better in one country than in another. Nonetheless, Hirschman, perhaps the economist who has most successfully utilized the concepts and findings of political science, has cautioned us about generalizations in that field.

In short, there is an increasing recognition that cultural, sociological and political factors affect financial and economic outcomes. This influence stems in part from their effects on the implementation of specific measures, and also from other-than-strictly-economic goals which may have an impact on financial and economic objectives. We recognize that those who have ignored such multidisciplinary factors often find that even presumably well-designed financial and economic measures do not always seem to be effective. We also have seen, however, that some of the most strongly held hypotheses concerning the effects of such other-than-strictly economic considerations have not been upheld. At this stage, a behavioral approach to finance and economics that is likely to be successful would entail a very selective approach to incorporating those other-than-strictly economic considerations. Such an approach should employ them in circumstances in which the knowledge of those making the applications is extensive and relatively profound.

An exception to such a highly circumscribed approach may be available in the case of the findings of certain areas of psychology. The new insights into decision making aid prediction and should regularly be introduced into the models of finance and economics. These psychological variables affect outcomes and even appear to affect objectives. As an example, if, in order to optimize, some problems require more information than ordinarily can be obtained and properly analyzed before decisions have to be made, then perhaps the objective should be thought of not as optimization, but as coping—coping in a manner that is likely to lead to results as favorable as possible under the particular circumstances, but coping nonetheless. Use would be made of formal and informal rules of thumb, which would hopefully be improved over time so as to improve performance, but which could not be considered to be tools for maximizing, for calculating optimization.[5]

Thus, psychological, cultural, sociological, and political considerations may affect the implementation of financial and economic measures, as well as our objectives in undertaking financial and economic measures. That influence, in the case of decision-making techniques, may lead not only to a modification of what is to be maximized, but also to a shift away from a maximization objective as such. Although it is difficult to generalize about the types of modifications in objectives that result from psychological and other multidisciplinary considerations, it is somewhat easier to indicate the degree to which goal maximization is being transformed into a more limited attainment of those goals—from profit maximization to a "high rate of profitability," for example. It is also easier to estimate the degree of deviation from the goal in its unrestrained form (to estimate, for example, the order of difference between profit maximization and a "high level of profits").

Professed, Implicit and Revealed Objectives

Whether or not multidisciplinary considerations alter the financial and economic objectives of individuals in all cases, we should distinguish between what we profess (and sincerely believe) to be our objectives and what our choices seem to reveal. Consider situations such as those in which a businessperson who has indicated that he or she seeks to maximize profits, and seems to be making a strong effort in that direction, is presented with a decision from a subordinate, calling for the layoff of a skilled employee with a long and dependable record and a large family. Sometimes, the businessperson decides against what he has calculated to be the maximizing measure. In reality, his objective is to maximize profits subject to constraints or conditions that are not always predetermined. Alternatively, some businesspeople view themselves as "socially concerned," but when faced with competitive pressures, they often make cost-minimizing, profit-maximizing decisions that might differ from what they would have anticipated in advance. In the latter case, there is a difference between the less-than-single-minded objective that is professed (and intended, at least in many cases) and that which is revealed. Finally, in some cases actions differ from those consistent with professed and intended objectives, not primarily because circumstances differ from what might have been expected, but because the consequences of alternatives were not adequately recognized (in some cases, could not have been anticipated) in advance.

Multiple Objectives

If businesspeople do not attempt to *maximize* profits, but only to obtain a high rate of profitability, it may be because of the extraordinary difficulty of doing so. It may also be because they have more than one objective. This is indeed likely if we take account of the wide range of multidisciplinary considerations. Economics seems to have dealt with this problem by viewing the goals emanating from those noneconomic dimensions as establishing boundaries, with maximization of the economic objectives taking place within those boundaries. Thus, moral considerations limit behavior, but within the limits established, everyone presumably seeks to do the best possible (i.e., to maximize). Most of the decision-making tools at the level of individuals and enterprises relate to maximizing something that has a common denominator—profits, perhaps sales (though that may merely be a proxy for profits in the long run), even utility, if it comes to that, though the use of a concept such as utility certainly raises the question of whether there is maximization in a sense anyone can verify. Note that most economists who dissent from the notion that businesspeople seek to maximize profits nonetheless focus on a single objective—that businesspeople seek to obtain a high level of profits, for example. Few delve into what, in addition to profits, might be sought and how that might be taken into account.

Alan Blinder, until recently the vice chairman of the Federal Reserve Board, has remarked, "Each of us, in our everyday lives, pursues multiple goals with a limited set of instruments. We understand intuitively that we must trade off one goal against the other, and we act this way in virtually everything we do."[6] Blinder's former job required him to agonize over the tradeoff between inflation and unemployment. Agonize is indeed the correct word, not only because of the human suffering involved in unemployment, but also because available economic analysis does not provide a common denominator between these two dimensions, particularly to the extent that one reflects other-than-strictly economic aspects.[7] We engage in numerous tradeoffs between alternatives, many of which do not have a well-specified common denominator. Some of the principal problems of our times reflect the inadequacy of our approaches to the existence of multiple objectives. For an example, see the opening statement of the introductory chapter.

The leading technical achievements of microeconomics depend heavily on the assumption that those who survive have a single objective that they maximize. How then does the discipline cope with the apparent fact that, in much of what we do, most of us have more than a single goal? While the challenge might seem to call out for a behavioral approach, incorporating elements from several of the social sciences (and perhaps biology and philosophy as well), there are still serious limits as to what can be achieved along those lines, and that integration of the disciplines certainly is not what mainstream economics attempts.

First, to the degree that the anomalies to economic analysis that have been uncovered reflect multiple objectives, it should be noted that mainstream economics insists that those anomalies are the exception, not the rule, and that the principal concern of economic theory should be to explain what is dominant so as to be able to predict satisfactorily. Some of the most traditional economists argue further that the anomalies have only been documented in laboratory experiments, not in the real world, and that the basic propositions of microeconomic analysis about prices, supply, and demand hold up well in the real world, at least in the long run. The claim that there is no real-world substantiation of anomalies ignores some evidence to the contrary, however.

Second, mainstream economics maintains that in giving doctors, lawyers and spouses the authority to make certain types of decisions without subsequent consultation, individuals and enterprises knowingly and willingly place constraints on themselves with respect to some choices in order to facilitate the expeditious functioning of everyday activities, while assuring the dominance of the most important goal or goals.

Third (and most clearly in response to the multiple objectives consideration), how do economists deal with phenomena such as drug addiction by the talented individual whose professional activity and health are endangered by taking drugs? Several approaches are employed. One is to assume that future damage to health is allowed for when the calculation is made that leads to the decision to take drugs. Another, more common approach has been the development of "two-self" models, with individuals shifting back and forth between objectives, maximizing first one objective, then another, without introducing much in the way of psychological explanations to explain the switch. (A variant of this in which psychological explanations *are* put forth is offered by recent work of Loewenstein, cited in Bazerman 1998, 90–91.) A third approach, and perhaps more convincing for the phenomenon of multiple objectives generally, has been to refer to "meta preferences" and second-order preferences (see Sen 1977; George 1984, 1993; and Hirschman 1981, 1982). Here, too, however, what is left unspecified is exactly what triggers the alternative preference systems.

Generally, economists assume a single dominant objective—in the case of enterprises, usually profit maximization—and the predictions, while not always on the mark in the short run, do not generally turn out badly for the long run. (This is despite such phenomena as the continuing, and perhaps even accelerating, errors in corporate earnings estimates, which are prepared by analysts using the most sophisticated estimation procedures available.) Whether or not all of the survivors attempt to maximize and succeed, most of those who fall by the wayside do not even try to optimize, or they do not have a single consistent objective.[8] Consider, however, that there are numerous deviations from optimization—on the part of individuals, enterprises and governments. Since several economists have shown that the cost to an economy can be quite high, even when economic agents employ techniques that reflect near optimization, one can only imagine the theoretical cost of using less maximizing techniques over a substantial period of time.

Part of any cost that an enterprise or an economy actually realizes would be attributable to an inadequate implementation of the profit-maximizing objective, of course. This aspect remains important, even though much more information has become available on how to upgrade technology and improve operational efficiency, and at significantly lower cost. (There are many well-documented cases of enterprises that have reduced costs per unit of output by as much as 50 percent and more in a year's time, sometimes without new investments. Only a few years ago, some prominent economists dismissed such a phenomenon as unlikely or one that did not amount to much in the aggregate.) Differences in objectives also must play a role, however. Consider, for example, the sizable variation in the average annual income of, say, the ten former students from any business administration school who, a dozen years after graduation, are considered by their colleagues to be the most successful in their class. Judging from the extreme range (and lack of sequence) of the incomes of those considered the first, second, third most successful, and so on, they probably did not all have the same, single-minded profit-maximization objective. That individuals might have multiple, partially conflicting objectives, not only from time to time, but in many situations and as a continuing presence, comes as no surprise to psychology. Indeed, that is part of what psychology is all about.

Some psychologists maintain that people have a hierarchy of needs, beginning with physiological needs, followed by needs for security, a sense of belonging, self-respect, and personal realization, according to Abraham Maslow. Empirical studies have not provided this theory with strong verification, perhaps because the concepts and the relevant tradeoffs are imprecise rather than because of error concerning the hierarchy of needs. The objectives of individuals and the nature of the tradeoffs might shift according to their income, wealth, professional attainment and family circumstances. Many individuals might attempt to do the very best that they can at certain (say, low) levels of income, and so on, but engage in a kind of constrained maximization, taking one or more other needs into account at higher levels of income.

Another line of reasoning among psychologists is in terms of response mechanisms. This approach encompasses aspects from physiological and cognitive psychology. The notion is that half a dozen factors affect sentiments, and it is sentiments that really influence actions. The factors include the level of sugar in the blood, images, smell and hormones as well as rational calculations. Undoubtedly, certain kinds of decisions are much more affected by some of these factors than by others, but if even two factors exert an influence on decision making and these vary for some types of decisions, then it is difficult to speak of "the objective" or to be precise about the optimal tradeoff. Ask an economist or a financial analyst in a social setting if he or she agrees that images and sexual drives can affect actions, and most would respond affirmatively, and quite sincerely so. Once the person was back in the office and working within the framework of familiar models that do not allow for such determinants, however, the same query would draw a smile (because of the apparent naiveté of the question) and a negative answer. The response might not be negative if the individual were a financial analyst who had become an investment adviser, however.

Various psychologists have referred to the underlying motivations of human action. Among the motivations that have drawn support from at least a group of their colleagues are the following: need for achievement, locus of control (the degree to which an individual feels he or she is in control of events), altruism, need for stimulus, and taste for a particular life-style (including any preferences for change—even implicit preferences such as might be expected from those who plan to continue educating themselves on topics outside their own area of expertise throughout their lives). Also mentioned as an underlying motivation of human action is an individual's time preference, which is said to be determined by such factors as the prevailing culture, the process of socialization, one's age, the locus of control, bequest motivations, levels of income—all of these in addition to the rate of interest that economists and financial analysts are prone to stress as explaining time preference. Beyond that, psychologists hold that emotions can trigger or give temporary importance to one or another of the motivations.

Many sociologists argue that some decisions may well be guided by logical, empirical considerations, but others are determined primarily by moral (normative) or affective concerns; they therefore reason that most decisions are subject to both influences. Anthropologists would argue that the relative importance of underlying motivations varies at least somewhat from society to society and from generation to generation.

Is it adequate, then, to deal with decision making in the financial and economic arena as if there were but a single objective, that we aim to maximize it, and that we are able to do so, or even come close to that? The first requirement and the usefulness of an objective as a guide to decision making depend on being able to evaluate the effects of decisions on the realization of the objective. This involves measurement, and one of the main reasons why many businesses may not maximize profits is that it is often difficult, if not impossible, to gauge the likely effects of particular actions on profits, or even to measure them ex post. Evidence of this can be seen in the experience regarding the phenomenon of major corporate downsizings about which there seem to be conflicting conclusions. Perhaps economics and finance should reallocate research efforts, devoting relatively less effort to the further refinement of already sophisticated techniques of optimization and somewhat more to other matters that are also critical to better decision making. One research effort might be to estimate the relative importance in some types of situations, and especially among successful enterprises and individuals of objectives that differ from profit maximization. This might be done by ascertaining the objectives that individuals reveal during the process of their actual decision making. A second research effort, taking account of that mix of objectives—profit maximization in some types of cases, and a mixture of considerations in others—might be to ascertain the manner in which unquestioned "survivors" implement those objectives. That accomplished, consideration might be given to what would be involved in moving *toward* a "best possible" solution, or at least a substantially improved solution to problems, both in the case of profit maximization and multiple considerations.

Rationality

Economics and finance assume that survivors behave rationally, that everyone should try to do so and that the way to get people to behave rationally and become survivors is to teach them the techniques of optimization. Learning—from formal instruction and from experience—is usually assumed to lead to increased rationality and thus, a tendency to make more nearly optimal decisions. Economics and finance define rationality in terms of *results*—actions that are consistent and that increase the utility of those who undertake them (which is generally understood to mean actions that advance material well-being). In psychology, the other behavioral social sciences and philosophy, rationality is defined in terms of the *process* employed to make a decision, whether or not it happens to lead to the best results. Behaviorally oriented economists take the process approach, favoring "procedural" rationality over what is termed substantive rationality. Many traditionally oriented economists do so as well in some of the personal, business and government decisions they advise on, even though they continue to teach the concept that rationality refers to substantive results. The importance of the way in which we define rationality will become clearer in the discussion of the implementation of economic and financial objectives in Part II. It can be noted for now that one of the most serious limitations of the traditional definition of rationality by economics and finance (and this would extend to the definition of rationality that refers to the processes employed as well) is the surprisingly frequent difficulty that humans have in being consistent, even in the case of relatively simple types of problems. This difficulty, moreover, extends to statisticians and econometricians.

IMPLEMENTING FINANCIAL AND ECONOMIC OBJECTIVES

Many traditional economists would be bothered by the preceding section on multiple objectives. While they recognize that human beings take account of many factors, they believe that for most of the problems on which economics focuses (microeconomics, in any event), the profit maximization objective is dominant enough so that an assumption that it is *the* objective leads to good predictions. Yet an increasing number of economists have come to advocate the use of a maximization approach to analyze all kinds of situations, even problems of marriage and the family and other primarily social concerns (in what even some of those same economists have characterized as economic imperialism). In any event, as already intimated, more traditional economists have become interested in behavioral developments because they have come to recognize that the difficulties of implementing "rational" objectives are much greater than was formerly imagined. It is not because they have finally become convinced that multiple objectives (or other-than-profit-maximizing objectives) are significant.

The Perception of Information

Assume, for a moment, that enterprises have a single, well-defined objective such as the maximization of profits. Assume, too, that they recognize the most important problems and opportunities confronting them, and the way in which both should be analyzed in order to maximize. The first concern, then, is to obtain the data needed to resolve matters, taking into account that they should gather more information only until the gains of securing additional information no longer exceed the cost of obtaining that data. Economists have devoted a great deal of attention to the importance of differences in access to information—data asymmetries—to explain why some decision makers fare so much better than others. However, it is not just access to data that matters. There are, in addition, differences in the way many individuals or enterprises *perceive* the same information, and these data perception asymmetries may vary for different categories of information or in different circumstances. As a consequence, a would-be optimizer may wind up trying to maximize a problem that varies from the one he or she actually confronts—perhaps by a good deal in some cases.

How much of a rise in interest rates is implied by an announcement that credit policies will be "tightened"? What is the exact price of steel of a given specification when prices are published, but with comments on prevailing discounts and adjustments that are "coded" and lend themselves to alternative interpretations by those with different experiences in dealing with such situations? What are the probable implications of a 25 percent devaluation of a country's currency for a company that produces components of a product that are exported as well as sold in the home market? (Real-world experience such as the contrast in the behavior of Argentine and Mexican enterprises in the late 1970s shows that firms with previous experience with devaluations perceive the implications of this information much better than those that have not.) And consider the task at hand for an engineer who understands the principles underlying a new production process, and knows the market price for the machinery incorporating them as well as the final price of the components, but has not yet grasped the range of undertakings for which the new process is likely to be technologically dominant. Problems in perceiving market, technological or public policy information accurately at the moment when a decision must be made (and the difficulties in recognizing the most important implications of such information), can interfere with the implementation of optimizing financial and economic calculations. Such problems of data perception involve an element of judgment, as does almost all perception.

Reasoning Processes, Judgment and Decision Making

The Limits of Rationality. Forty years ago, Herbert Simon noted two key limits to achieving perfect rationality. First, it usually is not possible to obtain all of the information relevant to a problem by the time a decision has to be made. (Although Simon did not quite phrase it this way, in view of his concern with perception, this might be restated: usually it is not possible to gain access to, and to perceive accurately, all of the information relevant to a problem by the time a decision has to be made.) Second, Simon insisted that, in general, it would not be possible to obtain the programs necessary to deal with all that information in a manner that would permit optimization. This may be less serious than at the beginning of the Computer Age, but it remains a problem, reflected, in part, by the phenomenon of "information overload" and by the psychological problems that sometimes accompany a sense of information over-load. These may directly affect some decision making negatively and even lead to "burnout" or the need of costly psychological counseling. The lack of nec-essary data and programs for optimization led Simon to maintain that the best that we could hope for was "bounded rationality." He characterized most de-cision-making processes as a type of "satisficing." He did not mean to imply that successful businesspeople were casual about their pursuit of profits (which the term *satisficing* might seem to suggest), but only that the operational im-possibility of optimizing profits (together with the observable fact that even successful businesspeople took objectives other than profits into account) led to decision making that did not conform to the traditional economist's definition of rationality.[9] The term *bounded rationality* later gained wide acceptance among economists and financial analysts, though in terms of a kind of con-strained optimization. In his role as a computer scientist, Simon has spent years working on decision-making aids called algorithms to help improve what he viewed as an (inevitable) process of satisficing by decision makers. In the end, he always rejected the notion that most solutions could approach optimization in the sense intended by many of the current users of the term *bounded ration-ality*.

Anomalies in the Decision-Making Process. How do people make decisions? Consider, first, consumers, and then, producers and investors (and not just any producers and investors but "survivors," i.e., "winners"). Consumers seek what they regard as good values; economists maintain that consumer decisions reflect their preferences, given the relative prices of goods and services and their budget constraints. Most economic models assume that those consumer prefer-ences are fixed in the short run.[10] Over the course of time, such preferences may shift, influenced by the family, religious and cultural factors, and by all manner of traditions and institutions of a society, not the least of which are advertising and the various other activities of active persuasion. Note that as much as a quarter of the gross national product (GNP) may be spent to influence the se-lection of goods and services,[11] and most of that extraordinarily large effort is spent to influence choices in the very near future. Some of that 25 percent of GNP persuasion effort funds a portion of the entertainment industry (or is viewed as entertainment in and of itself, as in the case of "catchy" commercial music). Thus, it contributes to the creation of additional services, but the point is that many choices come to reflect outside influences and pressures (informed and otherwise), or rather, new and short-term influences from outside, in addi-tion to the more traditional, longer term influences of culture, religious teachings and other societal institutions. Although it is the individual consumer who de-cides ultimately the degree to which to succumb to these influences, it would seem an exaggeration to refer to the overall process as reflecting undiluted con-sumer sovereignty, even in the short run. (Marketing matters!) Moreover, even in the short run, there are doubts about the role of preferences in determining choices.

Experiments suggest that our selections often help determine preferences; some choices are made only with great difficulty and without strong conviction, but the act of selection helps shape preferences. There are at least three reasons for this. First, perhaps only with choice and possession are product characteristics truly recognized and appreciated. Second, preferences may change after owning a product, even immediately afterward, even though the features of the product were well appreciated in advance, as economic theory usually assumes. One or more psychological effects appear to be at work. Among these is an "endowment effect," which is most readily comprehensible in terms of the loss that would be felt if one no longer possessed the item in question. The most important reason why selection helps shape preferences applies equally to producers and investors and is considered later.

Consumers attempt to learn from experience and to obtain more value from their choices over time, but the manner in which they do this or in which they make their initial choices raises doubts as to whether they are attempting to seriously implement anything that even remotely resembles an optimization objective—in any event, the maximization of material well-being. The "survivor" argument is particularly difficult to substantiate. Even many of the most successful producers make decisions in their role as consumers that would seem to reflect a lack of interest in careful calculation. Public and private programs designed to assist consumer decision making (such as consumer protection agencies or even business-funded Better Business Bureaus) seem to be a concern of the middle class in a small number of relatively high per capita income countries. Moreover, some surveys by economic psychologists and experts in consumer behavior reveal that most purchases of major consumer durables are made after obtaining only one or two direct price comparisons and further information from sales personnel, who can hardly be described as disinterested suppliers of unbiased information.

Among producers, decision making generally is undertaken with a more careful eye on cost and value, perhaps in part because the profitability of those decisions affects the capability of those involved to attain desirable levels of personal consumption. Certainly it is in large measure because there are checks on performance, both within an enterprise and externally, the external stemming from domestic and foreign competition, and in some countries, because of the threat of hostile takeovers of publicly traded companies. Even so, many studies show that most businesses do not press seriously in the direction of optimization until and unless they become subject to strong competitive pressures or to adversity. Perhaps the first study to document this lagging emphasis on optimization was Cyert and March 1963. Those authors referred to the nonmaximizing phenomenon as "organizational slack." Leibenstein and his followers spoke of it as x-inefficiency in order to distinguish it from the traditional concern of economists, efficiency in the allocation of resources, and they provided the beginnings of a behavioral explanation for the phenomenon, as well as some statistical support for its existence. In a somewhat earlier theoretical exposition,

Farrell had called it lack of technical efficiency, and it was the latter name and approach that was adopted by the small number of relatively mainstream economists who were concerned with the phenomenon.

Most of the models used in economic and business analysis have not attempted to incorporate the type of phenomenon described by Farrell, Cyert and March and Leibenstein, not even when the firms characterized by considerable organizational slack, x-inefficiency or low technical efficiency obviously have been survivors. For many economists, the development of the theory of rational expectations, though aimed primarily at explaining macroeconomic phenomena, has increased the emphasis on optimization. To the extent that economists who taught and wrote in terms of optimization of a single objective such as profits also served as advisers to government and business, they sometimes made ad hoc modifications to allow for more than a single objective, or less-than-completely maximizing behavior or, more commonly, to allow for limited success in implementing optimization objectives. At times the modifications were only apparent, with indication that the incomplete implementation of optimization was attributable to institutional constraints. It was often assumed that the institutional constraints could be eliminated without excessive economic cost, given only the application of sufficient will power (i.e., without consideration of what sociopolitical costs might be involved).

The strongest argument for developing a behavioral approach to economic and business analysis has come from the findings of decision analysts in psychology and from the kindred field work carried out by those in economics and business administration. These experimental or laboratory exercises subject a group of individuals (usually about 20, but occasionally up to 200), to a series of questions about financial and economic choices in a highly controlled laboratory setting. The individuals involved are most often students but sometimes businesspeople or other experts in the areas that are dealt with.

While the initial work in experimental economics confirmed many traditional propositions of the discipline, an increasing number of studies during the last two decades have tended to undermine some fundamental assumptions of economics and finance. Some experiments reveal that even individuals who are confronted with options much simpler and sharper than most real-world alternatives can have difficulty in detecting dominant choices, for example. Other experiments confirm work in psychology showing that many individuals who are risk averse with respect to gains are risk takers when it comes to losses. That might not seem unreasonable, the switch being to avert losses, but the lack of consistency in the attitude toward risk clashes with economists' usual definition of rationality. Models that take such less-than-strictly-rational but recurring behavior into account can improve predictions of financial and economic behavior. Even more troubling than the turnabout in many individuals' attitudes toward risk is that it is often possible to express quite a few of the very same changes as either "gains" or losses. Stated more generally, many of the preferences we reveal when we make choices vary according to the way in which the alternatives are framed and the choices are actually elicited. This is rather troubling for the simple, straightforward explanation of preferences and values that economics and finance have been built on. The problem applies to the decision making of all economic agents—producers and investors as well as consumers.

This should not be entirely surprising, however, if we consider human experience in general. Most individuals react somewhat differently to the same information when it is expressed in one manner than in another, even when the informational content is identical. Our interest in putting the best light on what we have to say is one of the reasons why we pay much higher fees for certain lawyers than for others, and it is obviously a very important consideration in matters of the heart. How likely is it, then, that we turn off a switch, so to speak, and completely ignore this human tendency to react to the *way* in which something is presented when it comes to economic and financial matters (which, moreover, may well have a variety of social and political implications)? Nonetheless, that is the nature of many financial and economic models; they are constructed in a manner that might make it seem as if only the values of hard data were relevant. This may begin to explain why their predictions are not always borne out and why this new work in psychology is beginning to have an impact on such areas as finance and organizational behavior.

There are other matters of concern as well. Studies demonstrate that most individuals tend to put too much emphasis on alternatives that are certain, but the remarkable fact is that this extends even to the *appearance* of certainty, as in those cases in which, for example, only the second of a two-step procedure involves such an outcome. Thus, although the overall outcome is not at all certain and should not be preferred to an alternative choice with the same expected value, even an appearance of certainty is often treated as something approximating certainty.

Several other seemingly irrational but frequently observed reasoning processes were noted in the Introduction. A few more are noted at this point.

- Consider a hundred dollars that could have been earned but was not, say because of a forgotten appointment or a broken promise. Despite the fact that the latter hundred dollars has the same value—reflects the same adversity—as a hundred dollars of costs actually incurred, opportunities that have been lost but do not involve out-of-pocket expenses are seldom regarded as comparable to the same level of costs actually incurred, even by most of those who have listened carefully to the teachings of economics and finance, explaining how the two are equivalent.

- Suppose it were possible to save the same $10 to $20 in the purchase of a big ticket item or a small one, in both cases by incurring the same extra fifteen minutes to travel to a more distant store, what would consumers do? Many individuals claim that they would make the shift if it were for something like a low- to medium-priced calculator, but few of them indicate that they would do so if the item in question were a TV or a CD player. Their reasoning is that the relation of the financial gain to the price of the large purchase is too minor to matter. The experiments indicate that the two cases would be treated quite differently despite the fact that the marginal costs and benefits are identical.

- Evaluations of decision options are often based less on calculations involving the respective probabilities than on rules of thumb (heuristics), which are quick and easy to apply and usually lead to results in the right direction. This is so even though they involve biases and thus bring about results that differ, sometimes significantly, from the techniques provided by financial and economic analysis. Nonetheless, we don't always attempt to identify the biases or to improve the heuristics.

- The first two of the examples just given contradict the teachings of financial and economic rationality, and the last, though possibly involving a cost-benefit justification, requires further elaboration in terms of psychology. Moreover, all of these anomalies refer to decisions that might be made in a point of time. Additional concerns arise when one considers decisions, the costs and benefits of which take place over the course of time. For example, many consumers purchase lower priced but more energy-using, and ultimately more expensive, durable goods than others. They pay as much as several times as large an amount as the interest on a consumer loan that would have enabled them to purchase the more energy efficient models, and an even greater multiple of the amount that many of them are earning on the same amount of money in a savings account during the same period of time. Second, in experiments at least, the interest rates that people insist on for delayed payments differ according to whether the sums of money involved are large or small. In addition, respondents in experiments indicate that the percentage adjustment of outstanding financial transactions that would be adequate to compensate them for a delay in fulfilling those obligations varies greatly according to whether what is involved is a gain or a loss. All of these results, which are surprising from the point of view of economics and finance, can be explained and predicted, with the help of the findings from psychology.

Learning

Economists, those in the other social sciences and management analysts all give learning considerable significance in explaining improved performance. The importance of the phenomenon is without question, but what constitutes an efficient process of learning? Economics is the discipline that deals with efficiency but has surprisingly little of a definitive nature to offer on this point, even after many recent laboratory experiments and computer exercises. Management experts offer advice to enterprises and governments derived in part from the empirical analyses of sociologists and psychologists, and in part from their own observations and experiences. The findings of psychologists, sociologists and management experts are not entirely consistent, but they represent the most serious efforts to date to pinpoint what is actually involved in the process of learning. At this stage, it seems that the development of useful guidelines will require a good deal more careful observation and inductive analysis based on that, with perhaps almost as much attention to unsuccessful as to successful cases of learning. A summary of some of the theories and empirical studies on learning is presented in Part II.

EXPECTATIONS AND EXPECTED PROFITS

Optimization techniques and analyses based on hard data from the past (with some extrapolation or modification of those data) constitute the main body of the economic and financial tool kit. The data deal largely with inputs and outputs, exports and imports, interest rates and financial flows, and the like. Generally, only the most anecdotal information is available concerning the underlying reasoning that led to the decisions reflected in the hard data or to the expectations that served as the starting point in the reasoning process or that reflected the product of the reasoning process.

Expectations of events and of profits are crucial to the analysis of financial and economic processes. Successful production and investment decisions are not likely to be guided by the results of the past, except insofar as they contribute to expectations about the future that, moreover, are borne out. Even so, only in the last few decades has the analysis of expectations received major attention. Economists have focused on whether or not expectations are rational—in some normative, optimizing sense—and on whether the data from the past confirm such a rationality of expectations in practice. Impressive theoretical constructs in favor of a rational expectations approach have been presented, and these have helped to explain the limitations of some macroeconomic theories dependent on assumptions that ignored the possibilities of learning, and thus predicted less well, the longer the period involved.[12] Nonetheless, the empirical analysis of the so-called rational expectations hypothesis, as an explanation of what actually has taken place, is quite mixed. The debate over rational expectations—or the circumstances in which rational expectations can be expected to prevail—may not be resolved until we understand how people, especially those who are successful, form their expectations and make their estimates of expected profits.

Psychology offers more than a single approach to expectations. The closest to a prevailing view states that people may base expectations (1) on a simple extrapolation from the past, (2) on an analysis of evidence from the past that reflects learning, (3) on an analysis of current information alone, or (4) on an analysis that each of the former can play a role in explaining expectations, with the relative weight of the three factors varying from situation to situation. The last certainly has a ring of common sense about it and contrasts with the approach that some psychologists attribute to alternative economic theories, which are alleged to base their analyses on only one of the factors to the exclusion of the others. Unfortunately, the presumably prevailing view of psychology just summarized provides only limited, qualitative guidance on when to apply any given weight to each of the three factors.

That eclectic contribution and the inconclusive verification of rational expectations by economists (along with the inclination of some economists to slip from one theoretical explanation to another) might lead to the conclusion that it probably would be useful for individuals with some knowledge of what both disciplines have been saying about expectations to behave like anthropologists.

They should perhaps watch, listen to, and question decision makers to detect what people claim their expectations to be and how they came to take the forms that they have. Economists sometimes develop models that improve the explanation of investment or other business decisions in the recent past or the prediction of such decisions in the near future. But even when such models capture the essence of *what* was done, often they do not reflect enough of the reasoning process employed, beginning with the way in which expectations were determined, to predict well beyond the short run or in a different environment characterized by different circumstances. In sum, expectations about profits are a key consideration in economic and financial decisions, but our efforts to explain profit expectations have focused on what is rational or at least seems intuitively reasonable; if that is not exactly the way in which even the most successful always determine their expectations about profits, then something important is missing from our guidelines for decision making. (This is all the more so if there is not always a clear definition of what is rational—or reasonable—as might sometimes be the case.)

GUIDELINES FOR FINANCIAL AND ECONOMIC DECISION MAKING

Most financial and economic decisions have multidisciplinary impacts. In some cases, the impacts are sufficiently clear and substantial that we have to find a way to allow for tradeoffs when one impact is at the expense of another (or alternative special consideration where the financial and economic impacts reinforce the others) if we are to make decisions that truly improve social welfare and that do so to a greater degree than would other decisions. As important as this consideration is, we are not in a good position to say much about how to go about determining these tradeoffs, though, as a minimum, we should periodically ask ourselves if our decisions are taking such noneconomic objectives into account.

Consider, however, the decisions that are dominantly financial and economic, particularly business decisions. Businesses are confronted with several categories of decisions. There are numerous ongoing routine matters that have to be determined almost immediately; more consequential but still secondary considerations, as well as investment decisions can be given more time; and complicated restructuring decisions involve ongoing actions over possibly a long period of time. Common general principles for handling these problems have been formulated. Basically, they state that actions should be taken only if the gains at the margin are at least equal to the costs, and if there is more than a single option, they emphasize that the one selected should offer the highest gains relative to costs. The problem, of course, is making that principle operational. Sophisticated techniques for doing so may demand too much data or time; they may require the involvement of more outsiders than is desired; or they may not be appropriate given the nature of the uncertainties involved. More general equilibrium approaches that consider the effect of everything on everything else, or at least, the impacts of the most important variables on each other, require models of behavioral interrelationships that are simply beyond our current knowledge and abilities according to many experts in that field. Comparisons of the initial results of the North American Free Trade Association (NAFTA) with the projections of general equilibrium analyses seem to confirm that.

In order to deal with major investments and other long-term decisions, the decision maker should be aware of the optimization techniques that economics and finance have developed. Some of these techniques may be directly applicable to the problems at hand. Modifications will be required in other cases; some are perhaps of a technical character, whereas others conceivably seek to introduce differences in the responses assumed on the part of suppliers or competitors or even those within the firm. Even in the case of major investments and particularly in the case of major restructuring, some second-best techniques may be required. Some such techniques may be formal and precise, others may be more informal. As for more routine matters (or even for major decisions that must be resolved quickly), use of rules of thumb will usually be required as surrogates for precise calculation.

The first implication of all this is that it is not enough to know the procedures for optimization or to hire a consultant who does. It is necessary to learn something about the second best approaches that are available, in particular those that successful enterprises use but also those used by less successful enterprises, and it is necessary to know why the potential promise of some of the less successful enterprises was not realized. Even in the case of the approaches employed by the survivors, it is important to learn the advantages and disadvantages of their approaches or the requirements for them to work reasonably well. It is also important to know the general direction of their biases from an "optimal" solution and the situations in which they function best and worst. Simon adds, "Standard decision theory has absolutely nothing to say about the search for alternatives—the whole process of designing possible courses of action—but this is in fact the most important part of the decision process. . . . Businesses spend much more time inventing courses of action than in choosing between them—and rightly so. There is no operational theory of optimization that deals with this process."[13]

What, then, can be said of the second-best approaches to problem solving?

First, as Simon implies, we need to develop guidelines that will help in the search for alternatives. At the very least, we need to be explicit about the search processes that are followed so that we can begin to document and deal with the biases that may be involved.

Second, in deciding between alternatives, we can consider algorithms and other sophisticated techniques to improve performance, though these are time- and resource-consuming to develop and often have large informational requirements. Such techniques, many of which have been developed by economists who advocate maximization, only promise local maxima—that is, in a sense, they are tools for satisficing.

The most common second best approach to problem solving has been the use of rules of thumb, often referred to as judgmental heuristics. (These are defined in Chapter 4, and discussed more fully in Appendix A.) Standard operating procedures fall under this heading. Some rules of thumb or heuristics are simple, and others are more complex. (In reality, many of the algorithms might be considered as more formal rules of thumb or heuristics.) Rules of thumb tend to be modified over time, though not all modifications may reflect improvements. Even when they do, the end results are not always better if the means of implementation are not adequate for the revised rules of thumb. The serious study of heuristics is a matter of only the last decade or two, but we are beginning to sense that there are many variants of the decision heuristics that psychologists and their colleagues in economics and business administration first enunciated (such as representativeness, availability and anchoring). These heuristics enable decision makers to move in the right direction, though with biases; biases are usually identifiable, thereby providing an opportunity to correct for extremes. Laboratory experiments and often more anecdotal evidence from field work have enabled us to learn more about the nature of those biases. What has become clear is that more efficient problem solving requires an awareness of these heuristics and their biases, as well as of optimization techniques, the latter of which have received the overwhelming amount of attention from researchers and management consultants. After all, heuristics are sometimes the best problem-solving techniques available; even where they are not, they are techniques in very common usage, the consequences of which we should take into account.

BEHAVIORAL FINANCE

Until less than a generation ago, many analysts (and even more investors) maintained that psychological factors were at least as important as financial and economic factors in explaining stock market fluctuations. Some of the most respected authorities on investment insisted that winners in the stock market could be selected by concentrating on what they characterized as enterprise fundamentals. In effect, they were maintaining that markets might reflect psychological or other factors at a given moment of time, and thus present the opportunity for successful selection by those who recognized that market prices did not necessarily reflect fundamental values at all times.

As greater rigor was brought to financial analysis and the economic analysis of finance in the 1960s and the 1970s, most of the experts in this area ultimately concluded that financial markets were highly efficient; this impression continued into the 1980s despite increasing evidence to the contrary.[14] It was being maintained, as one of the implications of that market efficiency, that it was not possible to predict future stock prices on the basis of present or past prices, or on the basis of any information from the present or the past. If there were momentary deviations of stock prices from their fundamental values, arbitrageurs would certainly bring about the indicated corrections.

Although a number of articles in the late 1970s and early 1980s paved the way, the revolution in finance probably dates to the 1985 Presidential Address to the American Finance Association by the late Fisher Black, once a Professor of Finance and at that time a partner in a leading Wall Street firm. Black insisted that many financial transactions were based on "noise," not news—on rumors, emotional factors, and a variety of considerations that did not amount to verifiable, hard data and the rational analysis of that data. He cited examples, as well as supporting evidence from financial analysts and financial economists, and he pointed to a number of startling implications. Note that this was at a time when individual investors in the financial markets were being replaced to an increasing extent by institutions, which were in a much better position to take advantage of increasingly complicated mathematical models and increasingly sophisticated computer analyses. Now it was not a disgruntled crackpot (or someone who was strictly an academic theoretician), but one of the most respected financial analysts was proclaiming that there was no reason to presume that financial markets were necessarily efficient, and thus, that the prices that prevailed in those markets reflected fundamental values. Black, the co-author of the most famous model for optimizing decisions in the short-term options market, and others who built on his work, maintained that the presence of noise undermined the ability of arbitrage to function effectively in correcting prices in all but markets of the shortest duration.

This triggered a further reexamination of what had been termed the efficient market hypothesis, and the findings that followed completely undermined what economists called the strong form of that hypothesis.[15] It was shown, for example, that the volatility of leading financial markets greatly exceeded what could be expected from financial and economic factors alone, and that there seemed to be little correlation between political upheaval that might be expected to lead to financial and economic changes, and the reaction of the markets to those political changes. Some major movements in the stock markets seemed to be virtually independent of such presumably rational considerations, while a number of economic trends and political events that might be expected to lead to significant economic and financial changes hardly caused a ripple in the markets. However, to say that the markets could not be well explained by economic and financial considerations alone is not to say that the changes could not be explained.

Allowing for overreactions to good (and bad) news, a common phenomenon described in part by psychologists as a failure to allow for reversion to the mean, studies began to show that it was possible to say something about future prices or at least about the relative profitability of groups of stocks defined by past performance as "winners" and "losers." In part, it was a demonstration that human reasoning involved more than financial and economic models allowed for—which many social scientists, philosophers and socially oriented economists had long maintained (and which might explain other matters even more than these). What was being discovered in the marketplace reflected irrationalities that psychology had been studying and that could be predicted. Some of those who had been examining broad financial and macroeconomic markets began to ask whether the decision-making results discovered in the laboratory experiments of economics and psychology might not help explain the surprising findings that they were uncovering. In the process, there was an outpouring of new work on contrarian investing and an expansion of applications in the financial markets. (The first important analyses of contrarian investment, incorporating the emerging findings of some of the psychologists referred to in this book, were published by the investment manager, David Dreman, as early as 1977 and 1979.)

These and similar phenomena appeared to extend to a broad range of markets. Anomalous behavior was documented in corporate and consumer decision making and in the presumably more competitive international as well as in domestic financial markets. Explanations were offered that could be characterized as rational only if one were to define rationality in a broader sense than that common to the prevailing models of economics and finance.

REFLECTIONS, IF NOT QUITE CONCLUSIONS

Recent work in behavioral economics and behavioral finance has uncovered much that seems to contradict traditional analyses, indeed, some fundamental precepts of both fields. There are qualifications, however. First, some behavioral findings are consistent with mainstream economics and finance. In fact, much theoretical work searches for rationality in what may be only apparently anomalous or paradoxical behavior. Second, where there are unquestionably anomalous results, some may not be so common or so important as to undermine the usefulness of the tools and techniques of the traditional, optimizing approach. Third, even where serious problems with economics and finance have been found—where the traditional theory strays too far from what is done by the most successful—it must be acknowledged that we have only the beginnings of a new paradigm to replace the old. (Moreover, some modifications of financial and economic theory would eliminate some of the earlier findings from the anomalous category.) Finally, many behavioral analysts believe that behavioral approaches will modify and complement, but not fundamentally alter, the traditional logic of financial and economic analysis. They seek recognition that normative models do not provide an adequate basis for describing actual decision-making behavior, and aim to develop models that will accomplish that.

As an indication of the possible tendency toward accommodation between behavioral and traditional approaches to financial and economic analysis, consider that although we now know that many financial markets are not efficient in a strict sense, that limitation seems to hold primarily for an "intermediate" time frame. In short run markets such as the 90-day options markets, arbitrage works well enough so that the markets function much as the models of rationality assume. While there is much that occurs over the course of time in markets that last for longer time periods that conflicts with what has been termed economic and financial rationality, the tendency is to correct the most serious irrationalities. Moreover, although psychology helps explain why (and where) economic rationality does not always prevail, fundamental values tend to prevail eventually, and what is overpriced tends finally to decline—though, alas, some of what is efficient but underpriced is driven from the marketplace.

Simon has acknowledged that the theory of rational decision making, about which he has serious reservations, nonetheless reflects improvements over what had existed previously and that many of those improvements were made in recognition of real world situations of considerable complexity. In addition, as noted elsewhere in this book, recent studies reflecting the rigor of traditional analytical methods have reduced some of the lack of realism of earlier mainstream models. Furthermore, when asked to tackle practical problems, many good orthodox economists show that they do not feel bound by the confines of the theory that they teach and see as the foundations of their discipline (much of which is greatly simplified for presentation at introductory levels). Still, in modifying their models and introducing assumptions about economic behavior or in allowing for differences in policy implementation that do not follow from traditional theory, the tendency is to incorporate information that they *happen* to have observed and that strikes them as appropriate to a given situation, or findings from another social science that they just *happen* to be aware of. These modifications are a type of behavioral economics, but they are even more ad hoc than what behaviorally oriented economists would hope to promote because they take account of a very small part of what is emerging from the behavioral social sciences. Moreover, the ad hoc modification of traditional models by talented and imaginative orthodox economists may lead less capable individuals to attempt the same "exceptions" with probably less favorable results. Behavioral economics and behavioral finance represents a more systematic effort to improve upon what the better orthodox economists already do from time to time, and to provide guidelines for how to go about doing it.

The significance of all this for policy recommendations seems great, at both the micro- and macroeconomic levels. As recently as 1994, few prominent economists were talking about this,[16] but a change finally seems to be underway.

NOTES

1. For a consideration of rationality in mainstream economic theory, see Part II, especially the first note to Chapter 2.

2. Akerlof 1983, 54, 62.

3. Akerlof 1991, 1, 6, 7, 17.

4. A recent review of earlier efforts to draw on psychology for the behavioral assumptions of economics notes that that discipline has become a focus of interest once

again, but the review calls for more attention to complex institutional shortcomings, social phenomena and the findings of sociology (Lewin 1996, 1293–1323, esp. 1319–20). See also Radner 1996.

5. What I characterize as coping is essentially what Herbert Simon meant by the term *satisficing* insofar as satisficing related only to the difficulties of maximizing profits (not to any doubts as to whether businesspeople really sought to do well in strictly financial terms). The conclusion that the objective might not be viewed as optimization also comes from Roy Radner. He states that the complexity of real-world decisions "raises serious problems for the concept of rational choice as we have presented it in terms of *optimizing behavior*. A mode of behavior that is not even *feasible* can hardly qualify as *rational*." See McGuire and Radner 1986, 17. Indeed, in chapter 9 of the same collection of articles, Radner observes that there is no generally accepted criterion of optimality—that the principal concern is viability. See Radner 1996 as well.

6. *Washington Post*, January 18, 1996, D11.

7. A further complication in this case is that many economists, among them the chairman of the Federal Reserve Board and the key staff members, believe that changes in monetary phenomena (the principal realm of concern of the FED) cannot influence the level of employment in the long run.

8. Herbert Simon maintains that it is debatable whether those who attempt to optimize have the best chance of doing so. "In Darwinian theory today it is generally acknowledged that the fitness terrain is very rough, with scads of local maxima. Few population evolutionists claim any more that anything is being maximized—rather that organisms that climb faster will likely survive better. But there is also much emphasis in contemporary Darwinian theory on the rapid changes in the environment that play a large role in determining who is going to survive." He adds, "Ability to move rapidly in new directions may be much more important to survival than optimization, even if that were feasible (which it almost never is). And heuristics [simple rules of thumb, see discussion in Part II]—especially heuristics that identify new problems and changes in the environment at an early point—may be what is required for rapid adaptation to change" (Simon, personal communication, February 10, 1997).

9. In fact, reconsideration of what exactly constitutes economic rationality is actively underway. See Arrow et al. 1996.

10. However, Gary Becker states: "The economist's normal approach to analyzing consumption and leisure choices assumes that individuals maximize utility with preferences that depend at any moment only on the goods and services they consume at that time. These preferences are assumed to be independent of both past and future consumption, and of the behavior of everyone else. The approach has proved to be a valuable simplification for addressing many economic questions, but a large number of choices in all societies depend very much on past experiences and social forces" (Becker 1996, 3–4). He goes on to extend the definition of individual preferences "to include personal habits and addictions, peer pressure, parental influences on the tastes of children, advertising, love and sympathy, and other neglected behavior." Such a list of other factors greatly exceeds what was common among mainstream economists for many years, but Becker adds that the resulting utility function is stable over time precisely because it includes measures of past experiences and social forces. He concludes that preferences both influence economic outcomes and are in turn influenced by the economy (Becker 1996, 18). This builds on the much-cited and highly controversial work by Stigler and Becker (1977).

11. McCloskey and Klamer 1995.

12. Arrow claims, however, that virtually every practical theory of macroeconomics is based partially on hypotheses other than rationality (see Zey 1992, Preface). Plott cites a number of irrationality assumptions in respected models of traditional microeconomic theory, some of which have proven useful in predicting decision outcomes. (See Arrow et al. 1996, comments to chapter 9.)

13. See note 8.

14. For contrary empirical findings, see Modigliani and Cohn 1979, which is referred to in Part II. The theoretical arguments were developed in a series of papers by Grossman and Stiglitz in the first half of the 1970s, culminating in Grossman and Stiglitz 1976, which showed that market prices never reflect all of the information possessed by informed individuals; that is, markets can never be informationally complete.

15. The notion of completely efficient markets had already been substantially undermined by Grossman and Stiglitz 1976.

16. For a complaint along these lines, see Knetsch 1995.

Part II

Economic and Financial Decision Making: A Behavioral Approach

Chapter 2

Behavioral Considerations

The basic assumption of most financial and economic models is that producers, investors and consumers seek to do as well as possible in financial and economic terms. This is sometimes qualified by brief reference to moral and other cultural constraints, but these constraints are not viewed as interfering with financial or economic maximization, except under highly unusual circumstances. Therefore, they are rarely mentioned in the traditional expositions of economics and finance. Even the recent addition of courses on business ethics has not altered the tool kit of techniques that is taught in most management training programs and recommended by consultants. Moreover, when the special ethical or cultural qualifications do come into play, it is usually insisted that it is still maximization that is sought, though maximization subject to the constraints indicated.

Leading authorities in both fields assume that the producers, and others who succeed—the survivors—possess such maximizing objectives and respond to incentives and risks in what the two disciplines regard as a rational manner.[1] They maintain that businesspeople in particular seek to optimize—to maximize the expected present value of future profits—and the more successful among them are those who come closest to doing so, some perhaps achieving full maximization at times as a consequence of learning and successful adaptation. Certainly, real-world experiences reveal that those who do not aim for a high rate of return and who do not seek profits in an energetic manner do not usually fare very well. Yet there is increasing recognition, quite aside from the matter of objectives, that the capacity to *implement* goals such as maximization often falls short of what is assumed. Some prominent mainstream economists concede that their models have not described what successful producers, investors and consumers actually do, to nearly the degree that they had expected.[2]

Perhaps the inclination of many economists and financial analysts to continue to use models that presume high degrees of rationality reflects what has been termed a conservative, status quo bias rather than an exercise in rational behavior on the part of the model builders.[3] Other considerations also may be involved, however, and these should be taken into account. Many behaviorally oriented economists and financial analysts believe that traditional, neoclassical teachings provide a useful framework and starting point.

The behavioral group seeks to *supplement* the traditional, normative models with others that replace optimization assumptions with the kind of behavioral assumptions that reflect the quasi-rationality of the "best practice" employed by survivors, and to determine the direction and the degree of bias from optimization involved in the use of such often successful, but not fully rational behavior. Second, behavioral economists and financial analysts hope to provide evidence that will help management experts determine better ways to reduce the gap between the near rationality of best practice and the still more approximate rules of thumb employed by most economic agents in many transactions. Third, some of the behavioral group also hope that their studies will help reduce the margin between the sophisticated best practice of survivors and full optimization (all the while recognizing that in most cases it will never be possible, or cost-efficient, to close that gap completely).

The Economist, a few investor publications, the *Wall Street Journal* and several general news magazines have run articles about behavioral economics and behavioral finance, and an increasing number have found their way into the leading professional journals. In addition, the first chapter of a major new graduate text in microeconomic theory takes note of several important elements of the behavioral agenda. Still, few texts in intermediate economic analysis, and none at the introductory level that this author is aware of, give attention to the possible implications of the behavioral assumptions that are being documented. Moreover, very few of the public discussions of economic policy do so—not those, for example, of the 1996 U.S. Presidential Election Campaign debate about tax reduction stimuli, nor those of a prominent development economist writing on the role of government in promoting economic growth in developing countries, and maintaining that neither of the two leading analyses alternatives are really adequate. On the other hand, changes are underway. Lawrence Summers, who contributed to the research in behavioral finance discussed in Chapter 7, has, in his position as U.S. Deputy Secretary of the Treasury, offered public testimony citing psychological factors as well as traditional economic reasoning for supporting several policy recommendations.

Indeed, a number of exceptions to the more general neglect can be observed in the area of finance, where behavioral ideas have become a major topic of academic research and have also contributed to several approaches of contrarian investing. An indication that it may be important to develop policy models that incorporate empirically grounded psychological findings into financial and economic models is suggested by the behavior of U.S. interest rates in 1994. Early in that year, analyses in the financial press predicted that a rise in short-term interest rates would have a stabilizing effect on long-term interest rates and might even lead to their decline as the financial community came to recognize that any excess demand for goods and services at that time would be repressed and the likelihood of inflation would be reduced. It was plausible enough, so it might have seemed, though it is not clear how many in the Federal Reserve System reasoned in that way. In fact, however, the Fed's increases in short-term interest rates in 1994 led to increases of rates in the long-term markets as well after all but one of its interventions that year. This suggests that other-than-strictly-financial factors were at work.

Another, not entirely unrelated incident also seems to cry out for the application of behavioral economics and behavioral finance. Leading experts in international economics such as Rudiger Dornbusch estimated that Mexico's peso was overvalued by 15, 20, perhaps 25 percent in late 1994, but the manner in which the devaluation was handled (and perhaps other factors) led to concerns that brought dramatic fluctuations and a devaluation that soon reached 50 percent. That was far in excess of all estimates of what had been required. Although it facilitated very large increases in the exports of a handful of enterprises with quality products that did not require export financing from the Mexican banking system, it also triggered much sharper declines in real income than had been anticipated. The interest rate fluctuated as much as 25 percent from one day to the next (real interest rates ranging between 25 and 50 percent). This led to an acceleration of unemployment and a severe economic recession from which the country has been much slower to recover than economists had predicted. This was the case despite the rapid and marked improvement of the balance-of-payments position and the recovery of financial markets.

The shifting estimation of financial and economic analysis may help explain the new interest in a behavioral approach. In the 1960s, professional analysts and the public in general had an appreciable confidence in the ever-more-rigorous techniques being applied in financial and economic analysis. This was certainly true with respect to the ability to rely on macroeconomic tools to control inflation and recession, which was reflected not only in the support of most professional economists, but also among an increasing number of policy-minded individuals, including perhaps even such unlikely figures as then President Richard Nixon, who declared, "We are all Keynesians now." (He made this statement just as real-world evidence and new theoretical studies were casting new doubts on the Keynesian approach.)

As for the economic analysis of the firm, the consumer and the investor, affirmation of the economists' approach came primarily from the economists themselves. It was also indirectly validated by the business community, which was hiring more economists than ever before. Their long debate as to whether businesspeople maximized profits seemed to be drawing to a close with the verdict that whether or not businesspeople in general maximized, survivors did.

Finally, whatever deficiencies or delays there might be in optimization on the part of individuals, one could always expect the markets to ensure that the best alternatives triumphed. In the case of financial markets in particular, several of the leading authorities held that given the continuing flow of information and the presence of arbitrage, market efficiency would prevail. A byproduct of this line of thinking was the conclusion that the prevailing prices of equities represented the best estimate of the fundamental values of stocks at any given time. Prevailing and past prices of equities could not be used to predict future prices. Whether or not the public at large really accepted the efficient market hypothesis, most people agreed that stock market prices were not predictable. Even so, for one reason or another, many investors purchased advisory services that predicted stock prices, some of which even advised on market timing. Most who purchased mutual funds diversified by choosing funds that employed the services of stock selectors rather than by buying funds based on leading stock market indexes. They did so even though the indexes outperformed the great majority of funds based on more expensive individual selection.

All this seems inconsistent with the assumption that people—investors in particular—are rational and, for the most part, risk averse. The sharp rise in long-term interest rates in early 1994 also does not appear to reflect a response to solely economic and financial phenomena. Nor does the extent of market reactions to the initial, December 1994 devaluation in Mexico. (Nor, it would seem, can economic and financial factors alone explain the extent of market reactions to the East Asian crises of 1997–98.) Consider half a dozen additional anomalies:

• More than ever before, those who went into business in the United States and those already in business who attended executive training programs were being taught about the concept of maximization and use of optimization techniques. They were aided in their evaluation tasks by more computer power than existed in the rest of the world, and they should have been pressured to use their capabilities more than before because of the greater access of women and minorities to business leadership. Nonetheless, much of U.S. business seemed to focus on short- rather than long-run maximization, and the country was losing its comparative advantage in an increasing number of industries. (That loss might be explained in part by the fact that Europe was just then regaining its prewar economic strength, and the Far East was first gaining access to much that was associated with industrialization, but that only makes the apparent focus on short-term maximization even more difficult to understand.)

• Increasing evidence of a "Winner's Curse" had been turning up: those who won at auctions or in hostile takeover bids seemed to pay more than any reasonable estimate of the true value of the assets they purchased.

• Many investors continued to reveal a preference for the stocks of enterprises that paid high dividends, in comparison with the shares of companies that reinvested more of their profits and registered capital gains sufficient to provide a comparable rate of total returns—and a higher rate of return after taxes. (This tendency weakened during the stock market boom of 1995 through October 1997, as capital gains increased dramatically and dividend rates declined sharply.)

• Even though it is not rational to take account of past expenditures when we are making decisions about the future, many people do so in decisions ranging from minor ones about the use of leisure time to larger and presumably much more important matters. (Minor decisions include Robert Frank's example of reticence to select an outdoor tennis court on an unexpectedly pleasant winter day because an indoor facility already had been paid for; more important ones include the inclination to continue with plans for an increasingly more dubious business expansion or the disinclination to sell stocks that have declined after having lost their initial luster.)

• Many people leave comparable tips at restaurants they have never been to before and to which they do not expect to return as at those where they dine frequently and from which they seek continued good service.

• Most people do not engage in a rational search for information, one that is guided by the magnitude of what is at stake. Reflecting the demand for information from those making purchase decisions, it is easy and inexpensive to obtain up to 100 pages of detailed information about the computer alternatives in the $1,500 to $3,000 range. Somewhat less information is available to orient the purchase of an automobile that may cost $15,000 to $50,000. And much less objective information is available or is generally sought for the purchase of a house that may cost 50 to 200 times as much as the computer. Computer technology has been changing much more rapidly than that of the automobile or the housing market, and this would explain the need for considerable information. Yet a great deal of evidence suggests that decisions in the automobile and housing markets have been so far from optimal that one might have expected a much greater increase in information search efforts, particularly given the infrequency of these purchases.

• Many individuals living in areas threatened by floods did not purchase the highly subsidized flood insurance that the U.S. government sold during the 1960s and 1970s, and the disaster relief programs that were offered after floods did not provide compensation that was sufficient (or timely enough) to explain the general lack of interest in that insurance. Even after these findings were disseminated in a wide range of publications during the last 20 years (and presumably the findings were summarized in some of the newspapers in areas threatened periodically by floods), subsequent inundations, such as those of March 1997, revealed that most of the people living in the endangered areas still had not taken out appropriate insurance (though, admittedly, the insurance was no longer so subsidized). Even risk averters seem to have difficulty in recognizing the benefits of risk management in certain situations; perhaps those living in flood risk areas were risk averters in many respects but not in others (an irrational inconsistency).

• The Money Illusion, the failure to recognize the difference between nominal and real values, or the tendency to continue to attach some importance to nominal values even though real ones are recognized, is common among most decision makers and remains persistent. It is not entirely eliminated even after substantial learning.[4]

What explains such phenomena, and what are the implications for formulating good policies for enterprises and for the public arena, as well as for preparing guidelines for consumer well-being? The answers to these questions are being influenced by new types of inductive studies in economics and by the findings from the other social sciences.

Observations and reflections dating back to the 1930s by an economist teaching in a law school stimulated a large number of analyses, though only after a lag of nearly four decades. Ronald Coase's work showed that more was needed to produce goods and services than the labor, capital and natural resources that entered into the diagrams and equations reflecting the long-standing production function analysis of economists. Because of the incomplete nature of most contracts—in part, their necessarily incomplete nature, given the impossibility of foreseeing all possible contingencies—a number of transaction costs also had to be considered in order to explain production processes. Among the most important of these transaction costs that Coase cited were those for legal services and employee supervision. This has become a major area of inquiry and has shifted the focus of analysis somewhat. Authorities such as Oliver Williamson now envision the business enterprise as a mechanism of governance and management as much as one of production. An understanding of transaction costs and underlying phenomena such as asset specificity and opportunism helped explain how firms might be able to achieve internally some of the functions ordinarily expected of markets and in some cases with greater efficiency. This has led to a greater justification of vertical mergers and to more concern with the phenomenon of coordination within enterprises. Antitrust law had been thwarting vertical mergers, whereas economics had long been faulted for ignoring coordination within enterprises. Studies in the last three years may have reduced the most extensive claims for transactions cost analysis, but the essential insights of this inductively spawned contribution to the theory of the firm remain.[5] The concept certainly lends itself to behavioral elaborations, even though they have not yet been those most emphasized.

Other economists such as Mancur Olson, Douglas North and many in the emerging area of law and economics have reflected on the experience of individuals, groups, and nations over relatively long periods of time and have helped explain how the legal and other institutions play an important role in determining the character of economic growth. For these writers, the word *institutions* refers not to associations and entities, but to the formal rules and informal constraints (the conventions and understandings) that prevail in a society, as well as to the terms by which the societies' activities are carried out. Institutions are seen as altering transaction costs and agency relationships, thus explaining the at-times-differing behavior of the same economic agents in different communities. This constitutes an important addition to economic analysis, but it has been carried out within a neoclassical maximizing framework. No consideration has been given to whether the findings of psychology and the other social sciences might help explain some of the differences in the institutional evolution. Might some formulation of the New Institutional Economics conclude not only that institutional arrangements affect economic behavior, but that they do so in part because of changes in how preferences are reflected, and also because of changes in the capacity for implementing objectives that result from those altered institutional arrangements? If so, such a revised neoclassical presentation would approach more closely the emerging behavioral economics based on the findings of cognitive psychology outlined in this book. The possibility of a rapprochement of the two is raised by a recent discussion of coordination within enterprises in an avowedly neoclassical text (Milgrom and Roberts 1992, 115–16). This work allows for a solution that has more in common with satisficing than optimizing, despite its initial statement that the analysis employed is that of maximizing, rational self-interest, neoclassical economics.

In the last two decades, attempts have also been made to modify the analysis of producer, consumer and investor behavior of a different character. These attempts have come not only from new challenges to the maximization assumption from the various social sciences and philosophy, but also from an increased awareness of the difficulties of implementing those or other objectives. The new doubts have arisen in part from the insightful applications of political science and political sociology, such as are found in the work of Albert O. Hirschman and more recently in the work of a larger number of economists writing on development, perhaps most notably, Dani Rodrik. These works, together with studies at the border of economics and political science by economists such as Charles Lindblom (beginning with his ''incrementalist'' characterization of government policy implementation), have had a major impact on policy analysis. Yet it is perhaps the recent micro work of the decision sciences, particularly the psychologists, that has most ably succeeded in leading to the incorporation of behavioral assumptions from psychology into economic models. These studies have extended arguments first expounded by the economist/psychologist/computer scientist Herbert Simon in the mid-1950s. Moreover, the psychologists have not simply waited for the economists to take up their new gospel. Rather, they have entered directly into the world of the professional economic journals, sometimes on their own and sometimes jointly with economists. They have produced empirical findings that challenge basic axioms that underlie the longheralded and highly touted rationality of economic and financial decision making. While relatively few articles of a behavioral character appeared in the leading economic journals for many years, *Econometrica*, the *Quarterly Journal of Economics* and the *American Economic Review* have played major roles in transmitting the breakthrough findings of the new inductively based challenges to traditional theory. The *Journal of Economic Perspectives* has been very important in this effort since its inception in the late 1980s.

NOTES

1. Perhaps the first to adopt the position of survivor rationality was George Stigler.
2. See, for example, the comments of Modigliani noted in Chapter 7, in the section ''Do Financial Markets Overreact?''
3. Samuelson and Zeckhauser 1988.
4. Shafir, Diamond and Tversky 1997.
5. For the original 1937 article by Coase, three later papers of his, and contributions by Williamson and half a dozen others, see Williamson and Winter 1991.

Chapter 3

What Do Individuals and Enterprises Seek? The Objective(s) Underlying Economic and Financial Decisions

THE OBJECTIVES ACCORDING TO ECONOMISTS AND FINANCIAL ANALYSTS

In most traditional economic and financial decision-making analysis, individuals and enterprises are assumed to be rational; that is, they are consistent. That consistency is applied to an effort to advance material or financial well-being to the extent possible. Thus, it is generally assumed that individuals and enterprises seek to optimize—to maximize over the long run.[1] There may be constraints, of course, in which case the objective is to maximize subject to those constraints. To the degree that not only known, well-defined risks, but uncertainty is present, calculation of what is involved in maximization presents problems, but it is assumed that as rational beings or entities, they are able to achieve something approximating maximization.

Although the most common formulations of economists and financial analysts consider risk in terms of variation from a mean value, there may be a problem with that approach. Most individuals and enterprises only regard downside risk as something to be concerned with; that seems reasonable, and efforts have been made to reformulate the models of rationality in those terms. Moreover, some authors insist that risk is multidimensional and involves the downside with respect to factors such as market share and reputation as well as profits and income. A survey of portfolio managers and relatively high-income individuals by one financial analyst concluded that investment risk is a function of (1) the potential for a large loss, (2) the potential for a below-target return, (3) the feeling of control (basically, control of the ability to limit loss), and (4) the perceived level of knowledge.[2] The survey did not attempt to ascertain whether the individuals' actual investment behavior was consistent with these factors, however, and the definitions of the categories may not be precise enough to permit adequate verification. Still, some economists as well as financial analysts are moving away from the traditional definition of risk as variance. That is part of what is behind the disagreement between Thaler and De Bondt and their critics that is considered in Chapter 7.

Most analyses that invoke a behavioral assumption of maximization do not bother to defend the assumption, but empirical findings on the point are available. Some reflect econometric studies of the effects of changes in incentives. A smaller, though rapidly expanding, number of analyses draw on experimental economics; many of these analyses support a maximizing tendency, at least with repeated experiments, but some are cautious about the degree to which such conclusions would extend to natural economic settings (Camerer 1990). Some of the findings of experimental economics do not support maximization. Critics have reacted by insisting that not all of the economic agents involved would be survivors, that the laboratory situations were improperly specified, that the periods covered were too short to reflect the market forces that the experiments sought to mimic, or that the incentives involved were not large enough to predict the way even the same individuals would react in real life. A limited amount of applied work in economics introduces other objectives, drawing on the analyst's judgment about particular circumstances or on findings from other social sciences, as, for example, in the use of sociology by a number of labor economists. The use of such often less-than-fully-maximizing objectives is the exception, however. Indeed, some prominent labor economists maintain that the reduced importance of labor unions in the United States is explained in part by the unions' tendency to maximize short term for their existing membership; Thus, what has happened to the unions has had a good deal in common with efforts by all who have had a degree of market power and have focused on the short rather than the long run.

How does this translate into the decision-making process of consumers, producers and investors?

First, let us consider the consumers. Economists assume that consumers attempt to obtain the highest level of satisfaction (i.e., they attempt to maximize consumer welfare) and that they tend to move toward this goal over time. Presumably, this sends the necessary signals to producers, and many producers go to great expense to detect consumer preferences. Consumers make their choices by exercising their preferences (generally assumed to be stable, at least at a point in time) in the light of the relative prices of goods and services and given their level of income (their budget constraint). Most models assume that each individual maximizes for himself or herself, though many mainstream economists take account of the entire family. More difficult for the traditional concept of maximization has been the argument of earlier economists, first Thorstein Veblen, and later, James Duesenberry and Harvey Leibenstein, that the relative position of people also is important in decision making (though consider the approach of Stigler and Becker), or the argument of Fred Hirsch and Robert

Frank about "positional" goods. These factors, along with various findings of sociology, psychology and anthropology, are considered in applied areas such as marketing, but some of the most successful of these multidisciplinary efforts appear to remain proprietary information and are not generally available for examination by those who would seek to understand what explains consumer decision making.[3]

Producers, Businesspeople in General and Investors. It is assumed that businesspeople and investors attempt to make optimal decisions and to learn from experience, so that more nearly optimal decisions are facilitated over the course of time. In the case of investment, the theory presumes that people attempt to take account of objective probabilities where these are known and to use these probabilities to help orient a subjective probability analysis that involves careful calculations and consistent behavior. Financial and economic theory assumes that producers and investors seek to maximize the discounted value of the stream of expected profits and that they take risk and uncertainty into account.[4]

The possible conflict of higher income and a less agreeable environment in the workplace is handled by tradeoff-type explanations at the individual level but does not appear to be well accounted for in explaining decisions and results at a more global level. Most economic models ignore the possibility of an alternative work environment that is not only less desirable, but so dangerous that it undermines the concept of a single objective such as that of profit maximization. There is at least one well-known exception that grapples with the issue, though only to resolve it in a way that may not generally hold. This effort, by George Akerlof and William Dickens (Maital and Maital 1993), borrows from the work in psychology on cognitive dissonance and maintains that with a sufficient remuneration advantage, workers gradually convince themselves that the work in question is not that dangerous (or, in any event, that it is not that dangerous for them). Therefore, the potentially troublesome dissonance is eventually overcome, the workers are left with a traditional maximization exercise and there is only the traditional need to determine the acceptable tradeoff between positions of different job characteristics. This assumes that higher compensation, rational reexamination of the adverse job characteristics or self-delusion are enough to overcome the dissonance caused by serious underlying concerns. That may sometimes occur, but the dissonance brought on by multiple concerns often seems to continue—and probably increases almost as often as it dissipates. The major impact of the Akerlof and Dickens article, however, was to awaken more economists to the realization that behavioral assumptions relevant to their analyses are available from psychology.

In general, the theory regarding business and investment decisions assumes that markets are highly efficient and that the decision maker seeks to obtain information up to the point at which the cost of obtaining additional information is equal to the gains from that information. Moreover, it follows from the rationality assumption that future incomes are preferred to present income only if the future incomes are large enough to compensate for the opportunity cost of deferring receipt of the income—that is, only if the person who forgoes income obtains a sum that is larger by an amount that is at least as great as he or she could obtain by investing the initial amount in the market.

THE OBJECTIVES ACCORDING TO SOCIOLOGY, PSYCHOLOGY AND THE OTHER SOCIAL SCIENCES

Authorities on culture, politics, sociology, psychology and philosophy maintain that many financial and economic activities have social, political or other objectives and that all have implications beyond the purely financial and economic.

Anthropologists sometimes present culture as a set of control mechanisms. They have cautioned us against expecting the same type or the same measure of response to given incentives in one society as in another because of differences in underlying values. That would seem to make sense, and certainly the analyses of economic anthropology are highly suggestive. But in this connection we should recall the seriously mistaken advice that was received from anthropologists about Korea (referred to in Part I).

A good deal has been written in recent years on philosophical considerations and how these considerations modify behavior. Most such matters are probably more important for circumscribing the limits within which financial and economic objectives prevail than for providing multiple considerations to be taken into account at all times. Nonetheless, this, even more than anthropology, sociology and political science, is beyond this author's competence; accordingly, the reader is simply referred to a few studies that deal with issues of philosophy and economics.[5]

Political considerations affect some financial and economic decision making, most obviously at the level of public entities and private associations whose actions influence public policy. Hirschman's work is replete with examples of how factors uncovered by political science have helped us to understand more fully and predict more satisfactorily decision making about "economic" policy. But, as noted, Hirschman has cautioned against generalization in this area. As with anthropology, the applications and whatever it is that can be said about objectives that they reflect seem to require great institutional familiarity and personal insight.[6]

Sociological factors appear to have had a major impact on many types of financial and economic decisions. To begin with, objectives reflect preferences, and, as sociologists have observed, individuals are not born with a set of preferences. These preferences are shaped by family and friends, religious institutions, community organizations and the customary ways of dealing with others in the locale and under the circumstances in question. An exposition along these lines that has received a good deal of attention is Amitai Etzioni's, *The Moral Dimension*.[7] Etzioni's most important theme, however, revolves around the idea that individuals have a continuum of motivations, ranging from the moral or normative/affective at one end of the spectrum to the logical/empirical at the other. The normative/affective limits the influence of logical and empirical considerations in certain activities insofar as some of the data used in analyzing the logical/empirical is collected in response to moral and affective motivations. In effect, Etzioni argues that maximization is unlikely to be the only consideration in a wide range of human actions, many of which have impacts on finance and economics. But how exactly would sociology modify this picture? In an article prepared for economists, the prominent sociologist, James Coleman, concludes, "We understand and are able to model behavior at the level of the individual but are seldom able to make an appropriate transition from these to the behavior of the system composed of those same individuals."[8]

The economist Robert Frank maintains that much of what is referred to as altruism only *seems* to be that, insofar as it is aimed at gaining the commitment required for long-term maximization. This does not explain all "acts of altruism," however. Apparently some important areas of financial and economic decision making are influenced by motivations that limit any tendency toward profit maximization. If we fail to take these areas into account, some of our analyses and predictions will likely go astray. The challenge is to indicate the areas or the kinds of circumstances in which this holds true and to estimate the magnitude of the constraint on what economics or finance would term an optimal result.

Perhaps a better explanation of the altruism issue emerges from Simon's recent analyses which build on the work of population biologists. Simon maintains that "a combination of bounded rationality and Darwinian selection for fitness will lead to large amounts of altruism, most of which will express itself in the form of sacrificing personal for group (organizational, ethnic, family) goals."[9] The altruism results from a trait Simon terms *docility*, which he defines as a receptivity and substantial responsiveness to social influence that may imply motivation to learn or imitate, or a willingness to obey or conform. He maintains that this trait is heritable and leads to the possibility for a society to cultivate and exploit "altruism," redefined somewhat from the most usual strictly self-sacrificing definition of the term as "enlightened selfishness." His argument allows for gains by those who are altruistic but insists that "many people exhibit loyalties to organizations and organizational goals that seem wholly disproportionate to the material rewards they receive from the organization or its success." Simon states, "I don't think you can account for the roles of large organizations in market/organization economies without this mechanism. The new institutionalists, Williamson et al., omit this mechanism, and thereby lay an unbearable load on contracting mechanisms" (Simon, personal communication, 1997). Simon adds that the strength of organizational loyalties is due not only to "docility," but also to cognitive factors.[10]

Finally, a number of psychological considerations need to be taken into account (in addition to Simon's redefinition of altruism). Whether these considerations are more important than those from the other behavioral social sciences, their amenability to empirical testing explains the relatively greater attention that the psychological factors have received.

Several well-known, late 19th-century economists believed that the behavioral assumptions of economic theory should reflect the findings of psychology. Other economists objected, and their position became dominant. Economics was particularly quick to abandon its interest in the findings of psychology as psychology began to reveal increasing doubts about utility theory. Psychologists had begun to assign importance to motives other than hedonism and to argue that behavior also was influenced by factors that were independent of motives and goals—that behavior might be affected by instincts and impulses. The limited tendency of economists to draw on psychology was further reduced after publication of Walras's mathematical analysis of equilibria. There were those, like the theorist J. B. Clark, who complained that economics often assumed behavioral relationships that simply constituted bad psychology, but such concerns were rare among mainstream economists. A few prominent figures like Irving Fisher wrote in a manner that did not necessarily exclude taking account of truly behavioral findings—but did not make explicit reference to them. Gone, too, were the psychological speculations of several late 19th- to early 20th-century economists about the reasons underlying intertemporal choice—motivational speculations in some cases and cognitive speculations in others. During the first half of the 20th century, most economists simply ignored psychology. Indeed, there was a small "behaviorist" tradition of experiments in economics which dealt with "revealed preferences" that proceeded completely and relatively unsuccessfully without any reference to psychology. Then in 1953 Milton Friedman declared in a much cited article, that economics did not need to consider the accuracy of behavioral assumptions as long as the models predicted well. The predictions he had in mind were not those about individual preferences with which microeconomic analysis begins, so much as those of market prices and quantities.

Even as Friedman was writing, a powerful challenge to the position just stated was underway, most notably from Herbert Simon and his colleagues, who developed the concept of bounded rationality. This concept accepts traditional economic rationality's emphasis on the need for consistent reasoning and the inclination to use that consistency in advancing material welfare. At the same time, it maintains that all that is done in the context of constraints that usually make optimization unattainable. As noted in Part I, Simon stressed incomplete information and the lack of programs to handle information adequately. Some of his writings also noted problems in perceiving even the incomplete information at hand. In addition, he conceived satisficing as attributable not only to the limits on optimal calculations, but also to a disinclination on the part of individuals to attempt the tremendous effort that might be required to obtain the very best results, as compared to just very good results, adequate for business and personal success. (A related matter was Simon's conviction that there was the possibility of goal conflict, principally between the individual members of organizations and also within individuals themselves.)

Nonetheless, even as late as the 1970s, very little work employing psychology appeared in the professional economics or finance journals. Simon's Nobel Prize may have helped bring about a measure of change, but the real breakthrough came as a result of the work of the psychologists Tversky, Kahneman, Slovic, Lichtenstein and a sizable group of others working on the analysis of decision making. Experimental economists reacted, initially doubting but then confirming and extending the anomalies that the psychologists had uncovered. Moreover, the success in utilizing what psychologists had developed in one area led economists to a more extended consideration of other fields of the discipline, especially as set forth by Earl in a leading survey article (1990). (In 1995, Earl authored a text on intermediate microeconomic theory for students of business administration that integrates important aspects of the applicable psychology into the main body of the analysis.)

A major new methodological challenge was underway. Perhaps the two individuals most responsible for bringing the new behavioral approach to the attention of a large number of researchers and students, as well as to the general public, have been Richard Thaler and Robert Frank. Frank made original contributions both in scholarly articles and in books aimed at a public broader than that of economists alone. He was the first to introduce the material into a text in intermediate microeconomic theory, though in "supplementary" chapters. Thaler's important work on anomalies reached much of the economics profession through his articles (a number written jointly) in the *Journal of Economic Perspectives*. The reissue of those lively articles as a hardbound, and later paperbound book reached a larger and more general audience (1992, 1994).

The ground for receiving the psychologists' work was prepared in part by Vernon Smith, perhaps the prime mover in experimental economics. Smith wrote that traditional economic analysis deals admirably with normative objectives such as profit maximization and with the techniques for achieving those objectives, but is incomplete and even misleading in suggesting the processes of convergence and in ignoring the costs of carrying out decisions. It begins badly, he contended, first by emphasizing consistent behavior and then by the manner in which it defines rationality.[11]

Simon observed that economists understand rationality in terms of the selections that people make. However, for psychology and the other social sciences, rationality is seen in terms of the decision-making process—reflecting *thought processes*, to add a subsequent comment by Plott (Zey 1992, 225). In *Organizations*, Simon and James March wrote about procedural rationality (the intent to be rational) but noted that the intent did not assure substantive rationality. For economics and finance, rationality is essentially error-free; insofar as there are errors, and if there is irrational behavior, these are random and cannot be predicted. Psychology does not make assumptions about the errors of human behavior. Rather, it studies the phenomenon, measures results, and tends to find systematic biases in what the economists and financial analysts refer to as irrational behavior, some of which psychology also would recognize as irrational. It may be useful to think of a continuum of rationality, with the traditional neoclassical economist's concept of rationality (perfect rationality) at one end and blatantly irrational behavior at the other. Simon's concept of bounded rationality would fall in between, though toward the perfect rationality end. The decision making captured in the studies of psychologists, which incorporate systematic biases, reflects what Simon may have had in mind when he explained the concept of bounded rationality, and probably other elements as well. Thus, the decision making reflected in the analyses of the psychologists also would fall in between the two extremes, though further from the perfect rationality end. Thaler has referred to such behavior as quasi-rationality.[12] Allais once indicated that he would define rationality in terms of revealed behavior. The argument for his position would seem to be strongest insofar as reference is to the behavior of those who are successful. Arrow argues for a reformulation of rationality in interactive terms, in which individuals pursue a goal of gradual improvement. He refers to interactive rationality as a procedural rationality that presupposes a strategy of improvement (Arrow et al. 1996). This might be viewed as a restatement of Simon's bounded rationality, consistent with his lifelong commitment to the development of measures to improve imperfect decision making.

Modern economics has much to offer in explaining how to combine resources efficiently, but it does not deal well with the phenomenon of inconsistencies among those who do not intend such inconsistencies. As Vernon Smith has observed, it also has little to say about what motivates and energizes human resources. (For example, consider the economists' generally positive assessments of the economic potential of India in the period following World War II and the more skeptical appreciation of the potential for more resource-constrained Japan—as well as the dire evaluation of South Korea's prospects in the late 1950s and early 1960s.)

Some of the behavioral social sciences' doubts about the assumptions of economics already have been noted, and more will be discussed. For the present, however, consider the often crucial matter of time preference. Economic analysis usually assumes that time preference is determined largely by the rate at which future benefits are discounted. Moreover, most models assume that even though there may be different time preferences between societies reflecting cultural differences, within a given community phenomena such as the rate of saving are determined largely by the level and changes in the level of the interest rate, given per capita income and the prevailing age distribution. (Elegant intertemporal optimization algorithims have been developed allowing for uncertainty and search, as Don Hester has pointed out to me in the personal communication referred to in note 1 to this chapter.) Although studies by economists demonstrate that personal saving is not as sensitive to interest rates as they once reckoned and that certain business activity is not especially responsive to changes in interest rates in general, these are but qualifications for the economist and financial analyst. Those in the behavioral social sciences tend to approach time preference in qualitatively different terms. The inclination is to think that while a prima facie preference may exist for immediate consumption, that preference may vary according to the maturity of the individual (including his or her degree of self-control), the degree and type of socialization in a community at the time, the awareness of detrimental effects of certain types of consumption, considerations about the future and possible emergencies that might arise, motivations to leave bequests and even behavior modification measures. Those from outside economics and finance firmly believe that changes in any of these variables may be as important in altering time preference as a change in the rate of interest. A psychologist or a sociologist would not assume that changes in time preference probably reflected changes in the interest rate.

In the introduction to a text on economic psychology used in business administration programs in a number of European universities, W. Fred van Raaij lists eleven factors or areas in which psychology affects economics and business behavior:[13]

1. Motivational factors—biological, social and cognitive.

2. Values and norms—developed through socialization, which guide and constrain economic behavior.

3. Information processing—including both that from individual memory and from the external environment.

4. Attitudes—as a means individuals develop to judge objects, persons and ideas.

5. The social comparison of one's own input, output and situation with that of other individuals, and the social influence of others.

6. Rules or heuristics for combining information, weighing benefits and costs and assessing the value of choice alternatives.

7. Attributions of success and failure to causes and learning from this for future behavior.

8. Affect (emotional factors) in perceiving and evaluating information and in guiding behavior.

9. Bargaining and negotiation processes in competitive and cooperative games.

10. Learning processes.

11. Expectations.

These factors are not equally important to all economic and financial phenomena, nor does psychology offer unequivocal findings in all cases. Nonetheless, the mere listing of all these possibly relevant considerations from the field of psychology suggests how complicated an analysis of economic and financial phenomena might have to be in order to provide true understanding and to predict well on a regular basis. Attention is given here primarily to items 1, 3, 6, 10 and 11. Several of these are among the most conceptually justified and among the best supported empirically. In the case of expectations, empirical considerations are the more important, and the topic is so critical for economics and finance that it can hardly be ignored.

Antonides (1991) endeavors to incorporate these elements in two models of economic behavior. It acknowledges that the models are only suggestive (and I would add that they do not seem entirely consistent). Undoubtedly, psychology has many important insights to offer toward an understanding of economic behavior, but quite a few of the interrelations have not yet been fully worked out. The incorporation of psychology into economic analysis is warranted but is best restricted to those psychological theories that have been well supported empirically. It might be desirable for economists to do some of their own testing of "economic psychology." Some might profitably even become applied psychologists in much the same way that a number of economists have become applied mathematicians. (And it would seem warranted for all to study economic psychology, just as all are required to study a certain core level of mathematics.)

The possible impacts of family and community values, religious institutions, individual socialization and maturation, and the individual's position relative to others on preferences and objectives have been noted. Those impacts reflect largely the considerations of sociology and anthropology. Psychology's contribution to explaining preferences and objectives derives from that discipline's analysis of motivations and emotions.

First, some maintain that individuals possess a basic personality but that their preferences may vary according to circumstances; that is, some motivations are intrinsic and internal and other motivations are influenced by the environment.

Second, as mentioned in Part I, there is the intuitively appealing contention that individuals have a hierarchy of needs, beginning with a need for the physical necessities of life and advancing to security needs, a sense of belonging, self-respect and personal realization, with some tradeoff between these factors so that the hierarchy is not strict.

Third, as also noted, some psychologists have referred to "response mechanisms," maintaining that individuals respond to factors such as the level of sugar in the blood, images, smell, and hormones as well as to rational calculations. These factors are said to lead to sentiments which, in turn, lead to actions. This overlaps the first category of intrinsic and environmentally influenced preferences.

Fourth, and apparently the most seriously considered approach among psychologists is one that makes reference to seven or eight motivational factors:

1. Need for achievement
2. Locus of control
3. Sensation seeking and risk taking
4. Altruism
5. Time preference

6. Cognitive system

7. Life-style. To which might be added:

8. A preference for preference change

1. *Need for Achievement* has attracted a great deal of attention, but remains a controversial concept, even among psychologists. It maintains that when they are young, the individuals of a society develop a motivation toward accomplishment that greatly influences what the majority of them attempt later in life. The motivation toward accomplishment is determined to a considerable degree by the stories told to young children in each society. Some empirical studies seem to substantiate this contention. While the methodologies they have employed have been criticized, the concept of a need for achievement, shaped by the traditions of a society, has some appeal. The implication seems to be that for most individuals, it would take a generation to bring about a change in the need for achievement. Yet those associated with the concept have developed training programs to modify the participants' need for achievement in as little as a month or two. The improved entrepreneurial activity by those who have taken such courses is impressive. Still, the degree to which the changes attained reflect a revised need for achievement is not entirely clear; they may reflect a number of other factors. Among these factors are the way in which information is perceived, the tendency to insist on fuller explanations, the manner in which judgments are made, the strengthening of entrepreneurial confidence and the development of a greater sense of personal responsibility for outcomes (see also the following discussion of locus of control). The Entrepreneurship and International Business Development Program courses organized by the United Nations are the latest and perhaps most successful of such courses, but the scale of that program (referred to internationally by its Spanish acronym, EMPRETEC) is quite limited. The selection process for participation in the program also explains a measure of the successes achieved, particularly in some countries.

2. *Locus of Control.* According to this concept, individuals are motivated differently according to whether they believe they themselves or outside forces shape most of the events of their lives, that is, whether the locus of control is basically internal or external. Successful entrepreneurs are regarded as having an internal locus of control. A strictly rational approach might lead an individual to reject either extreme and recognize that in some circumstances he or she has (or could come to have) more control over events than others. As a description of how people behave and a positive theory of how survivors come to survive, however, the concept of locus of control certainly has a place. The principal problem probably lies in the difficulty of ascertaining internal as against external locus of control.

3. *Sensation Seeking and Risk Taking.* Writings by the economist Tibor Scitovsky, drawing on the work of physiological psychology, have maintained that diminishing marginal satisfaction and boredom are potentially important influ-

ences on economic activity. Satiation in consumption is a consideration to be reckoned with, Scitovsky insists. Moreover, the response of individuals to incentives is influenced by the degree to which stimulus influences motivation. This observation might seem to conflict with the dictum of Alfred Marshall to the effect that the greatest return of monopoly is the quiet life, but perhaps Scitovsky would reply that a monopolist needs more stimulus if he or she is to move beyond that quiet life and undertake further activity. Note that the recently accentuated openness of markets to foreign competition, the challenge/opportunity of technological change and the threat of antitrust prosecution may provide the requisite stimulus. Implicit is the notion of an optimal level (and perhaps an optimal type) of stimulus. Added risk may sometimes provide the level or type of stimulus necessary to reach that optimum.

It would be quite difficult to quantify what exactly constitutes the optimal stimulus, however, and the differences in the optimal level and the optimal type of stimulus would be likely to vary, especially from one individual to another. The successful design and implementation of financial and economic incentives appear to be as much art as science.

4. *Altruism.* It would be naive not to recognize that some seemingly altruistic acts are aimed at gaining the commitment required for long-term maximization. It would be equally mistaken to ignore the idea that altruism does motivate some actions. Some altruism probably is innate, but much appears to be influenced by the environment. Indeed, Simon redefines altruism as an enlightened selfishness that many individuals exhibit in groups, especially in families and in organizations. What we have traditionally meant by the term *altruism* may not motivate much financial and economic activity,[14] but the redefined altruism, the enlightened selfishness that reveals itself in organizations, probably is important and needs to be taken into account.

5. *Time Preference.* For psychologists, many factors in addition to the interest rate enter into the determination of time preference, and the time preference that results from this mix of stable and fluctuating factors is an element in motivation. Economic analyses should probably pay more attention to this conclusion of psychology than they have to date.

6. *Cognitive System.* Psychologists believe that the capacity to differentiate the environment and integrate information influences motivation. However, the most important impact of differences in cognitive systems may be in the ability to implement objectives, which is dealt with in Chapter 4.

7. *Life-Style.* Life-style may be a motivational factor, but motivations also influence life-style. Attempting to disentangle this idea may not be easy at this stage and may not lead to an understanding of motivations that is sufficiently improved to warrant the effort in most cases.

8. *A Preference for Preference Change.* This element of motivation may be important for some people. It may be reflected generally by the continuing interest of many individuals in wide-ranging education, even after they become adults. It does not seem to be a very tractable factor, however.

To what extent do emotions affect preferences, either directly or through their impact on one or more of the motivational factors just mentioned? Most economists and financial analysts would be inclined to say that such emotional factors may sometimes affect the preferences and decisions of individuals, but that the aggregate effect is likely to be small, in particular because the emotions of individuals are likely to cancel each other out. In some situations, however, the emotionally influenced preferences of key decision makers have had a major impact. Of more general application, economic and financial models do not allow for the adverse effect of stress on rational decision making, and medical studies have demonstrated that the negative impact of this factor is quite marked. Perhaps even more consideration might be given to the role of stress under the subject of the implementation of objectives.

In sum, economics and finance are likely to benefit by considering the possible importance of several of these elements for certain problems or groups of people, but doing so complicates the analysis. The benefits of doing so would not always justify the costs. The incorporation of the contributions of psychology into financial and economic analysis should be selective and probably should emphasize the work related to the implementation of objectives.

PERSONAL DECLARATIONS CONCERNING FINANCIAL AND ECONOMIC OBJECTIVES

Up to this point, we have focused on the objectives of economic and financial decision making according to authorities in those fields and on the contention that it might be desirable to modify the views of economists and financial analysts to take account of the findings of the behavioral social sciences and philosophy. No one would claim that we ought to accept at face value people's declarations concerning their objectives.[15] Perhaps, however, some attention should be given to them, particularly if follow-up inquiries can be used to clarify answers and thus reduce the phenomenon of responses that are misleading, not because of a lack of candor but because of the way the questions were posed, the special circumstances of the period when the questions were asked or simply because the respondents may have "gotten up on the wrong side of the bed" that morning.

Many researchers have asked people about their financial goals, but even when objectives are essentially the same, the responses sometimes vary according to the culture involved, the general situation of the community and the personal circumstances of those involved. The intended message may be the same, but Argentines voice it differently from Mexicans, and the citizens of a given country often respond differently in years of prosperity and optimism than in years of recession or increased uncertainty. People who have come into wealth often answer differently than when they were struggling, even in those cases when their objectives remain the same.

Some insight into the problems of using businesspeople's responses to reveal their objectives may be provided by the results of interview-based studies conducted over a two-year period in Uruguay, involving more than a hundred enterprises. (See Appendix B.) Differences were found to exist between what businesspeople say when asked to state, in their own words, the objective of their enterprise's activity and what they indicate when asked to check off their objective(s) from a previously prepared list. Moreover, when that list includes a statement about merely maximizing profits over the long run, or over the course of five years, the maximization alternative does not receive as much support as when the alternative is rephrased, "to produce a high quality product and maximize over the long run" (or over the course of five years). Furthermore, a greater number of firms claim a cost-minimizing, profit-maximizing objective in the midst of greater pressures and adversities. Perhaps the most notable aspect of the findings, however, is that some firms claiming a maximization objective employ guidelines for resolving certain kinds of problems that are not consistent with optimization. Even among those who follow through with more-nearly-maximizing guidelines such as the use of strategic planning and cost-benefit analyses, the search for information to implement those guidelines is frequently undertaken in a manner which, though following often plausible rules of thumb, falls far short of optimization.

REVEALED OBJECTIVES: JUDGING OBJECTIVES BY WHAT INDIVIDUALS AND ENTERPRISES ACTUALLY DO

What are the goals of individuals and enterprises as revealed by the decisions actually rendered? Do businesspeople truly maximize profits, and how much does it matter whether they maximize or just seek to earn a high level of profits and do better than their competitors?

A survey of English businesspeople in the late 1930s unleashed a three-decade-long debate about what businesspeople actually do. The controversy that followed dealt not only with what they did, but also with what they *sought* to do (and what they *needed to do* to ensure their survival). No one suggested that businesspeople were indifferent to profits, but it can make a great deal of difference to individuals among them and to the society at large whether they attempt to maximize and whether they are able to implement that objective. Some observers held that while businesspeople attempted to maximize, what they sought to maximize was revenue or some other objective. Mention of some of these seemingly different objectives may just have reflected the recognition that implementation of a long-run profit maximization objective was so difficult that revenue maximization, for example, was pursued as a means of ensuring a customer base that made long-run profit maximization more nearly feasible. Currently, many engineers, scientists or doctors in new business ventures seem to show more interest in technological breakthroughs than in maximizing profits, though for a number of these people technological breakthroughs may serve as a proxy for long-run profit maximization. Still, many enterprises that have given primary emphasis to technology—sometimes explicitly, other times implicitly by maintaining scientists or technologists in the principal positions of management—have lost ground competitively or have been taken over by more traditionally oriented businesspeople when the profitability (or promise of future profitability) of the enterprise lagged. Moreover, if businesspeople come close, but do not actually maximize (i.e., do not do all that is necessary to achieve that objective), then even though they might fare almost as well as if they had been able to achieve optimal results, there could be a substantial cost to the society as a whole (Akerlof and Yellen 1985). That cost would be significantly lower if, as in economic experiments, market interactions were to compensate for less-than-fully maximizing behavior on the part of individuals.

Several categories of studies may be considered. First are those that attempt to ascertain whether given businesspeople or enterprises have endeavored to maximize profits. Second, there is evidence on the search process—that of businesspeople already referred to and that of consumers—engaged in an effort to improve their welfare. Third are studies of the kind of inefficiency that traditional economics texts used to assume did not even exist and that still is not reflected in the diagrams or equations of those texts: studies of organizational slack (also known as x-inefficiency and a lack of technical efficiency). Fourth, there are the experimental studies—laboratory or experimental economics, for the most part, augmented by efforts to design experiments in field environments. Finally, there is formal and informal work on how people confront situations in which the choices seem so difficult that one must question whether there could conceivably be a single, overriding objective. (Note that management authority James March maintains that managerial behavior can be generally characterized as that involving multiple and conflicting goals.)

The Maximization Debate

The British economists, Hall and Hitch, concluded that English businesspeople, generally employed a system of mark-up pricing—that they determined prices by adding a certain percentage to their costs. That's a rule of thumb that would almost never be consistent with profit maximization. But perhaps many of those firms were not survivors, and perhaps the apparent frequency of such business behavior in Great Britain helps explain why the country lost the strong economic position it once held. Among the studies that followed was one in the 1950s showing that certain decisions of a successful U.S. airline reflected marginal cost pricing and thus revealed profit maximization (at least in the activities considered). Such evidence contributed to the conventional wisdom that whether or not everyone maximized, survivors tended to do so.

The Search Process

Consider the following responses of Uruguayan businessmen confronted with substantially increased competitive pressures, first, from firms in the much larger economies of Brazil and Argentina as a consequence of economic integration (MERCOSUR), and second, from firms worldwide, following the dramatic reduction of local import duties and other barriers to trade.

Among those enterprises stating that they sought to maximize profits, only two appeared to use reasonably precise cost-benefit analyses to evaluate even some of their decisions regarding the search for additional information (neither of which appeared to make adjustments to allow for general equilibrium-type considerations). Three firms placed a good deal of reliance on the advice of outside consultants but were not always aware of the guidelines those advisers used. Five firms stated that they employed a cost-benefit mentality but did not actually make calculations; two relied to a considerable extent on an analogy with information search experiences in the past; two collected information on what they regarded as key variables; three stated that they collected information until their leading doubts were resolved; and one firm stated that it collected data as long as time permitted. Three firms appeared to employ varying guidelines, only sometimes reflecting a cost-benefit mentality. Twelve firms had no clear guidelines—certainly none that they could verbalize; they simply mentioned the categories of information about which they regularly gathered information, or they mentioned several different considerations that they usually took into account, or they stated that they did not have any consistent guidelines for their information search. Except for a few of the firms in the last group, most of the search processes probably helped improve enterprise decision making, but they undoubtedly differed greatly in the efficiency with which they achieved that result.[16]

Such far-from-maximizing search behavior is consistent with that identified in an earlier case study by another author of decision making in a metalworking industry, but it is at odds with the more nearly optimizing behavior reflected in the search guidelines observed in the relatively less complicated environment of laboratory experiments. Considering industry and the services at large, it is clear that even some of the most successful survivors have not always employed as optimal a search process as possible. Whether that is due to lack of motivation or to problems of implementation is not certain.

When it comes to the consumer's information search, economic psychologists and marketing specialists have shown that in making decisions about television sets, dishwashers and the like, most consumers do not attempt to obtain more than one or two price quotes. Moreover, much of such product assessment as they do seek comes from the very persons selling the items under consideration (notwithstanding the relative accessibility of an increasing number of well-known independent sources of information such as *Consumer Reports*). Then too, when consumers do look further afield, there is sometimes a disturbing disparity in the information available (i.e., the information for which there is an effective demand), with less available for many large-budget items than for others of intermediate size. None of this is to deny that consumers have demonstrated an interest in improving their decision making to some degree.

Studies of Organizational Slack, X-Inefficiency and Lack of Technical Efficiency

The traditional exposition of microeconomic analysis assumes that the basic challenge is to allocate resources efficiently among competing uses. That is no small or easy task, as the complications of the analysis reveal. Unfortunately, the analysis of resource allocation makes the simplifying assumption that wherever the resources are employed, they are used well. One might attempt to defend the assumption by concluding that such efficiency in the utilization of resources comes to prevail over time, and relatively quickly at that. If that were true, much of what is taught in business schools and much of the work of management consultants would be superfluous. And it is not true, of course. Studies by Cyert and March in the 1950s and 1960s showed that business firms have a great deal of organizational slack. They do not press to use their labor, capital and natural resources much more efficiently until they are subjected to adversity or to substantially increased competitive pressures.

Later in the 1960s and throughout the next two decades, Leibenstein used the expression "x-efficiency" to deal with somewhat the same phenomenon and dedicated a great deal of effort to explaining it, increasingly in motivational terms. He and his followers also provided some empirical verification of their construct. A more traditional economist, Michael J. Farrell, already had written about what he called "technical efficiency." That terminology was employed in the documentation of the same phenomenon that was accepted by more neo-classically oriented economists (see, e.g., the studies of Howard Pack). Those neoclassical economists who recognized the frequent lack of technical efficiency did not necessarily attribute the sometimes extraordinary gaps in efficiency that they uncovered to motivational considerations. This, too, helps anticipate the material that follows from implementation problems.

The Experimental Studies

Although some "field studies" of actual economic phenomena have been done, most experimental studies have been undertaken in a laboratory setting. Even in those cases in which this can be performed well enough to capture the essence of decision making, there is a serious question as to whether the results from such settings—settings much simpler than those actually confronting individuals and enterprises—can be taken as serious indicators of motivations.[17] Moreover, there is the case of the prominent statistician, Leonard J. Savage, who, while he failed to answer certain queries of the type used in experimental economics in a manner consistent with the economist's (and statistician's) definition of rationality, failed for reasons that had nothing to do with motivation but everything to do with the then insufficiently recognized difficulties of implementation. That raises the question of whether much of the material outlined in this section on "revealed" motivations does not have more to do with implementation problems than with motivation.[18] It may help explain why traditional economists, who have been somewhat concerned by the anomalies turned up in the experiments, do not feel that it is necessary to alter the assumption that maximization/optimization is *the objective*.

Decision Making So Difficult As to Suggest the Multiplicity of Objectives

Perhaps the evidence that most seems to undermine the assumption that people seek to maximize a single objective comes from the way people cope with situations characterized by strong conflicts (concerning which see the discussion in Part I).

A SUMMING UP

What do individuals, particularly successful businesspeople, seek? Economists and financial analysts maintain that when it comes to activity in their realm, the objective of individuals, particularly businesspeople and investors, is to act rationally. As they have defined it, this means to make the kind of decisions that will attempt to maximize profits (i.e., to maximize the expected present value of the stream of future profits). Psychologists, sociologists and other behavioral social scientists maintain that human objectives are broader (which economists acknowledge) and that these broader objectives affect the full range of human activity, including what are ordinarily characterized as financial and economic decisions (which the more traditional economists would tend to deny).

Many businesspeople declare that they seek profits—indeed a high rate of profitability—but they insist that they do not attempt to maximize. Rather, they seek to maximize only after taking account of other objectives—a constrained maximization.[19] Perhaps it does not quite reach constrained maximization because usually there is not a visible demarcation of the point at which the other objectives begin to hold sway, or a precise delineation of the tradeoffs between profitability and those other considerations. Many would therefore maintain that they have multiple objectives. At the same time, some of the most successful do seem to have an objective that more nearly approximates cost minimization/ profit maximization, and that has become more apparent with increased competitive pressures. Even companies that were once famous for lifetime employment relationships engage in downsizing operations that often involve major layoffs and significant setbacks in social and psychological terms.

Still, there seem to be variations between tasks in the degree to which a maximization objective dominates, as can be seen in some production and investment activities, particularly in certain cost-cutting operations. Many of the most highly successful producers seem to react in a qualified manner when faced with situations involving serious hardship to their personnel or the communities in which they are located. Perhaps the reticence to lay off workers is somewhat less common than before, but it continues. The only denial of the importance of a hesitancy to take drastic downsizing measures would be to insist that such decisions only *appear* to reflect affective motivations. In reality, they represent efforts to provide a measure of assurance to those who continue to work in the company, guarding against undue loss of morale and a weakening of their productivity. That may describe some situations, but it is hard to believe that it applies to all. As a result, such not-solely-maximizing objectives should be taken into account in a financial and economic analysis that attempts to describe actual behavior. Even a normative analysis that focuses on how to maximize should consider such matters, showing exactly what to expect from a world in which many producers and perhaps most consumers do not attempt to fully optimize.

Estimates might be ventured, moreover, of the cost to society, not only (a) when economic agents fall just a little short of optimizing behavior, but (b) how this is changed when some specified economic agents seek a good deal less than full optimization. Objectives involving substantially less than an effort to optimize undoubtedly might have some adverse affects on efficiency, but insofar as that considerably-less-than-full optimization usually reflects less than full exploitation of other actors, even in the absence of any well-labeled moves toward cooperation, might not the costs of such less than full optimization be offset by a greater sense of trust and perhaps an evolving implicit cooperation? Experimental economics has shown that individuals are not always as strictly rational as the logic of economics would expect them to be, and yet the result is sometimes a larger overall economic pie.[20] It might be possible to design better public policies if we were able to gauge the costs to society that are actually realized when objectives reflect alternative deviations from maximization. Finally, there is an undisputed cost to the community of being unable to *implement* optimization objectives. That is the subject to which we now turn.

NOTES

1. This note deals with three points: the components of rationality, as viewed from a relatively orthodox point of view; the growing effort to redefine rationality, and the third, the so-called indiscriminate use of superrationality.

The Components of Rationality. In a personal communication dated November 1, 1997, Mordecai Kurz of Stanford University stated:

The issue of rationality has three fundamentally different components . . .

(I)   Do economic agents maximize in their static, non-random choice patterns?

(II)   Can static behavior under uncertainty be explained by principles of rationality?

(III)   Are expectations of agents "rational" in some sense?

Item (I) covers the simple issue of maximizing behavior when there is no uncertainty and no considerations of the future. Discussion of this type of rational behavior . . . resulted in what is known as the "weak axiom of revealed preference" as a minimal condition of rationality. The typical set-up to this question is the pattern of purchases of a household given a fixed and certain budget. It does not take much to find out that that optimizing behavior is difficult and emotionally demanding. . . . [A]lthough there are probably some agents that may not be able to solve this optimization problem each time, empirical household studies have exhibited very limited violations of the basic axioms of demand theory.

Item (II) is the most celebrated since the failure of the expected utility theory in the static context (i.e., no expectations about the future are involved and the decisions are made in real time) is easily replicated in experimental studies.

I deal with Kurz's discussion of this matter in the next-to-last chapter of the book, except for his comments about financial markets. Kurz maintains that the decisions of the latter involve large stakes that are not based on human intuition, but rather, are guided by

models into which one feeds such things as, probability distributions of returns, covariance matrices, risk aversion parameters etc. and the computer makes the calculations of the optimal portfolio. Similarly with regard to the pricing of derivative securities using Black-Scholes theory. Others insist that they use consultants . . . who are asked to follow textbook procedures. Hence, most of the pitfalls of human intuition are avoided by forcing the process to become computerized and impersonal. The human choice is used to select *the model* to be employed but not to make the actual calculations.

This position is supported by many prominent economists, but Chapter 7 on finance introduces evidence from others in the field suggesting that money managers do not always act in such an impersonal and traditionally rational manner. Even so, a few references to studies that support Kurz's position are cited, affording the reader a basis for making his or her own determination.

Item (III) is very controversial. Brief note is taken of certain material from Kurz's interesting contribution to this area in Chapter 6.

Recent Efforts to Redefine Rationality. The issue of what constitutes economic rationality is being reopened, however. See Arrow et al. 1996, especially the comments of Arrow and Roth, and also Radner 1996. Arrow contends that rationality must be redefined as interactive rationality and ought to include the pursuit of gradual improvement. (Perhaps the concept of interactive rationality also would allow for Simon's "enlightened selfishness" definition of altruism and would take into account the more-than-occasional differences between the performance of individuals in economic experiments—particularly in repeated experiments—and the performance that would be expected from the more traditional rationality of game theory—even in repeated games.) Roth argues that it is necessary to consider the environment in order to define what is rational. (Moreover, at the level of the individual, Sen has long maintained that the rationality of decisions is best assessed in the light of what a person is trying to achieve.) Radner expresses several concerns, among them the uncertainty that economic agents have about the logical implications of the information they possess.

The "Indiscriminate Use of Superrationality." Some of the models of financial decision making are, as the Spanish saying goes, "more Papist than the Pope." The motivation of Markowitz, in preparing his pioneering work, *Portfolio Selection* (Markowitz 1959), was open-ended inquiry, as Don Hester has reminded me. It was "to understand whether actions by investors are consistent with their beliefs about means, variances and covariances. He didn't assume that they were [and] in interviews found that they were not" (Private communication, May 27, 1997). (Elsewhere, I mention Tversky's comments on the significance of this type of divergency.) Note also that Modigliani 1988 complains of the "indiscriminate use of superrationality" in many financial models— this more than a decade after publication of Grossman and Stiglitz 1976 and nearly a decade after the empirical demonstration of continuing irrationality in financial markets by Modigliani and Cohn 1979.

2. Olsen 1997.

3. For a multidisciplinary approach to decision making that extends beyond economics and finance, see Kleindorfer, Kunreuther and Schoemaker 1993, which is summarized in Chapter 9.

4. A recent addition to the theory, Dixit and Pindyck 1994, shows that because of the irreversibility of some investment decisions, incorrect guidance may result from use of the net present value rule—similarly, with respect to following the textbook recommendation that firms should enter a market (or expand) as long as prices are above long run average costs and exit or contract when prices are below average variable costs. Though important, these qualifications do not incorporate the type of observations in this volume; all the same, they lend more weight to the material presented here regarding risk and uncertainty.

5. See, for example, Kahneman, Knetsch and Thaler, "Fairness as a Constraint on Profit Seeking: Entitlements in the Market," and Kahneman, Knetsch and Thaler, "Fairness and the Assumptions of Economics," both in Thaler 1991; also, Rawls 1972; Redman 1991; Elster 1983, 1984, 1986; and Sen 1987.

6. In a recent review, Dani Rodrik states: "A political scientist or historian may well find much of the economics literature on the political economy of reform naive or simplistic. However, what is encouraging about this literature is that economists are now doing their political economy analysis explicitly, rather than implicitly as used to be the case. Most economists have now come to the realization that good economic advice requires an understanding of the political economy of the situation. . . . The bad news is that the habit of attributing myopia or irrationality to political actors—whether explicitly or, more often, implicitly—persists" (Rodrik March 1996, 38).

7. Etzioni 1988. See also Zey 1992.

8. Coleman 1984, 267–68. For additional material on the overlap between sociology and economics, see Smelser and Swedberg 1994 and Piore 1996, 741–54.

9. Simon, personal communication, February 10, 1997; Simon 1990 and Simon 1991, esp. 34–38.

10. In "Organizations and Markets," Simon raises a number of additional points that should be noted. First, he reasons that given the proportion of people who work in organizations and the importance of decisions in organizations to those in the market, modern industrial societies might be termed organizational economies rather (or as much as) market economies, and he attempts to provide a theory of an organizational economy. The key, that of the motivation of individuals in organization, is explained in terms of (1) authority, (2) rewards, (3) loyalty or identification with organizational goals emerging from "docility" and cognitive factors, and (4) coordination. Unfortunately, Simon's insightful discussion of coordination was not included in the 1992 presentation of Milgrom and Roberts on the same subject (which does refer to a number of other contributions of Simon, however).

11. Nonetheless, Smith later wrote a review of the Hogarth and Reder conference volume, *Rational Choice* (1987), strongly criticizing what was being done to modify traditional economic analysis by the cognitive psychologists and those in economics who were following their lead (Smith 1991).

12. Thaler's work on quasi-rationality is dealt with throughout this presentation. Note should be taken here of an important survey article, "Why Bounded Rationality? (Conlisk 1996). This article first distinguishes between bounded rationality and the unbounded rationality that has dominated the models of economics, and notes direct and indirect

evidence of bounds on the rationality of decision makers. Second, it documents the ability of bounded rationality models to meet the first concern of neoclassical economists and improve explanation and prediction, at least in some kinds of situations. Third, it refutes the "as if" arguments for unbounded rationality—the argument that whatever it is that runs through their minds, people, in particular survivors, act as if they were completely rational. Fourth, the article explains the logic of bounded rationality in terms of the fundamental concern of economics, scarcity. That is, it incorporates into the analysis, the cost of attempting to optimize or to improve decision making (see also Pingle and Day 1996).

Conlisk makes it clear that in some cases results are greatly improved by the use of bounded rationality models, though that is not always so. Perhaps the time has come for economic research to reallocate research efforts, away from the question of whether bounded rationality exists and what might explain it, and toward the relative importance of different types of bounded rationality models in different types of situations. It may be possible to do some of that on a deductive basis and some through the use of currently emphasized, rigorous empirical tools (econometrics, experimental economics). Perhaps it is time, however, to develop a few more solid case studies of what happens in different, complex, ongoing real-life situations so as to develop hypotheses of the relative importance of bounded rationality models in different types of situations. Such studies might look at some cases of failure as well as some cases of survivor success.

13. Van Raaij, ch. 1, Introduction, in Antonides 1991.

14. A sophisticated presentation on this topic, not yet reflected in this text, is Stark 1995.

15. This rushes past the most interesting and disturbing message of Kuran 1995.

16. A fuller account of this study is given in Appendix B.

17. Ward Edwards is critical of the experimental studies in psychology. He recommends surveys of larger numbers of persons that make use of more than one method of questioning respondents, followed by a discussion of inconsistencies in the answers, a revision of the questions, a reconciliation of results, and the use of multiple criteria (multi-attribute) decision analysis. The last-named method has also been subjected to serious criticisms, however.

18. Consider, too, the conclusions of the psychologist, Tversky: "The rational theory of choice appears to provide a much better account of people's normative intuition than of their actual behavior. Indeed, when faced with violations of dominance, transitivity, or description invariance, people often modify their behavior in accord with the rational model. This observation indicates that people's choices are often in conflict with their own normative intuitions" (Arrow et al., 1996, 195).

19. However, in interviews I have had with manufacturers over the course of many years, some veteran producers have stated that they believe they have come closer to realizing maximum profits than earlier in their careers. The reasons, they explain, are their greater awareness of more of the relevant information, their better perception of the significance of information, and their use of better procedures for making decisions—all reflecting the potential role of learning in improving substantive rationality even if complete maximization never quite becomes the objective.

20. See Camerer, "Behavioral Game Theory," ch. 13 in Hogarth 1990. For the most extensive account of behavioral game theory, see Camerer 1997. This is also supported in the published and unpublished work of Hofman, McCabe and Smith.

Chapter 4

Implementing the Objectives: Characteristics of the Process

INTRODUCTION

Whether individuals and enterprises truly seek to optimize may not be entirely relevant if such a goal often cannot be implemented. Indeed, implementation problems play an important role in explaining the growing awareness of anomalies of economic and financial theory.

Economic rationality involves two elements. Actions must be consistent, and they must advance economic well-being. Economists see rationality in terms of outcomes, in terms of the results of the actual choices people make. The intent to employ a rational approach does not assure substantive outcomes that are optimal or that tend toward optimality. That may not happen for a number of reasons. A decision maker may not have access to the necessary information or the programs to employ that information efficiently, the information may be perceived incorrectly, mistakes may be made in using decision-making procedures and rules of thumb may be used without adequate allowance for the decision biases incurred in using such approximate measures. Exogenous factors may intervene, and more.

A major characteristic of rational decision making is reflected in what is termed *transitivity*. If someone prefers the theater to movies and movies to concerts, then the person should prefer the theater to concerts. Yet this rational ordering does not always prevail. To begin with, there may be alternatives that are too similar to be recognized by some individuals or in some contexts; the differences may be fuzzy, they may not "register," there may not be a Just Noticeable Difference.[1]

More importantly, one alternative may seem preferable to another simply because of the manner in which it is presented or because of the way a decision about the choice between the two is elicited. Even when each of these alternatives is absolutely clear, the *manner* of presentation may affect choice. The frequency with which this happens appears to vary among individuals and categories of circumstances. Some of this inconsistency is quite predictable—robust and systematic. It may turn out that we have reversed our choices, our apparent preferences, without having experienced any changes in our underlying attitudes and inclinations. Some preference reversals involving a lack of transitivity have been documented, but most simply reflect differences in the way the choices are presented or the way information about choices is elicited. This is only one factor interfering with smooth implementation of objectives, but it is one that had not even been recognized as a logical possibility until quite recently, at least not in the context of economic and financial decision making.

Many decision makers are inclined to assume that the data for implementation of objectives are what they seem to be when they first become aware of the information. Problems in data perception are referred to from time to time, but almost none of the literature of economics and finance indicates how one might conduct a "reality check" of the true value of data. The way in which data verification is done tends to vary, if it is undertaken at all. Moreover, if data perception leads to difficulties, what of the problem of risk perception and of perceiving the significance of alternative situations of uncertainty, where there is no objective standard to relate to (only vague boundaries at best)?

Often people attempt to implement their objectives without taking into account that they are imperfect calculators, especially when the problem seems similar to others that were manageable "on the back of an envelope" but are much more complex. The use of calculators and computers may help, but we sometimes fail to recognize steps that we skip, or we turn to the instruments of precise calculation only after having made assumptions critical to the final result. Those often critical short cuts seldom reflect even an informal cost-benefit justification for not undertaking more careful calculations at the outset. Or when we take short cuts that are justified, often we are unaware of the magnitude, and sometimes even of the direction, of the biases that may be involved and we do not consider them.

Many casual observations suggest that people have difficulty in implementing a maximization objective—any maximization objective, not just profit maximization—and that this holds even when they are provided with market incentives to do so and penalties for not doing so. There are also casual observations that go the other way, suggesting that maximization tends to prevail, certainly that producers and investors who stray far from maximization do not survive. Nonetheless, those who insist that individuals or enterprises who stray far from maximization do not survive are conceding that some measure of failure in moving toward maximization is consistent with survival.

Efforts to verify the implementation of maximization objectives are available at the level of the individual and the marketplace. Those relating to financial markets are dealt with in Chapter 6. Evidence about individual behavior in natural settings remains sparse, but Chapter 5 deals with the escalating findings of laboratory experiments. These experiments point to the difficulties of implementing a maximization objective, though they also reveal that substantial movement toward its realization can be achieved after several replications. Unfortunately, many important types of financial and economic events are relatively unique events. A final disturbing note: while fuller information about the environment (including the information held by other economic agents) sometimes helps lead to optimization in experiments, it actually impedes such a result in other cases.

THE PROCESSING OF INFORMATION

Basic Considerations

The point most often stressed is the lack of information, particularly asymmetry of information—that is, the relative lack of information on the part of one or more of the parties involved in any transaction. To this should be added the imprecision or uncertainty about the meaning of some information. Even so, complaints are often heard about "information overload." That is just another way of stating Herbert Simon's observations concerning the difficulties of achieving maximization because of the lack of adequate programs to deal with even such information as is available and the lack of adequate intelligence to deal with the problems, even adding artificial intelligence to human intelligence. In any event, the standard exposition of economics and the set of tools that have been most refined by the discipline are suitable for dealing with a well-defined set of alternatives. Yet as Richard Nelson and Sidney Winter (1982) have indicated, exploring a poorly defined choice set, such as frequently confronts decision makers, is a vastly different activity than optimizing a clearly enunciated one. Indeed, Simon has noted that a truly major challenge may lie in the search for the alternatives that comprise the choice set. Even available programs for scientific discovery are not optimization programs. Alternatives often have to be invented or designed.[2]

Beyond that, even the consequences of well-defined alternatives are not always fully grasped, and search processes take place in the context of the particular problems that are faced, or, more accurately, in the context of the problems that appear to prevail. What constitutes optimal search may not be at all obvious, and many second-best solutions may be sensed only during the course of experience. Indeed, they may be molded by an evolutionary process. That evolutionary process is influenced by the historical and cultural context of a society, though not dictated by it. It is also affected by the approach of particular management cultures to the search process, as well as by the fact that the costs of retaining what is obtained in search are lower than the costs of initiating search. Perhaps the disconcertingly far-from-optimal implementation of the search process among both enterprises and consumers is not entirely surprising.

What follows is somewhat taxonomic, but it is a checklist of factors, many of which are often overlooked. A possible framework for a socioeconomic model of decision making within an organization can be found in Tomer 1992, which discusses decision-making steps in information processing and categories of decision strategies, organizational influences that regularize decision-making behavior, and organizational circumstances that can foster high mental activity, intuitive as well as logical.

Information Processing Biases[3]

Problems may arise in acquiring information, in initial processing, or in dealing with feedback. Biases in the acquisition of information may arise from the nature of information availability, considerations of perception, frequency, concreteness of information, and data presentation. Biases in information processing may arise because of errors in applying statistical techniques, inappropriate use of certain techniques, or incorrect understanding of probability, inconsistency in applying judgment standards, employment of useful but only approximate rules of thumb or heuristics, the way the information is framed, consistency of information sources, presence of stress and social pressures, and even illusion of control or wishful thinking. Feedback biases may arise from a misunderstanding of chance fluctuations, logical fallacies, hindsight bias, and the frequency and fidelity of the information feedback.

The Acquisition of Information

Availability. Biases may arise because the ease with which specific instances can be recalled from memory affects judgments about the relative frequency and importance of data. This leads to overestimation of the probability of well-publicized or dramatic events (or those involving the decision maker or his or her family and acquaintances), or recent events along with the underestimation of less recent, publicized or dramatic events (or those not involving the decision maker, his or her family and friends). A prominent example of the availability bias is the belief of most people that homicides (which are highly publicized) are more common than suicides, but, in fact, the reverse is true. The availability heuristic has elements in common with the theories of attention that some writers in psychology and management have emphasized.

Perception. Imperfect perception of the true value of market, technological or public policy data at the time a decision is made is likely to lead to an effort to solve a problem that differs from the one confronted. Yet various studies show that a good deal of information is imperfectly perceived at the point in time when a decision is made. This difficulty in perceiving information accurately is a general phenomenon that affects everyone. It is accentuated by the fact that many people perceive some data differently than others because of differences in their educational background, their life experiences and even their basic personality. Note, too, that anticipation of what one expects to see may influence what is perceived. People tend to disregard or underweight conflicting information and seek that which is consistent with what they expected or what their initial information revealed (or what the information obtained by their organization revealed). Finally, certain information simply may not register until one has the appropriate framework in which to place it.

Frequency. People often take greater note of absolute than of relative frequency. More information is available on successes than on the ratio of successes to overall attempts. Even when both are available, sometimes a ratio does not register as well as the image of the successes. It seldom occurs to baseball fans that a league-leading slugger fails to deliver two-thirds of the time, even though that is precisely what a batting average of .333 signifies.

The Concreteness of Information. Concrete, vivid information tends to be sought more than "abstract" information or "statistics."

Data Presentation. The order of data presentation (such as being first or last rather than somewhere near the middle of a list) can affect one's ability to access information.

Biases in Information Processing

Incorrect Understanding of Probability. People overvalue certainty and even the appearance of certainty. In general, they treat certainty (as well as extremely low probabilities) quite differently than probabilities of a less extreme range. However, difficulties can also arise in distinguishing between probabilities in a fairly broad range, particularly a broad middle range such as between 0.4 and 0.6. (Note, though, that, some individuals seem unable to verbalize probabilities of certain events but make choices that are similar to those of persons who are able to estimate probabilities.) Studies concerning natural disasters reveal the tendency to ignore very low probabilities—that is, to treat the probabilities of such events as if the likelihood of their occurrence were essentially zero. Then, after an earthquake, hurricane, flood, or the like takes place, the tendency is to treat them as if they had probabilities higher than reality, though gradually such people slip back to seriously understating their likelihood. Two other problems may arise. First, while an event may be so unique that it is not possible to assign a *precise* probability, it is sometimes treated as if it had a probability well beyond any plausible range. Second, many people believe that they can influence probabilities, that they can alter them (part of what is understood in the phrase "managing risk"). This applies to individuals with formal instruction in probability analysis as well as to those without such instruction. While there is something to this for ongoing dynamic processes, the tendency is to exaggerate the degree to which the probabilities can be changed.

Errors in Applying Statistical Techniques. First, there is illusory association or correlation. People sometimes mistakenly conclude that phenomena are correlated just because they have observed a common occurrence of the same phenomena on a few previous occasions. Second, as Ward Edwards has shown, judgments frequently are not revised to the extent indicated by probability analysis after the receipt of new information (Kahneman, Slovic and Tversky 1982, ch. 25). Third, linear extrapolation is often used where it is not appropriate. When it is clear that a linear approach is not acceptable and it is not used, incorrect approaches in estimating nonlinear extrapolation are often employed.

Inconsistency in Applying Judgment Standards. Most of us are unable to apply a consistent judgment strategy in extensively repeated circumstances. Models based on the enunciated criteria of experts predict better than do the very same experts, and even relatively simplistic linear models tend to predict better than experts operating on a case-by-case basis. Among the most important studies on this point have been those of the psychologist, Robyn Dawes. Another major inconsistency results from the different way in which most people value the same dollar amount of gains and losses. This phenomenon (to be amplified later) is compounded by the framing phenomenon.

Employment of Rules of Thumb, Simplifying Strategies or Heuristics. A heuristic has been defined as "any principle or device that contributes to the reduction in the average search to solution" (see Newell, Shaw and Simon 1962, 85, cited in Nelson and Winter 1982, 132). Short-cut rules of thumb or heuristics often are justified by cost-benefit considerations, but such short cuts involve biases from what would be indicated by the use of statistical techniques and optimization measures. Frequently, the extent of the biases is not recognized or is not taken into account. Two major lines of work have been done in this area for dealing with complex decisions. (It has generally been assumed that simple decisions are handled by routines without careful calculation.) The first has emphasized "attributes," and here the psychologists developed "compensatory" and "noncompensatory" decision rules. In some cases, it has been maintained that personal attitudes are combined with a normative social component and that the two forge the intentions that lead to behavior. The compensatory decision rules stress tradeoffs between the desired attributes, while the noncompensatory decision rules are based on the assumption that it is not possible to compensate for low values of a desired attribute with high values of another (in contrast to the marginal rate of substitution concepts of traditional marginalist economics, though perhaps not wholly unlike the conceptualization of linear programming). The noncompensatory approach includes conjunctive and disjunctive rules, as well as lexicographic rules which rank attributes of interest to the decision maker, leading, in some cases, to "elimination by attributes." Usually, the disjunctive rules assign overriding importance to a single attribute. These approaches sometimes lead to intransitivities in choices. Few economists have been attracted to this approach to date,[4] but fuller accounts can be found in Earl 1990 and Baxter 1993. Quite different, however, has been the economists' reaction to the contribution of psychologists of the heuristics, especially availability, anchoring, and representativeness.

Availability. The ease of recall of certain information (e.g., a dramatic or well-publicized event) may affect the valuation of that information. For this reason, Peter Lynch, the extraordinarily successful former head of the Fidelity Magellan Mutual Fund, tended to avoid the stocks that analysts and writers were celebrating on the grounds that such "availability" increases the likelihood that the shares of those companies were overvalued.

Anchoring and Adjustment. Judgments sometimes involve essentially mechanical adjustments from a starting point such as recent historical data (last month's inflation data, for example). The resulting assessments are often characterized by unwarrantedly high levels of confidence.

Representativeness. Judgments of the likelihood of an event or an identification may be based on its similarity to a class of events (or a group of characteristics). This kind of stereotyping often leads people to ignore even contradictory probability data that may be available. In one experiment, the participants concluded that a sizable share of those in the small, seemingly random sample were librarians because those of the group that they interviewed appeared to possess certain attributes that were often associated with that profession. The judgment was rendered despite the fact that the participants were provided with information in advance, indicating that the proportion of librarians in the group was much lower. Representativeness tends to entail a statistically invalid reliance on small samples (the so-called law of small numbers); a failure to allow for "reversion to the mean" (to allow for the fact that so-called hot streaks, for example, in sports or in business, may be just that and not indications of new expected mean values); and reasoning by analogy, according to which judgments are based on the similarity, or seeming similarity, of a situation to one that was faced before (or that another—particularly successful or particularly unsuccessful—individual or enterprise is believed to have confronted previously). This heuristic often leads to unwarranted overconfidence.

Judgmental heuristics, framing and the related anomalies outlined in Chapter 5 are also discussed in Appendix A. Readers not very familiar with heuristics will find it helpful to turn to Appendix A at this point. While the evidence is quite strong that heuristics such as availability, anchoring and representativeness enter into decision making, few efforts have been made to document the kind or mix of heuristics that different individuals or enterprises employ in alternative types of natural decision-making situations. Yet this seems critical to the development of the descriptive behavioral economics toward which the economists and psychologists involved aspire. This type of effort is particularly important, moreover, because some of the heuristics may lead to different results. Timur Kuran (1995, 362) has observed, for example, that the availability heuristic sometimes works at cross purposes with the representation heuristic. (Note that the discussion of this volume understates the possible importance of an alternative kind of heuristic, represented by the matching law and melioration.[5])

An outlier in all this, but one that receives a great deal of attention in a recent study by Zur Shapira (1995), is a tendency of managers (and lottery ticket purchasers) to value particularly striking outcomes more than the probabilities of those outcomes—outcomes such as multimillion dollar rewards, but particularly worst case outcomes such as bankruptcy. Shapira's findings are based on surveys of businesspeople in Israel and the United States. Finally, the above all refer to the reasoning of individuals, albeit taking into account the influence of others. Yet another phenomenon is that of "group reasoning," and a related phenomenon is the reasoning of organizations.[6] The characteristics of group thinking do not seem sufficiently well identified as to merit regular application of the concept in the analysis of economic and financial decisions at this point, but the day of such applications may not be far off. Both group and organizational reasoning appear to rely heavily on "enlightened self-interest" rather then on individually maximizing self-interest, while, at the same time, making extensive use of special heuristics with significant biases. That is, both follow lines of reasoning that differ in important respects from the traditional definitions of rationality.

Framing. Changes in the wording or framing of a question or incentive that do not change the fundamental underlying values of what is at stake can nonetheless lead to very different responses. The framing phenomenon is widely recognized in much human activity. Note, for example, the high compensation that lawyers get because of their ability to skillfully arrange and present evidence that many lower-priced attorneys also could obtain. But until recently, economics and finance did not even consider the phenomenon, presumably because it conflicted with the rationality axioms of the two fields. If, a decade ago, one had asked a good neoclassical economist if he or she would alter a selection between investments in the event that the same cost-benefit data were presented in two different ways, but with the relevant values obviously the same, the individual would have stared incredulously at the questioner for having asked what would have been regarded as such a foolish question. That was before experiments showing that the way data are presented can influence financial and economic choices. In laboratory experiments, a good deal of the disturbingly irrational framing effect seems to disappear when the identical situation is repeated several times. How much that result depends on repetition in a short time period is not clear, however. Nor is it clear whether the framing irrationality can be expected to be reduced nearly as much when even slight variations are introduced in the repeated experiments. Most important decisions involve variations, often major variations with respect to the situations confronted in the past. Therefore, the fact that repeated experiments of an identical character have greatly reduced the framing effect is not of much consolation.

Many problems can be phrased in either a positive or a negative manner, with the choices often varying according to the context. Two examples involve experiments in which identical data were given—in one case, concerning policy to deal with an impending catastrophe, and in the other, concerning treatment for a group of the seriously ill. In the latter case, experts (physicians) were asked to make the judgments. In both experiments, the options were framed alternatively in terms of survival rates and mortality rates. And in both, the recommendations for the manner in which to address the situations varied according to whether the data (*identical* in both cases) were labeled ''survivor rates'' or ''mortality rates.'' As important as framing appears to be, there is not yet, any theory of framing (Shiller 1993, 19). Nor have there been systematic experiments or case studies to ascertain the differences in the types of outcomes that have been associated with particular kinds of framing variations in the past, which might help in the formulation of a theory. Still, it would be difficult to exaggerate the importance of the work on framing for the analysis of economic and financial decision making. We will return to this topic in Chapter 5.

Presence of Stress and Social Pressure. These factors alter the care, consistency or criteria with which people select and process information.

Illusion of Control and Wishful Thinking. The locus of control aspect of motivation leads some people to disregard actual probabilities or prevailing realities.

Information Feedback

Misunderstanding of Chance Fluctuations. This is exemplified by the heads and tails ''gamblers' fallacy.'' Moreover, many people who recognize the fallacy in objective questioning (they realize that the odds of ''heads'' coming up on, say a seventh flip of the coin following six ''tails,'' are still only 50–50) nonetheless act differently in similar real-life situations. The gamblers' fallacy is recognized more easily by those who have had a course in statistics than by others, though it is not clear if the actions of those with the background in statistics reflect the same comparatively more rational tendencies in real-life situations.

Logical Fallacies. An inability to recall the details of an event leads to erroneous reconstruction of reasoning processes, often in addition to incorrect recall of some relevant data.

Hindsight Bias. People often claim that they are not surprised by results that they did not predict, sometimes specifically refrained from predicting or even predicted incorrectly. Yet the claimed lack of surprise is often sincere.

Fidelity of the Feedback. This refers to the ability to recognize the degree to which feedback data reflect the phenomenon in question and are not mixed with other information. The frequency of accurate feedback and the frequency of the phenomenon in question also may be critical to a good revision of judgments.

Summary

If much can go amiss in acquiring information, in processing it and in dealing with information feedback, then even if an individual or an enterprise does possess a single objective that he or she seeks to maximize, the probability of being able to do so must generally be very low. The main hope for the eventual triumph of optimization would be as a consequence of market interaction—or with the assistance of learning.

LEARNING

Learning can be defined as the understanding gained, usually over a period of time, which is retained long enough to lead to some change in behavior for the activities to which it applies. This definition would rule out lessons seemingly learned, perhaps even leading to good repetition and application on examinations, but that are not applied subsequently in real-life situations to which they are relevant. However, most definitions of learning would not require that the changes in behavior be permanent. Langley and Simon have defined learning in complex systems as any process that modifies a system so as to improve, more or less irreversibly, its subsequent performance of the same task or of tasks drawn from the same population.[7] Learning may change preferences, and it may change the way of carrying out processes. It may be reflected in innovations, which have become an important topic of economic inquiry, especially by the neo-Schumpeterians.

In the basic economic model, there is perfect knowledge and perfect rationality so that there is really no role for learning. Economists have moved beyond that and have long acknowledged learning in a variety of ways, in particular, as a lagged reaction that improves the ability to achieve technical efficiency over time, or to advance that and realize technological change. The theory of rational expectations recognizes the possible existence of mistaken expectations but maintains that errors are random. In that framework, there is no learning to improve behavioral predictions from errors such as those that psychologists have been documenting. Rational expectationalists have a place in their framework for learning, but it is strictly to help improve rationality for those who otherwise would not be among the survivors. Mainstream economists have often referred to learning by doing—by producing, by exporting or by realizing some active experience—but the discipline of economics that so emphasizes efficiency has had little to say about how one can (or should) achieve or assess an efficient process of learning, particularly if the underlying conditions are changing, as they usually are. Joseph Stiglitz has written of "learning to learn." An effort to integrate the analysis of learning into the general framework of economic analysis can be seen in Young Back Choi's observations that even the decision-making process involves learning (some decision making, I would maintain) inasmuch as it reflects a successful search for a paradigm to cope with a situation that we could not make sense of before (Choi 1993).

Even as economists find themselves grappling with the question of learning, most seem to be ignoring much of the work that is being done in psychology on the subject, particularly certain work in cognitive psychology. To what extent can psychology help economics and finance to understand and thus make the appropriate assumptions about learning?

Psychology offers half a dozen lines of thought on learning. These can be categorized as

- Stimulus and Response
- Cognitive Learning
- Social Learning
- Learning by Programmed Instruction
- Latent Learning
- Organizational Learning

Stimulus and Response. The classic studies in this area analyzed simultaneous stimulus and response. The work in the second half of the 20th century has dealt with reinforcement (operant conditioning), which has involved the use of repeated stimuli, with the ensuing responses characterized as instinctive. Skinner and his followers obtained results independent of the findings of physiological psychology or cognitive psychology. Also under the heading of stimulus and response has been the work in behavior modification, first with electric shock and, increasingly in recent decades, with drugs, as more and more problems have been analyzed in terms of chemical imbalances. Many psychologists have adopted one or another of these stimulus and response approaches (see summaries in Lea 1992). Few economists have done so, the most notable exceptions being the Alhadeff in the early 1980s and the recent work on animal behavior.

Cognitive Learning. Cognitive learning deals with insights, reasoning and imagination and emphasizes retrieval and extraction, association, repetition, recognition and the solution of problems. Some psychologists have pointed to the difficulties of learning, in particular the need for suitable feedback, and to the phenomenon of negative or incorrect learning. (This might be juxtaposed to some of the work of Olson and other economists who have maintained that institutions do not always improve in terms of their economic impact—contrary to what one might expect from a survival-of-the-rational-optimizer line of thinking). While the earlier work in cognitive learning recalls names such as Piaget, and often difficult verbal constructs, an entirely new tradition has been evolving. This new tradition has developed in part from work with computer simulations and computer tutor programs, from the use of visual imagery in thinking, from what are referred to as connectionist learning schemes[8] and adaptive production systems and from various special protocols including one in which individuals are asked to ''think aloud'' while they are solving problems—that is, they are asked not to ''introspect'' or ''retrospect.'' This work, dealt with at somewhat greater length below under the heading, The New Research in Cognitive Learning, is being used in the field of management science and seems to offer important applications for economics.

Social Learning. The term *social learning* refers to cognitive processes backed up by reinforcement. It has been broken down into direct learning, indirect learning, and imitation and emulation. One of the leading applications has been by those interested in marketing. Shiller, several of whose studies are discussed in Chapter 7, is receptive to the use of psychology in economics but has observed that social learning is difficult to predict.

Learning by Programmed Instruction. Learning by programmed instruction draws on a variety of theories and received a great deal of attention in the mid-1960s. Although the results were less successful than expected, the programs have become more interactive and have been greatly improved.

Latent Learning. This term refers to phenomena such as the learning of rats in a labyrinth and to unplanned (unpremeditated) learning that draws on earlier general education. An example of the role assigned to latent learning that draws on earlier general education can be seen in the conviction of some individuals and enterprises that a strong primary and secondary school (and perhaps college) education that provides general tools, together with an inquiring frame of mind, are more important for success in business than training in specific skills or analytic tools.

Organizational Learning. Organizational learning has not received a great deal of attention from psychologists, but this neglect may come to an end as recent works in psychology have explained some of the central ideas of economics and business administration to researchers in the field. At the moment, the major text emphasizing the importance of coordination internal to the enterprise, Milgrom and Roberts 1992, refers primarily to the importance of "routines," a concept introduced into the economics and management literature by Nelson and Winter. An effort to introduce the concepts of organizational behavior into economic analysis has been made by Tomer 1987. (See also Chapter 9, Postscript.)

The New Research in Cognitive Learning. Much of this subsection is likely to seem rather foreign to economics and finance, but the reader should not skip the last three paragraphs, in any event.[9]

In 1975, Simon wrote that learning does not refer to a single, simple set of human cognitive processes and does not involve one kind of change, or a change in one component of the system. He offered eight considerations for researchers to bear in mind, particularly those dealing with the learning processes of students:

1. The kinds and degree of understanding that a student achieves in solving a task can have important consequences for his or her retention of skill and knowledge, ability to transfer that knowledge, and the speed and efficiency with which additional knowledge is acquired.

2. Understanding has many facets.

3. An important component of problem-solving skills lies in being able to recognize salient problem features rapidly and to associate promising solution steps with those features. (In a later study of Simon the example is given of a chess master being able to recall the position of pieces in well-defined game situations much better than the novice, but not being much better in recalling the position of randomly placed pieces.)

4. Limits of short-term memory may prevent application of a problem-solving method that is understood.

5. Understanding generally requires not only storage of adequate semantic information but also availability of problem-solving schemata of a general and a specific character.

6. Syntactic may often be substituted for semantic processing, and vice versa.

7. Understanding processes entails being able to construct representations of problem situations.

8. It is becoming increasingly possible to determine in detail what understanding any specific matter involves. Thus, it has become possible to write computer programs that specify what a person who understands knows, what processes he or she has available for solving problems and acquiring new knowledge in that domain and how his or her knowledge is organized in memory.

Research has been shifting back and forth between the attention given to performance and that given to learning processes. Research in cognitive learning has attempted, first, to understand human performance, how the human brain stores and processes various kinds of semantic representations and then to incorporate that information into computer programs. Importance has been given to the recognition of patterns. A number of experiments have shown that students learned high school mathematics as well when they were presented with carefully chosen sequences of problems and were asked to work out the examples, as when they were offered instruction on the basic principles involved. (This finding seems to lend support to the contention that educational institutions have determined their teaching methods by use of very rough rules of thumb, without any deep understanding of learning processes.) The students in the mathematics learning experiment acquired knowledge from examples in what is referred to as "productions," which are defined as sets of conditions leading to actions.

The students first discovered conditions under which the actions were appropriate and then elaborated the conditions to increase the efficiency of their actions. Researchers do not appear to know how close the results of the traditional teaching methods or the approach using worked-out examples are to achieving the most efficient mathematics learning results. A similar comment can be made with respect to the experiments that move to "adaptive production systems"—systems that reprogram themselves (computer programs that learn by generating new instructions that are annexed to existing ones). Among the other issues that arise are the respective roles of logical reasoning, on the one hand, and selective search processes (search algorithms) using mental models in problem solving, on the other. Other concepts include proceduralization, composition and the building of efficient productions that recognize useful configurations, all of which have quite precise definitions. Finally, experiments have supported the intuitive proposition that the efficiency of learning mechanisms differs according to the learner's native abilities and prior learning experience.

Langley and Simon (1981) lists the characteristics of a good explanation of learning to learn as involving a "set of invariants," but also as

1. Explaining a variety of phenomena
2. Being more basic than the phenomena it explains
3. Being simpler than those phenomena
4. Being free of ad hoc components

Two conclusions emerge. First, we are just beginning to understand the guidelines for improving the efficiency of learning. We have no notion about how to maximize learning processes, and we are only beginning to develop reasonable guidelines for satisficing, though we do seem to have a much better basis for avoiding learning disasters. Second, work in economics that attributes importance to learning is not even using available heuristics that might at least avoid serious error and perhaps facilitate satisficing.

In sum, although a much better understanding of learning is critical to good economic analysis, psychology seems to offer almost too many explanations (see, e.g., the chapter on learning in Antonides 1991). Considering cognitive psychology alone, while economics has begun to devote a great deal of attention to the findings of this subfield in the area of decision making, the new research on cognitive learning, which is turning up improved new heuristics, does not yet seem to have attracted much attention from economists.

Sociology may offer some assistance with respect to learning at the organizational level, but here, too, economists do not seem to be paying much attention. A disconcerting phenomenon is that even if people learn, they do not always apply that learning beyond the immediately subsequent period. This may just be a matter of the proper definition of learning rather than what might superficially seem to be a need to consider retention as well as learning. Furthermore, many decisions are made too infrequently to provide a good basis for learning, or if made more often, they do not allow for a quality of feedback that is conducive to learning. Much of the learning required for economic and financial decision making involves much more than what is required in some of the psychologists' and computer scientists' experiments about propositions in secondary school mathematics (for which the solutions are well known). Finally, psychologists have shown that the confidence of individuals tends to increase with experience—regardless of the character and quality of the judgments made over the course of that experience (i.e., regardless of whether their learning has advanced commensurably).

CONCLUSION

Implementation difficulties make the probability of realizing a maximization goal very low, unless market interaction and learning provide a major assist.

The study of learning by psychologists is yielding heuristics that might enable finance and economics to move further toward substantive rationality, but the two disciplines do not seem to be taking much advantage of these advances. The need to do so seems great, however. In *The Handbook of Experimental Economics*, Camerer concludes that learning is very difficult except in simple deterministic situations and that learning stochastic rules is especially difficult. He reports that even experts in various fields routinely violate rationality in their use of readily observable information (Kagel and Roth 1995, 611–12). Moreover, we do not know how to design experiments or specify models capable of capturing the learning of individuals with a great deal of tacit information that is not easily explicable. Yet the learning of such individuals probably provides the key to understanding many types of important decisions, not the least of which are those involving technological innovation.

NOTES

1. Schwartz 1987; Mas-Colell, Whinston and Green 1995, ch. 1.

2. Simon, personal communication, February 10, 1997. In a recent interview the author of this book held with a successful enterprise in a technologically sophisticated industry, a key executive stated that if, in hiring for an important engineering position, he had to choose between two individuals, one superior in traditional engineering skills and the other, comparably better in "horizon scanning," he would select the second without hesitation.

3. Except for the observations on perception, this section draws heavily on Hogarth and Makridakis, "Forecasting and Planning: An Evaluation," ch. 9, in Earl 1988 and Bazerman 1998. Presentations on biases and framing, with colorful examples, can be found in chapters 2 and 3 of the Bazerman volume. A brief exposition of the availability, representativeness and anchoring and adjustment heuristics is given in chapter 1 of Bazerman, with illustrations of the three throughout the text.

4. The work of Slovic, Tversky, Kahneman and Sattath on the "construction" of preferences referred to in Chapter 5 may begin to change that, however.

5. The matching law refers to the tendency of animals (and apparently many humans) in experimental situations to equalize average rates of return from competing alternatives; "it calls for a match between the ratio of behavioral investments to the yield of those investments across all competing alternatives. . . . The process of comparing the rates of return and shifting toward the alternative that is currently yielding the better return is called melioration. . . . Melioration has the inevitable effect of stabilizing in the vicinity of the matching law, and it also seems to be the process that most people spontaneously invoke when they are asked to describe their own choice" (Herrnstein 1991, 361–62). See also Herrnstein and Prelec 1991.

6. The reader might check out four sources: March and Simon 1993, 1–19; Simon 1991; Simon March 1994; and Milgrom and Roberts 1992, chs. 1–4 and 16. See also Chapter 9 of this book.

7. Langley and Simon 1981.

8. Connectionist learning schemes postulate networks that learn by changing the

strengths of their interconnections in response to feedback. See Simon and Associates 1992.

9. This subsection draws on the following references: Simon June 1975; Simon 1986; Zhu and Simon 1987; Zhu et al. February 1996; Larkin and Simon 1981; Langley and Simon 1981; and Simon, *Models of My Life* (New York: Basic Books, 1991).

Chapter 5

Major Anomalies and the Presumed Rationality of Financial and Economic Behavior

INTRODUCTION

Vernon Smith acknowledges that although laboratory economics has made major contributions, it is not without its problems (Smith 1994). Nonetheless, drawing in part on work in psychology, experimental economics has raised serious questions about basic tenets of economics and, by extension, about areas of business administration that have drawn heavily on the logic of economic analysis. The tenets that follow, most of the explanatory examples, and the first sentences of interpretation are taken (in most cases, verbatim) from an analyis by Thaler that brings together the contributions of many researchers in this area[1] though I have added several qualifying observations, some of which he might not agree with.

Neoclassical economics is based on the premise that models characterized by rational, optimizing behavior capture the essence of human behavior. In the 1950s and 1960s, Allais and Ellsberg provided striking counter-examples to the normative theory of choice under uncertainty, the expected utility theory of von Neuman and Morgenstern. According to the expected utility theory, rational decision making was based on a multiplication of the values of possible outcomes by the probabilities of their occurrence. A modified version, subjective probability analysis (subjective expected utility or SEU), called for multiplying the values of outcomes by the probability of their occurrence as estimated by the individual decision makers. This view of rationality still dominates economic and financial analysis.[2] However, as early as 1954, psychologist Ward Edwards had maintained that people do not use expectation rules in making choices among risky prospects. In the 1960s and 1970s, Edwards' students and several other investigators uncovered considerable evidence to support that view. In the late 1980s, Thaler drew upon the increasing body of laboratory experiments to evaluate fifteen principles of rationality used by economists to describe actual choices. What follows, though summarized and simplified from the material published in economic journals, is a bit more abstract than the rest of this volume.

The essence of Thaler's study is that laboratory experiments show violations of more than a dozen important principles of economic analysis, even in the presence of financial incentives to act in the manner that the teachings of economics indicate is rational. The next section of this chapter, The Basic Anomalies, outlines the tenets, explains the violations and attempts to assess the frequency and seriousness of these findings for the basic paradigm of microeconomic analysis. A paragraph of overall conclusions and implications follows the discussion of the fifteen tenets.

Thaler expresses his doubts that rationality would improve even if the incentives were extraordinary, given that many people do not appear to be particularly rational (or to seek qualified professional assistance) in making many of the most important decisions in life, but that is just speculation. Surely, some improvement in rationality can be expected if there is sufficient time, which, unfortunately, is not always available, or if an identical situation is repeated and perhaps even if a very similar situation is presented (see also the discussion of Tenet 1 that follows).

THE BASIC ANOMALIES

Thaler lists the fifteen principles or tenets of rationality under the categories of choices involving decision weights, values, framing, deterministic choice and judgment. They will be explained briefly following this initial listing (phrased, in a few cases, slightly differently than in the original article):

Decision Weights

Tenet 1. Cancellation. The choice between two options depends only on the difference between the options, or on the states in which those options yield different outcomes. When one alternative is preferred to another, that preference will hold if the same amount is added to both or subtracted from both.

Tenet 2. Expectation. The utility of an outcome is weighted by its probability. There should not be a preference between two alternatives that are equivalent. If uncertainty is involved in both equivalent alternatives, the origin of the uncertainty should not influence decision choices and change the indifference between the two.

Values

Tenet 3. Risk Aversion. The utility function for wealth is concave and risk averse. (There is a diminishing marginal utility of wealth.)

Tenet 4. Asset Integration. An individual's utility is determined by the final state of a transaction or a set of transactions specified in advance to be interrelated. (Overall utility is not determined by adding up the utility at intermediate or component stages.) Wealth is the gauge and carrier of value.

Framing

Tenet 5. Preference Ordering. Preferences are independent of the method used to elicit them. People have transitive preferences, and there is no "preference reversal." (The reversal of a preference ordering does not occur without a change of conditions or the passage of a significant interval of time.)

Tenet 6. Invariance. Choices between options are independent of their representation or description.

Tenet 7. Dominance. If Option A is better than Option B in every respect, then A is preferred to B.

Deterministic Choice

Tenet 8. Opportunity Costs. Willingness to pay equals willingness to sell (in the absence of income effects and transaction costs); opportunity and out-of pocket costs are equivalent.

Tenet 9. Marginal Analysis. Choices are made to equate marginal costs and marginal benefits.

Tenet 10. Sunk Costs. Fixed, historical and other sunk costs do not influence decisions.

Tenet 11. Fungibility. Money is spent on its highest valued use. Money has no label.

Tenet 12. Domain of Utility. The willingness to pay for a good depends only on the characteristics of the good and not on the perceived merits of the deal.

Tenet 13. Economic Opportunities. All legal economic opportunities for gains will be exploited.

Judgment

Tenet 14. Rational Expectations. Probabilistic judgments are consistent and unbiased.

Tenet 15. Bayesian Learning. Probabilistic judgments are updated by the appropriate use of Bayes's rule.

Tenet 1. Cancellation. The choice between two options depends only on the difference between the options, or on the state in which those options yield different outcomes. When one alternative is preferred to another, that preference will hold if an identical amount is added to both or subtracted from both.

This seems straightforward, but it does not always hold. Consider a pair of problems to which the overwhelming majority of respondents in laboratory experiments give inconsistent answers.

Problem 1 (the Allais Paradox). Choose between:

A. $1 million with certainty
B. $5 million with a probability of .1, $1 million with a probability of .89, and $0 with a probability of .01

Problem 2. Choose between:

C. $1 million with a probability of .11 and $0 with a probability of .89
D. $5 million with a probability of .10 and $0 with a probability of .90

Most choose answers A and D, but the only difference between the choices in the two problems is that an .89 probability of $1 million has been subtracted from both A and B to give C and D.

Consider a similar set of problems with smaller amounts of money:
Problem 3. Choose between:

A. $2,500 with a probability of .33
   $2,400 with a probability of .66
   $0 with a probability of .01
B. $2,400 with certainty

Problem 4. Choose between:

A. $2,500 with a probability of .33
   $0 with a probability of .67
B. $2,400 with a probability of .34
   $0 with a probability of .66

In Problem 3, 82 percent of the participants chose B, whereas in Problem 4, 83 percent chose A. Yet A and B of Problem 4 are obtained by eliminating a .66 chance of winning $2,400 in A and B of Problem 3. As above, the combined choices violate the independence axiom. In both sets of problems, certainty prospects are overweighted relative to gambles involving probabilities of less than unity. Some laboratory trials show that this tenet of economic analysis does not always hold. The question remains whether the tenet would fail to hold very often if the incentives were very large, that is, if the situation were regarded as important. (Thaler's views on that matter have already have been indicated, but recent experimental evidence shows that the size of incentives does matter; it increases the cost incentive to calculate more carefully.) Suppose, too, that the problem were a recurring one and the feedback quite good. Would learning make a difference? Referring to all fifteen tenets, Thaler expressed skepticism about the likelihood that learning might alter the results very much, but subsequently, evidence showed that some of the anomalies are attenuated with repetition. The degree to which this is true seems to vary a great deal with respect to the various tenets under consideration and seems to be influenced by the relevant institutions.[3] These considerations need to be remembered as we note the apparent failure of the other fourteen principles of economic analysis to hold in other laboratory experiments.

Tenet 2. Expectation. The utility of an outcome is weighted by its probability. There should not be a preference between two alternatives that are equivalent, and if uncertainty is involved in both equivalent alternatives, the origin of the uncertainty should not influence decision choices and change the indifference between the two.

In the experiment, the subjects were induced to exhibit a preference between two alternatives that were not clearly distinguishable in terms of probability.

Problem 5. There are two urns containing a large number of red and black balls. Urn A is known to have 50 percent red balls and 50 percent black balls. Urn B has red and black balls in unknown proportions. You will win $100 if you draw the color ball of your choice from an urn. From which urn would you choose a ball?

Many subjects express a strict preference for Urn A with the known proportions rather than the "ambiguous" Urn B. This is indifferent for red or black balls, indicating that the subjective probabilities of each are the same and presumably equal to .5, the known proportion in Urn A. Nevertheless, most subjects feel that the ambiguous urn is in some sense riskier. This preference for the known urn violates Tenet 2. Moreover, preferences in the context of ambiguity appear to depend on both the signs and the magnitude of outcomes, so a complete description would necessitate abandoning the independence between the decision weights and the outcomes. (Other investigators have concluded that preferences in the context of ambiguity also are influenced by the degree of confidence that decision makers have in their own judgment skills.[4]) This type of situation seems less likely to be improved by learning than the first because elements enter into it that are not of an easily quantifiable nature.

Tenet 3. Risk Aversion. The utility function for wealth is concave and risk averse. There is a diminishing marginal utility of wealth.

Tenet 4. Asset Integration. An individual's utility is determined by the final state of a transaction or set of transactions specified in advance to be interrelated. (Overall utility is not determined by adding up the utility at intermediate or component stages.) Wealth is the gauge and carrier of value.

Thaler notes, to begin, that risk aversion is neither an axiom of rationality nor a necessary component of economic analysis, but that the risk aversion assumption is commonly used.

Problem 6. Choose between:

A. An 80% chance to lose $4,000
B. A certain loss of $3,000

The overwhelming majority of people prefer a certain gain of $3,000 to an 80 percent chance to win $4,000 (i.e., an outcome with an expected value of $3,200). This reveals a strong risk aversion. That is only in the realm of gains, however. In the experiment using the previous example, 92 percent indicated a preference for the 80 percent chance of losing $4,000. In the domain of losses, a preference for risk seeking is revealed. Thaler contends that it is necessary to reformulate the utility function to reflect the fact that the attitude toward risk and utility depends on the sign of the perceived changes in wealth, in violation of Tenet 4.

Consider the following pair of problems:

Problem 7. Assume yourself richer by $300 than you are today. You are offered a choice between:

A. A sure gain of $100
B. A 50% chance to gain $200 and a 50% chance to gain nothing.

Problem 8. Assume yourself richer by $500 than you are today. You are offered a choice between:

A. A sure loss of $100
B. A 50% chance to lose $200 and a 50% chance to lose nothing.

In Problem 7, 72 percent of the participants selected A and 28 percent, B, whereas in Problem 8, only 36 percent chose A and 64 percent B. Since the two problems are identical in terms of final asset positions, the inconsistency between the choices demonstrates that subjects tend to evaluate prospects or possible outcomes in terms of *gains and losses* relative to some reference point rather than the final states of wealth.

This is taken from the seminal article, "Prospect Theory: An Analysis of Decisions Under Risk" (Kahneman and Tversky 1979) and from their article "Rational Choice and the Framing of Decisions" (see Hogarth and Reder 1987). The formulation of the value function was intended to incorporate three important behavioral regularities observed in the study of both perception and choice:

1. People seem to respond to perceived gains or losses rather than to their hypothetical final wealth positions, the latter of which is assumed by expected utility theory;

2. There is a diminishing marginal sensitivity to changes, regardless of the sign of the changes; and

3. Losses loom larger than gains. This is referred to as loss aversion, the sharp disutility associated with perceived losses, and may be a more useful concept than that of risk taking for the same phenomenon. It must be stressed, however, that it reflects risk taking. Behavior often considered to be motivated by risk aversion, such as unwillingness to accept low-stakes gambles at better than fair odds, is more accurately characterized as loss aversion. Some studies suggest that in real-life situations, entrepreneurs in small to medium-size enterprises do not exhibit the same tendency toward loss aversion as the general population. (This statement refers to those who can be characterized as entrepreneurs, not to the overall group of businesspeople in small and medium-size enterprises.) If the results can be duplicated, the policy implications are important, but the real-life nature of such incidents seriously limits the controls one can apply and thus also the measure of confidence in the conclusions.[5]

Tenet 5. Preference Ordering. Preferences are independent of the method used to elicit them.

Studies in this area by Slovic and Lichtenstein led to documentation of preference reversal, which has shaken up the economics profession a bit. In the initial experiments, subjects were asked to choose between two alternative bets: (1) the P bet, with a high probability of winning a small amount of money, and (2) the L bet, with a smaller chance of winning a larger amount. The expected values were about the same. The subjects also were asked to value each bet by stating the minimum amount they would accept to sell each of the bets if they owned the right to play them (or alternatively, the maximum amount they would pay to buy the gamble).

Most of those who preferred the P bet assigned a larger value to the L bet, and vice versa. The results were replicated with real money in a Las Vegas casino. In a review article on the subject, economist Thaler and psychologist Tversky note that preference reversal implies either intransitivity (preferring A to B and B to C but not preferring A to C), or the failure of what economists call procedure invariance (see Tenet 6), or some deficiency in the payoff scheme used to elicit the cash equivalence of preferences.[6] Studies show that potentially very disconcerting lack of transitivity is rarely the cause of preference reversal. Usually the explanation is procedure invariance.

Thaler and Tversky state that preference reversal challenges the traditional assumption that the decision maker has a fixed order of preferences and that the same preference orderings should be indicated whatever the manner of asking about them (whatever the solicitation procedure). The authors show that different methods of elicitation could change the relative weighting of the attributes and give rise to changes in the preference orderings. People do not have predefined preferences for every contingency, they contend. Rather, preferences are constructed during the process of making a choice or judgment. Moreover, the context and procedure involved in making choices or judgments influence the preferences that are implied. Thaler and Tversky maintain that behavior is likely to vary across situations that economists consider identical. They have not indicated the nature of those variations, however.

Preference reversal experiments have been replicated extensively by both psychologists and economists, and the debate has shifted from whether the phenomenon exists to what explains it.[7] Nonetheless, as Vernon Smith (1994) has reported, laboratory studies published in 1990 and 1992 indicate that in certain well-specified settings, in third, or at most fifth reiterations—after participants have had an opportunity to see the implications of their choices or equilibrating market mechanisms begin to exercise more of a role—much, and in some cases, all of the inconsistency in choices is reversed. Unfortunately, we do not get three to five shots at most decisions. In sum, where there is a tendency toward preference reversal, its significance will vary according to such factors as feedback and the nature of learning. However, it is not likely to disappear in moving from one important business decision to another—though it could tend to be eliminated in recurring, virtually identical routine situations.

Tenet 6. Invariance. Choices between options are independent of their representation or description.

Consider the following three problems:

Problem 9. Which of the following options do you prefer?

A. A sure win of $30

B. An 80% chance to win $45

Problem 10. Consider the following two-stage game. In the first stage, we have a 75 percent chance to end the game without winning anything and a 25 percent chance to move into the second stage. If you reach the second stage, you have a choice between

C. A sure chance to win $30.

D. An 80% chance to win $45

Your choice must be made before the outcome of the first stage is known. Problem 11. Which of the following outcomes do you prefer?

A. A 25% chance to win $30

B. A 20% chance to win $45

The participants in the experiments answered as follows:

Problem 9: 78% chose A, and 22% chose B

Problem 10: 74% chose C, and 26% chose D

Problem 11: 42% chose A, and 58% chose B

Since Problems 10 and 11 are identical in terms of probabilities and outcomes, they should produce consistent responses. However the participants appeared to treat Problem 10 as equivalent to Problem 9 rather than Problem 11. The attraction of Option A in Problem 9 is explained by the certainty effect. In Problem 10, the attractiveness of Option C is due to the illusion of certainty created by the two-stage formulation. This is referred to as the *pseudo-certainty effect*. This type of response inconsistency due to differences in framing probably is common.

While the essence of the framing and preference reversal phenomenon has been dealt with in the discussion of Tenets 6 and 7, and in previous chapters, the importance and yet still incompletely resolved character of this area leads me to offer some extracts from three articles by psychologists, along with a few additional comments of my own.[8]

In an article published in 1988 aimed at psychologists, Tversky, Slovic and Sattath wrote: "Preference can be inferred from direct choice between options or from a matching procedure in which the decision maker adjusts one option to match another. Studies of preference between two-dimensional options (e.g., public policies, job applicants, benefit plans) show that the more prominent dimensions loom larger in choice than in matching. Thus, choice is more lexicographic than matching. This finding is viewed as an instance of a general principle of compatibility: The weighting of inputs is enhanced by their compatibility with the output."[9]

Referring to earlier studies, they insist that "people often do not have well defined values and beliefs," that observed preferences "are actually constructed in the elicitation process" and that "choice is contingent or context sensitive. It depends upon the framing of the problem and on the method of elicitation." "Different elicitation procedures highlight different aspects of options and suggest alternative heuristics, which may give rise to inconsistent responses." As Tversky, Slovic and Sattath maintain, choice and matching are likely to involve different heuristics, and many real-world problems can be expressed either as a direct choice or a pricing (i.e., matching) decision. Discussing the compatibility principle, they note that the pricing of gambles is likely to emphasize payoffs more than probabilities because both the response and the payoffs are expressed in dollars. When there is a lack of compatibility, additional mental processes are required. Compatibility may be induced by the nature of the information (e.g., ordinal or cardinal), the response scale (grades vs. ranks) or the affinity between inputs and outputs (where common features loom larger in similarity than in dissimilarity judgments). The article deals with options with two attributes but notes that studies have not yet resolved what happens if three or more attributes are involved.

Two years later, writing for economists, Tversky, Slovic and Kahneman stated: "Observed preference reversal (PR) cannot be adequately explained by violations of independence, the reduction axiom, or transitivity. The primary cause of PR is the failure of procedure invariance, especially the overpricing of low-probability high payoff bets. . . . PR and a new reversal invoking time preferences are explained by scale compatibility, which implies that payoffs are more heavily weighted in pricing than in choice."[10]

With respect to the gambling study cited in the beginning of the discussion of Tenet 5, Tversky, Slovic and Kahneman state that the payoffs determined the buying and selling of gambles, whereas choices between gambles (and ratings of attractiveness) were influenced primarily by the probability of winning and losing. Thus, participants chose one option and set a higher price on the other. Experiments also showed inconsistencies over time. Summing up other findings, they note that alternative framings of the same option (for example, in terms of gains or losses or in terms of survival or morality) produce inconsistent preferences, and alternative elicitation procedures (for example, choice and pricing) give rise to a reversal of preferences. They conclude as follows:

Indeed the failures of description invariance (framing effects) and procedure invariance (elicitation effects) pose a greater problem for rational choice models than the failure of specific axioms such as independence or transitivity, and they demand descriptive models of much greater complexity. Violations of description invariance require an explicit treatment of the framing process, which precedes the evaluation of prospects. . . . Violations of procedure invariance require context-dependent models . . . in which the weighting of attributes is contingent on the method of elicitation. These developments highlight the discrepancy between the normative and the descriptive approaches to decision making. (Tversky, Slovic and Kahneman 1990, 215)

Three decades of research on preference reversals are recapitulated succinctly in Slovic May 1995. What has been involved, the article notes, has been an effort to understand the mental operations associated with judgment and decision making; it underscores the difficult questions that have been raised about the nature of human values. Slovic observes, "Different frames, contexts, and elicitation procedures highlight different aspects of options and bring forth different reasons and considerations that influence the decision" (p. 369). In addition, "decision making is a highly contingent form of information processing, sensitive to task complexity, time pressure, response mode, framing, reference points, and numerous other contextual factors" (p. 369). A section that should be of interest—indeed, of concern—to economists working with cost-benefit evaluation is one on contingency valuation, which criticizes that methodology in terms of the discussion just given, but also offers suggestions for an improved approach. Finally, the concluding section, given the perhaps provocative title, Preference Management, states, "The experimental study of decision processes appears to be forging a new conception of preference, one that may require serious restructuring of normative theories and approaches toward improved decision making" (p. 370).

Plott has offered a discovered preference hypothesis, contending that rationality can be understood as a process of discovery, whereby preferences are gradually determined and responses redefined as an individual accumulates experiences (Arrow et al. 1996). Although some observers have deemed this to be inconsistent with the constructed preference hypothesis, both considerations may often be relevant.

A few psychologists have recommended decomposition as an aid to problem solving unless the interconnections are great—though, in fact, they often are in matters of economic policy. Others have cautioned about biases resulting from overly simplifying complex phenomena. The first reaction of many economists to experiments that reveal preference reversals as often as 40 percent of the time is one of skepticism, accompanied by a conclusion that the experiments in question probably did not deal with representative market phenomena. Even findings a quarter as high would be deeply disconcerting, however, especially since most studies have emphasized options with only two attributes. In most real-world situations, many more attributes are involved, and that increases the chances that decision makers will not be able to maintain the consistency necessary to avoid preference reversal. Moreover, in many real-world situations we are confronted with choices in which some of the possible consequences are not well understood. This further undermines the notion that preferences between options are well defined and can be ascertained in advance with confidence. It makes framing and elicitation even more important than in the kinds of experiments that the psychologists and economists actually have run, in which the consequences of the options ordinarily have not been an issue.

All that said, the psychologists and experimental economists could do more to help. First, even with respect to two-attribute options, experiments could be undertaken to catalogue the relative importance of preference reversals for each type of contextual consideration mentioned. It would be valuable to know if certain contexts tended to lead to preference reversals in 40 to 50 percent of the selections made, while in other categories, reversals seemed to occur less than 5 percent of the time. Note, too, that while Tversky, Slovic and Kahneman have shown that framing considerations can explain intertemporal reversals of preference, some of the authors referred to on that topic contend that small changes in framing have major impacts on the discounting employed and thus on the preference reversals observed. Moreover, in their article, "Money Illusion," Shafir, Diamond and Tversky (1997) argue that alternative framings of the same financial options can give rise to different degrees of money illusion that leads to different choices. They also link money illusion to other decision phenomena discussed in this volume, such as anchoring, mental accounting and loss aversion. Finally, some of the researchers concerned with intertemporal rationality (economists and financial analysts more than psychologists) are optimistic about individual and institutional efforts that can be undertaken to reduce preference reversal in that dimension.

Tenet 7. Dominance. If Option A is better than Option B in every respect, then A is preferred to B.

The following set of problems illustrates how both invariance and dominance can be violated.

Problem 12. Imagine that you face the following pair of concurrent decisions. First examine both decisions; then indicate the options you prefer.

Decision (i): Choose between:

A. A sure gain of $240
B. A 25% chance to gain $1,000 and a 75% chance to gain nothing

Decision (ii): Choose between:

C. A sure loss of $750
D. A 75% chance to lose $1,000 and a 25% chance to lose nothing

Responses: A: 84%, B: 16%, C: 13%, D: 87%

Problem 13. A majority indicate risk aversion in the domain of gains and risk seeking in the domain of losses. A total of 73 percent of the subjects selected A and D, while only 3 percent chose B and C, the latter of which actually dominates A and D. The problem can be reformulated, subtracting a .75 chance with respect to $240 in A and D, and a .25 chance with respect to $750 in B and C.

Thus,

E = A & D = 25% chance to win $240, 75% chance to lose $760
F = B & C = 25% chance to win $250, 75% chance to lose $750

Responses: E: 0%, F: 100%

The violation of procedural invariance and dominance in Problems 12 and 13 raises two important points. First, since invariance and dominance are fundamental to any model of rational choice, no hybrid, nearly rational choice model can possibly capture this type of behavior. Second, Problems 12 and 13 illustrate the useful distinction between choices that are transparent and those that are not quite so easy to visualize. All subjects choose the dominant option in Problem 13 because the dominance is so easy to detect. The dominant choice is not so clear in Problem 12, however. If all real-life problems were transparent, behavioral approaches would have much less relevance to economic and financial analysis. Expected utility theory is often an accurate representation of choices only when they are transparent.

Tenet 8. Opportunity Costs. Opportunity costs and out-of pocket costs are equivalent; Willingness to Pay equals Willingness to Sell (in the absence of income effects and transaction costs). This discussion also draws on other articles by Thaler, notably one written jointly with the economist, Jack Knetsch and the psychologist, Daniel Kahneman, on the endowment effect, the status quo effect and loss aversion.

Nobel Prize winner Ronald Coase maintained that goods and services that are not received are worth as much as the payments made for the same quantity of the same goods and services that are received. This is essentially a reaffirmation of the principle that opportunity costs should be valued the same as equivalent out-of-pocket costs. Moreover, Milton Friedman, also a Nobel Prize winner, insisted that whether he was a buyer or a seller of an item depended on the price; above a certain price he would be a seller, and below that price, a buyer. Yet, most people do not estimate a gain forgone to possess as high a value as an expenditure or a loss of the same amount. (Recent studies have substantiated casual empiricism on this point.) Moreover, that is ordinarily the way the courts rule in resolving disputes. Changing the viewpoint only somewhat, people often act as if they would not sell an item they own for less than a certain price, but if the item is lost or stolen, they are unwilling to replace it at that price or even somewhat less.

In an early experiment of this phenomenon, half of the subjects were given tickets to a lottery and the other half, $3. The first group was given the opportunity to sell their tickets for $3, and the second group was permitted to buy the tickets for $3. Of those given the ticket, 82 percent decided to keep them, whereas only 38 percent of the other group sought to buy a ticket.

Repeated experiments have shown that, when dealing with articles that an individual purchases for his or her own use (not as stock to be resold in regular, ongoing commercial transactions), there are very large differences between the value that the individual places on those articles (the willingness to accept, or WTA) and the value that most prospective buyers place on those same articles (the willingness to pay, or WTP). Eliminating any influences that may be attributable to transactions costs, income effects, or a natural bargaining inclination of sellers to want to sell high and buyers to buy low, Kahneman, Knetsch and Thaler found the difference between the WTA and the WTP to be of the order of 2–1 to 3–1, and sometimes higher (Thaler 1992, ch. 6). Subsequent experiments by Smith and colleagues narrowed but did not eliminate this difference (Smith 1994) and did not deal with the extreme disparities that are referred to as enhanced loss aversion. Disparities between buying and selling prices such as are shown in the experiments raise serious problems for practitioners of cost-benefit analysis, who are confronted with the challenge of placing monetary values on goods not traded in markets.

This result, which has become known as the endowment effect, appears to occur as soon as one comes into possession of an article. It is not restricted to what might be considered "valued possessions" but extends even to such commonplace items as beer mugs and ball-point pens. Nor is it a matter of discovering the qualities of an object because most of the experiments have allowed careful examination of the articles by all parties at the moment of their distribution. Since the negotiations take place within minutes after distribution of the articles, the endowment effect is virtually instantaneous. Moreover, when sellers are placed in the position of buyers, they are not willing to pay the minimum prices that they demanded as sellers.

The effect seems to be attributable principally to the pain of letting go of something. It reflects the loss aversion mentioned in explaining risk seeking in the domain of losses of people who reveal themselves to be risk averse when it comes to possible gains. This inconsistency in valuation violates what economists and financial analysts term *rationality*, whether or not it reflects rationality in some other sense. Some economists have suggested that the endowment effect may be part of a general "status quo bias," which affects problems not necessarily framed in terms of gains and losses and that extends to the exchange of articles intended for rapid turnover (unlike the endowment effect) and to all types of economic and financial dealings.

The loss aversion effect may also help explain why the level of transactions falls so much when the prices of real estate or stocks on an exchange decline, even though lower prices would ordinarily lead to a higher level of transactions. There are many still unanswered questions. Do changes in one's endowment alter preferences? (Should one's tradeoff between two articles be influenced by whether or not the person owns one of the articles in question if he or she is well aware of the product characteristics?) What are the implications of loss aversion for the selection of employment alternatives, each of which offers certain disadvantages with respect to the other? What are the implications for valuing a decline in real wages in a period of inflation?[11]

Tenet 9. Marginal Analysis. Choices are made to equate marginal costs with marginal benefits.

One application of marginal analysis is to optimal search—about which some doubts already have been raised. Experiments have shown that most subjects say that they are willing to experience the cost of a 20-minute car ride to save $5 (mid-1980s dollars) on the cost of an inexpensive item that they planned to buy (for example, a $15 calculator), but not a significantly more expensive item (a $125 jacket or a $500 TV set). They mistakenly relate the benefit to the total price of the item rather than the marginal benefits. In informal experiments in microeconomics theory classes at the Federal University of Paraná in Curitiba, Brazil, this anomaly was upheld in one case, at the beginning of a course, but not toward the end of another course, after much more time had been spent on explaining marginal analysis. In any event, and apropos the comments on contingency analysis and the followup questions and answers in both classes, it might not be possible to predict the actual behavior of many of the students simply from the answers that they gave. Repetition probably does lead to learning and a tendency for equivalent marginal costs to be considered the same (and for a marginalist analysis to apply in general). However, even slight variations in the repetitions seem to prevent the tenet from being upheld with quite the frequency that might be expected, given the logic involved and the instruction on the point in economics and finance.

Tenet 10. Sunk Costs. Fixed, historical and other sunk costs do not influence decisions.

Several experiments and many examples have been used to show that this principle is often violated. One illustration is revealed by the type of response given by sports enthusiasts who have purchased tickets to an athletic contest in a city several hours away and who decide to drive to the event because they have purchased the tickets (a sunk cost), even though travel conditions have worsened and are sufficiently disagreeable or dangerous so that they would not travel there if they had to purchase the tickets on arrival. Another example, already referred to, concerns the use of indoor versus outdoor tennis facilities. In general, individuals, households, enterprises and governments behave as if they had what Thaler terms an implicit mental accounting system; sunk costs are costs that have not been ''mentally amortized'' and are coded as losses. Several violations of Tenet 10 are cited in Chapter 7. Violations of this rationality principle are frequent, and whereas some seem to be attenuated by learning, others are not. (Little has been done to determine which type of violations fall into each category.)

Tenet 11. Fungibility. Money has no labels and is spent on its highest valued use.

Common examples of people's failure to guide themselves by this principle can be seen in actions such as failure to pay a credit card balance in full, incurring an interest rate charge of 18 to 21 percent and even higher instead of removing the necessary funds from a savings account that pays perhaps a quarter of the credit card rate. Two problems used to test the tenet were:

Problem 16. Imagine that you have decided to see a play where admission is $10 per ticket. As you enter the theater, you discover that you have lost a $10 bill. Would you still pay for a ticket to see the play? (88% replied affirmatively.)

Problem 17. Imagine that you have decided to see a play and have paid the admission price of $10 per ticket. As you enter the theater, you discover that you have lost your ticket. The seat was not marked and the ticket cannot be recovered. Would you pay $10 for another ticket? (Only 46% responded affirmatively, and the other 54% negatively.)

In Problems 16 and 17, the loss of the $10 affects the choice of whether to buy a ticket only when it is coded in the same account. A key question in the investigation of mental accounting systems is the relationship between costs and losses. When is a cost a loss? (Surely when it is considered excessive, but does that vary according to circumstances or the institutional environment, as well as from person to person?)

Violation of this tenet of economic and financial rationality is much greater for household decisions (including the investments of households) than for decisions made by businesses.

Tenet 12. Domain of Utility. Willingness to pay for a good depends only on the characteristics of the good or service and not on the perceived merits of the deal.

An example cited is that of several people on a beach on a hot summer day when one of them offers to get up and bring back some ice cold beers. How much are the others willing to pay for the beers if they are obtained from a nondescript local grocery store, and how much if they come from a nearby gourmet restaurant, well known for its ambiance? In both cases, the beers will come ice cold and in the same unopened bottle. The answers and the differences between the willingness to pay tend to vary a good deal.

Perhaps a more convincing example, and one that has received a great deal of attention from economists, concerns what is regarded as fair, or at least acceptable, in splitting money in an arrangement in which the one who proposes the split is allowed to keep what he proposes for himself only if the other person accepts the proposed split. Neither party receives anything if the proposed offer is rejected. Whether or not such extreme situations (ultimatums) are common, it is clear that perceived merits do appear to have played a role in many negotiations between persons from different cultures.

Tenet 13. Economic Opportunities. All legal economic opportunities for gains will be exploited.

On the one hand, something less than all legal opportunities may be exploited insofar as social norms imply additional constraints. Most people will sacrifice some financial gain for social acceptance, even if it does not necessarily contribute to greater profits in the long run. On the other hand, the extent to which laws limit efforts to obtain gains is sometimes determined by the relation of the fine or penalty (modified by the probability of being caught) to the benefits of avoiding the law. This affects certain types of transactions, but in the case of industrial espionage involving new technologies, the imagined benefits may be so large that moral constraints and social norms may be the most important constraints. Beyond that, violation of some laws (such as tax laws) is treated as a sport and is openly admired in some societies, which raises other considerations.

Among the examples and experiments have been several relating to tipping in restaurants. In one case, a businessman travels to a distant community, and after having lunch in a town to which he has never been and to which he never expects to return, he leaves a tip. In another case, this one used in experiments, people have indicated that they would leave tips almost as large in restaurants they go to on a single occasion as in those which they frequent a great deal. However, the latter may exemplify what people say they would do (and what they might actually do in some experiment), but may not necessarily be what they would do in a natural economic situation.

Tenet 14. Rational Expectations. Probabilistic judgments are consistent and unbiased.

Tenet 15. Bayesian Learning. Probabilistic judgments are updated by the appropriate use of Bayes's rule (Subjective Probability Analysis).

Rational expectations are treated at somewhat greater length in Chapter 6. Suffice to note two points here. First, some economists have objected to the use of rules of thumb or heuristics, because, as they state, use of such measures and theories of expectations that are not based on the rational expectations model can make sense only if there is a theory that would explain systematic mistakes. Barro and Fischer once took such a position, but that was prior to the widespread publication of work on psychology's decision analysis. The findings of the latter provide the beginnings of just such a theory of systematic errors or deviations from rationality. In addition, even many survivors often employ such rules of thumb or judgmental heuristics and follow procedures that violate the dictates of subjective probability analysis. They give, for example, too much weight to one or another category of information, attributing to small samples the characteristics of large populations and failing to take account of important phenomena such as regression to the mean. Heuristics have already been discussed in Chapter 4 and are dealt with further in Appendix A. In short, both the tenet on expectations and the tenet on the use of subjective probability analysis often fail to hold.

Implications and Conclusions

Thaler notes that the real challenge is how best to describe the behavior of economic agents in complex environments (Thaler, Conclusion in Roth 1987). The power of traditional economic theory helps in analyzing many phenomena, but the rigorous analytical tools become a handicap when economists restrict their investigations to those explanations consistent with the existing paradigm. As an example Thaler refers to the remarks of an editor of the *Journal of Financial Economics*. The editor had commented that to explain the "January effect" in the stock market (whereby small firms appear to earn particularly high returns in that month), it would be necessary to explain the seemingly strange effect in terms consistent with rational, maximizing behavior on the part of all actors in the model. The degree to which the principles of economic and financial analysis are violated seems to vary. The problem appears more serious for consumer than for business and investment behavior, and the anomalies probably are much more common for some of the tenets than for others. What remains an important issue is the degree to which adverse experiences following less-than-fully rational decision making can alter behavior or the degree to which more active efforts of behavior modification can do so. Psychologists such as Kahneman are skeptical, as is Thaler, but note the findings reported by Vernon Smith referred to above, and the comments of the late Fisher Black, who claimed that he observed such shifts toward the development of improved heuristics in process in the world of finance (see the section "The Recognition of Noise" in Chapter 7).

INTERTEMPORAL CHOICE

Almost all of the discussion of anomalies presented so far has dealt with reasoning concerning rationality and expected utility in a point of time. There are also some very disturbing anomalies related to intertemporal decision making—decision making that involves costs or benefits distributed over more than a single time period.[12]

The starting point of any discussion on intertemporal choice is the presumed tendency of most people to give too much attention to the present and not enough to the future. Most individuals save less than they should (certainly less than they wish they had when the future rolls around), they spend too little time in activities that develop skills (employment skills and skills that will later yield pleasure such as music and art appreciation), and they overindulge in activities with indirect negative effects that will impact mainly in the future.[13] The irrationalities extend far beyond discounting future benefits too steeply. They also involve discounting the future benefits of some goods and services more than others, using discount rates that are not constant through the entire stream of benefits, and acting as if we are obliged to discount future benefits at rates much higher than is truly the case.

One of the most common intertemporal anomalies can be seen in the purchase of household appliances. Consumers frequently decide to save $50 to $100 in the initial purchase price, even though a more expensive, energy efficient model might offset the initial difference in as little as two or three years of an eight- to fifteen-year expected life of the equipment, due to lower operating costs. The irrationality of such decisions—sometimes implying that an individual is acting as if he or she would have to pay an interest rate of more than 50 percent to borrow funds to purchase the energy efficient model—is striking, especially for those who have access to consumer loans at a bank or credit union for only 10 to 12 percent, but even for those who would have to charge it and pay off a credit card balance at 18 to 21 percent.

The message of financial and economic theory is clear. First, a rational individual should apply a discount rate that reflects the cost that he or she has to pay to borrow. Second, the rate of discount should be consistent among the various decisions that involve more than a single time period. People are much more impatient about immediate delays than about future delays of the same amount of time, as Camerer 1990 puts it. There is a great deal of what has been called hyperbolic discounting—discounting that follows a hyperbolic rather than an exponential form over time (Ainslie 1991). When faced with an inferior early option and a superior later option, the hyperbolic discounter tends to prefer the later, but to switch to the inferior option as both approach in time. This tendency is aggravated if the options become physically visible, particularly if the inferior, early option becomes visible while the other does not.

Actual decisions often imply discount rates that differ greatly from the cost of money to the individual. This can be seen in the consumer appliance purchases just referred to as well as in many decisions to refrain from purchasing more insulation or from replacing existing windows with a more insulated type. (Note, however, the tendency to go to the other extreme and overinsulate after certain emergencies such as the dramatic but temporary escalation of energy prices in 1974 and then again in 1979. This recalls the irrationalities of under- and then overinsurance against low-probability natural disasters events referred to earlier.)

At the same time that they make decisions implying an extraordinarily high rate of interest, many of these same individuals make other decisions that imply much lower, and, in some cases, even negative rates of interest. Many teachers elect to receive their salaries in twelve monthly payments rather than in nine, receiving no compensation for delaying the receipt of their income. Millions of U.S. citizens receive tax refunds regularly (instead of making adjustments in their withholding arrangements or estimated tax payments that would eliminate their overpayments during the year). Some people still join Christmas Clubs, savings plans that offer zero interest and often penalize early withdrawals. For many people, consumption tends to increase steadily over the course of their life until they retire. Moreover, most surveyed indicated that they would prefer to receive the same quantity of lifetime salary income in a rising stream rather than have the larger salaries come in the earlier years, even though their expected value would be considerably larger. There are several possible explanations for this thinking (e.g., attributing utility to the act of anticipation, valuing present consumption in terms of past consumption), but that does not make it any more rational in terms of traditional economic calculation. While some of the more flagrant irrationalities such as saving in Christmas Clubs are declining, other, not-too-dissimilar decisions and preferences continue with little modification. (Note that some psychologists do not regard a negative time preference as necessarily irrational.)

Experimental studies show that the rates of discount that individuals apply to decisions vary according to the length of time involved, the amount of money involved and whether the amount is a gain or a loss.

People who require a certain premium if they are to receive a sum of money in a year instead of at once do not generally insist on proportionately as large a premium for receiving money in two years instead of one. This would seem to suggest a declining rate of discount as the period of time is lengthened and creates possibilities of preference reversals reflecting intransitivity.

Other experiments reveal that individuals do not require proportionately as large a premium for a year's delay in receiving, say, $5,000 as they do for receiving $50. A disparity also exists in the reaction toward gains and losses. In one experiment, with the same time period delays involved, foregoing a gain of $10 required a compensation of $21, whereas to avoid a loss of $10, a future compensation of only $15 was deemed adequate. Such decisions are consistent with the discussion of decision making in a point of time which found that a given amount of money is valued more if it represents a loss than if it represents a gain.

Some analysts have attributed particularly high rates of implicit discounts to the temporary emergence of certain "appetites." Emotions (passions) are used to explain various actions that might not seem to correspond to rational self-interest, some of which are harmful in the long run, and others of which reflect a kind of enlightened self-interest and are beneficial to both the individual and the community over time. A prominent psychologist writes that the lure of immediate self-gratification at every moment establishes competing interests within the individual that struggle within themselves for dominance. Several economists and psychologists extend that notion and attribute various anomalies to individuals' having multiple personalities. All of this brings us back to the phenomenon of addiction, which has been explained in each of the following ways:

1. Addiction is a disease and does not involve choice.

2. Addiction is like entering on a primrose path; one enters slowly and unknowingly, but it is then very difficult to extract oneself.

3. Addiction reflects a divided self—multiple selves.

4. Addiction involves long-term negative effects, but overall the addict is better off than he or she would have been in the absence of addiction.

The disconcerting nature of many temporal anomalies is more firmly established than the explanations for them. However, framing appears to play an important role in bringing about anomalous results, as do expectations in natural economic situations. Some psychologists argue that small changes in framing can have major impacts on the rate of discount, as noted earlier. A number of psychologists maintain that the preference reversals that arise from other-than-exponential discounting can be overcome, that consistency in behavior can be learned. Both individual and social mechanisms of self-discipline are cited, some of a cognitive character and others of a rather different nature (e.g., "using the momentum attached to emotions"), with most economists relying not so much on corrective mechanisms as on the establishment of conventions and institutions to offset the irrational individual behavior. Among the institutional arrangements are social security systems, employer pension plans and artificially steep wage profiles designed to help people achieve a desired intertemporal consumption profile. Robert Frank, the author of the last remarks, argues that there is a need of remedies for societal problems, which he concludes reflect suboptimal time discounting. In addition to low savings rates, he lists low corporate rates of investment, ballooning private and public debt, abysmal educational attainments, AIDS, environmental degradation, high rates of infant mortality, crime and teenage pregnancy. He insists that the economic approach to intertemporal choice provides few useful insights into these problems (Frank, ch. 15 in Loewenstein and Elster 1992). Elster writes of the need for far-sighted public institutions to exert a learning effect and a "displacement effect," fulfilling needs related to the future and leaving individuals free to pursue more short-term goals (Loewenstein and Elster, 1992, ch. 2). While virtually everyone would share Frank and Elster's, concerns, the guidelines for rational government intervention in these activities are not always clear. The notion that government intervention can be relied upon to be far-sighted just because private initiatives may not be is certainly in doubt.

Perhaps the last observations extend too far beyond the main thrust of this presentation. Returning then, to the initial focus, we can state that if individuals make such inconsistent intertemporal decisions, what are the macroeconomic implications of those inconsistencies, particularly since evidence of the market's ability to overcome the anomalous behavior of individuals is mixed?[14] Should our concerns be less if such intertemporal inconsistencies apply much more to private consumption decisions than to those involving investment? Is it possible to generalize about the type of decisions that are most subject to intertemporal anomalies? Is experience (or instruction) likely to be more successful in reducing these anomalies than those referring to expected utility in a point of time? Clearly, the issue of intertemporal irrationalities raises many major concerns, and a broader approach is needed to help resolve them.

NOTES

1. Thaler, "The Psychology of Choice and the Assumptions of Economics," in Roth 1987, 99–130. The excerpts and adaptations are reprinted with the permission of Cambridge University Press. See also Russell and Thaler 1985.

2. Simon and a group of associates (George B. Dantzig, Robin Hogarth, Charles R. Plott, Howard Raiffa, Thomas C. Schelling, Kenneth A. Shepsle, Richard Thaler, Amos Tversky and Sidney Winter) prepared a report for the National Academy of Sciences, which termed SEU

a sophisticated mathematical model of choice that defines the conditions of perfect utility maximization rationality in a world of certainty or in a world in which the probability distribution of all relevant variables can be provided by the decision maker. . . . It has nothing to say about how to frame problems, set goals, or develop new alternatives.

What chiefly distinguishes the empirical research on decision making and problem solving from the prescriptive approaches derived from SEU theory is the attention that the former gives to the limits on human rationality. These limits are imposed by the complexity of the world in which we live, the incompleteness and inadequacy of human knowledge, the inconsistencies of individual preferences and belief, the conflicts of value among people and groups of people, and the inadequacy of the computations we can carry out, even with the aid of the most powerful computers. . . . To bring it within the scope of human thinking powers, we must simplify our problem formulation drastically, even leaving out much or most of what is potentially relevant. (Simon and Associates 1992, 33–34)

Economists deal with expected utility or decision utility. Some psychologists such as Kahneman also consider *experienced* utility, which can conflict with what was anticipated and used in decision making (Arrow et al. 1996).

3. For a summary of the effects of the size and frequency of incentives, see Kagel and Roth 1995, 661–65, esp. 663–65.

4. See Kagel and Roth 1995, 644–49.

5. Bewley maintains that entrepreneurship in general can be understood as ambiguity neutral. See T. F. Bewley, "Knightian Decision Theory: Part I," Cowles Foundation Discussion Paper No. 807, New Haven, CT, 1986, cited in Kagel and Roth 1995, 649.

Support for prospect theory from experimental economics can be found in Myagkov and Plott December 1997.

6. Thaler 1992, ch. 7. See also Tversky 1996.

7. Appraisals of the preference reversal experiments can be found in Kagel and Roth 1995, 68–75 and 658–65.

8. See also Kagel and Roth 1995, 658–61.

9. Tversky, Slovic and Sattath 1988, 371. All the quotes in the following paragraph also are from p. 371.

10. Tversky, Slovic and Kahneman March 1990.

11. See also Kagel and Roth 1995, 665–70, esp. 668–70, which explains the endowment phenomenon in terms of five other possible effects, only one of which is dealt with in this text.

12. This section draws particularly on Thaler and Loewenstein, "Intertemporal Choice," ch. 8 in Thaler 1992 and Loewenstein and Elster 1992.

13. On the contrary, insist Becker, Grossman and Murphy. People who consume drugs are aware of and take into account the negative effects that are likely to follow (Loewenstein and Elster 1992, ch. 14).

14. "Market theorists assume that expected utility predicts preferences at the market level," writes Dorla Evans, "even as evidence mounts that it predicts poorly at the individual levels. The arguments for better-predicting markets are grounded in the assumption that individuals respond to the competition of the markets. . . . I conclude that expected utility does indeed predict better in markets, but analyses suggest that improved performance may be due to the statistical role played by markets introduced by market price selection rules" (Evans 1997).

Camerer, reviewing a larger number of experimental studies, sounds a somewhat more optimistic note, concluding that while it depends on the particular type of market, in general, market experiments tend to reduce Bayesian judgment errors (Kagel and Roth 1995, 605–8, 675–76). Holt observes that double auction experiments whereby both buyers and sellers post and accept prices publicly, seem particularly effective in reaching market efficiency (Kagel and Roth 1995, 368–72). In a section entitled "The Relevance of Experiments to the Study of Industrial Organization," which discusses the pros and cons of the issue, and the charge that laboratory experiments cannot duplicate natural settings, Holt concludes, "Experiments are usually not suited to address empirical issues about the underlying structure of industrial markets. An experiment can be used to test the behavioral assumptions of a theory that relates structure to performance, to stress-test a theory by introducing small violations of its structural assumptions, and to search for stylized facts or patterns in laboratory markets. The particular objective affects the degree of parallelism between the experimental design and the motivating theories or natural markets" (Kagel and Roth 1995, 355). Finally, consider the often disappointing results of those markets with the best feedback data of all, financial markets, as discussed in Chapter 7.

Chapter 6

Expectations and Expected Profits

Investment decisions should be based not on the results of the past, but on expectations about the future. Unfortunately, it is much easier to evaluate the efficiency of past or even current allocation of resources than it is to deal adequately with expectations and, in so doing, transform good guidelines for decision making into decisions that increase the likelihood of successful results. This chapter provides a brief review of what strikes me as the disappointing status of the work in this area, beginning with the approach of economics and finance, and inquiring, then, whether help is to be found from psychology.[1]

HOW DO ECONOMISTS EXPLAIN EXPECTATIONS?

Although expectations are not observable, many economists attempt to base expectations estimates on objective data. Most attention is focused on aggregate data, given the frequent assumption that many individual data tend to cancel out. Basically, there have been four lines of argument.

First, a good deal of work by economists on expectations has involved extrapolations from the past. Sometimes this has been accompanied by explanations and a careful effort at justification. More often, however, the use of extrapolation has been more in the nature of an assumption that the future will be much like the past—the immediate future, in any event.

Second, and more commonly, expectations have been estimated by offering a modified extrapolation that reflects learning from past experiences and that endeavors to take recent changes into account, even introducing certain changes in economic relationships in an attempt to evaluate recent trends—in birth and mortality rates, technology, and so on. Most weight is usually given to recent data, and sometimes an effort is made to take certain types of biases into account. Such approaches to expectations are often quite eclectic and ad hoc, and they vary from one another.

A provocative and highly dissident approach was the potential surprise theory of G. L. S. Shackle, which insisted on the potential of discontinuous change and the lack of any capacity to predict. It has had very few followers. (For a recent summary and critique, see the bibliographical listings under Earl, particularly Earl 1995.)

Fourth, there is the theory of rational expectations (TRE), associated particularly with the names of Muth, Lucas and Sargent. Authoritative presentations can be found in texts on macroeconomic theory. As a general comment, although TRE has been extraordinarily controversial, its high level of influence probably is due to its success in explaining the inability of Keynesian theory to predict well beyond the short run, as learning took place and the assumed irrationality of certain economic agents in the Keynesian framework tended to be overcome.

- TRE assumes that all of the relevant information is available and that the calculations based on that information are rational.

- TRE assumes that the deviations between expectations and actual events are minimal and random.

- TRE concludes that since there are no substantial deviations between predictions and future events, expectations can be based on hard data; there is no need to measure expectations directly. As such, it is possible to replace "expectations" with some fixed function derived from past and contemporaneous variables that can be observed.

Comments on TRE:

1. In its initial formulations, TRE implied that measurement of expectations was not required; subsequently, some adherents have attempted to verify the theory.

2. It is sometimes said that TRE implies that businesspeople have little difficulty in making calculations that take economists months. While that may seem like a serious criticism, certainly a difference exists between making calculations and behaving in a way that enables one to arrive at the same results. Milton Friedman used to refer to the billiard player who behaves *as if* he were aware of the mathematics and had made the maximizing calculations necessary to sink his shots. More recently, Thomas Sargent has affirmed that a key group of late 17th-century English bankers behaved in a manner consistent with TRE (unlike their French counterparts a hundred years later, in his telling of what took place).

3. Whether or not TRE really describes the way in which expectations are formed, if people act on the basis of certain expectations (e.g., rising inflation), those expectations tend to be realized.

4. Efforts to verify TRE have been less favorable than its proponents predicted but more successful than its harshest critics anticipated.

5. The TRE theory is consistent with the perfectly rational behavior of optimization/ maximization. In that sense, it is conceivable as a normative theory—but it seems

inadequate as a description of how those who are successful behave. Note needs to be made of both its strengths and weaknesses for policy purposes.[2]

Finally, expectations are strongly influenced by the way in which risk is viewed.[3] Economists are aware that people's perceptions of risk are influenced by sociological, cultural, ethical and political factors as well as by psychological factors. However, since little of this has been formalized, economists tend to ignore such factors, with the exception of those who are country risk analysts. Serious problems are involved in ascertaining the facts needed to assess risk (i.e., difficulties in perceiving information accurately and in making judgments about the relative importance of the various types of information). The multiple characteristics of risk and the different ways in which the various characteristics often are weighted further complicate matters. This along with the endowment effect considerations referred to previously explains the alternative valuations of natural resource projects with nonmarket benefits. Such valuations also are quite sensitive to a variety of special effects and contextual factors, as well as to the way in which the proposals are framed and information elicited. Many risks tend to receive attention disproportionate to their importance—too little in some cases, and too much in others. In particular, there seems to be an irrationally excessive aversion to imprecisely understood risks. (Such an aversion perhaps can only be understood in terms of assigning high probabilities to worst case scenarios.) Finally, in evaluating risk, excessive weight tends to be given to the possibility of errors of commission as compared to errors of omission, which also distorts expectations. This is more important for certain categories of decisions than others. It seems imperative that more of the findings from the emerging empirical studies of risk in different situations be incorporated into the presentations on expectations.

CAN PSYCHOLOGISTS HELP US UNDERSTAND EXPECTATIONS?

Basic Considerations and the First Results

Toward the end of the Second World War, most leading economists were predicting a pronounced postwar recession (relying on models in some cases and on reasoning by analogy with what happened after the First World War, in others). The psychologist, George Katona, was skeptical. He decided to survey consumers, basically to ask them how they viewed the country's prospects and their own, and to ask them about their plans for purchases. This simple and direct approach was the birth of the Index of Consumer Sentiment and the Indexes of Producer Sentiment and Intentions.

The information obtained in those surveys was introduced into the economic analysis and greatly improved predictions, becoming a standard part of much macroeconomic analysis. The results were particularly notable with respect to inventories and were more successful than alternative approaches in detecting periods of economic turnabouts. A concern, however, has been that the surveys predict better for the general level of purchases than for specific commodities about which inquiries were made. Refinements in these surveys have included increased attention to expectations at the individual as well as the aggregate level. In addition, a distinction was made between what were regarded as routine situations and new ones, with changes in expectations leading to shifts in the "normal" relation between income and consumption.

What underlies the Indexes of Consumer and Producer Sentiment? Katona and his followers (among whom were economists and sociologists as well as fellow psychologists) concluded that expectations were inherently uncertain. They maintained that expectations involved conscious reasoning along with imitation and affect, that they reflected knowledge and opinions, evaluations and feelings, as well as a tendency to try to prepare for events in advance and even to control them to the extent possible. Katona and his followers contributed a great deal to improved prediction of macroeconomic results. They were able to explain the relation between variables quite well as long as the variables were relatively stable, but also to catch many of the shifts to new relationships— though they did not succeed in clearly ferreting out the basic factors underlying those relationships.

Attitudes

Some psychologists have given considerable attention to "attitudes" ("an individual predisposition to evaluate an object or an aspect of the world in a favorable or an unfavorable manner," according to Antonides 1991, 89) to help explain expectations and other phenomena. Empirical verification of attitudes has not yet been strong, perhaps in part because of difficulties in specifying the concept. It does not seem to be a promising contribution for behavioral economics at this point.

Moods

Emotions have been touched on in the discussion of motivation and preferences. A mood refers to a relatively enduring emotional state. Moods and, in particular, shifts in moods may help explain expectations, leading, for example, to changes in decisions about saving, consumption and the purchase of stocks (or certain groups of stocks such as "technology" stocks or biotechnology stocks). There are differences in moods between persons and groups, and shifts can take place from one time to another for the same person. Closely related to this notion is the concept of waves of optimism and pessimism at both the personal and societal level. While moods and waves of optimism and pessimism may well have important impacts, as in the case of attitudes, the concepts are not yet operational for other than highly speculative economic analysis—perhaps more for developing behavioral hypotheses than for exercises in verification.

An Eclectic View

Writing on expectations and TRE, the Swedish psychologist Karl Erik Wärneryd (1997) stated that expectations are formed on the basis of (1) extrapolations of past experiences, (2) learning (based on the degree of success of past experiences) and (3) new information about the individual's environment. He maintained that the weight of each component should vary according to the conditions or situations. Ordinarily, he maintained, psychologists would include all three components, whereas the rival economic theories have tended to include only one or another type of information in their explanation of expectations. He concluded that this may be about to change, however, inasmuch as several recent studies by economists suggested that what is rational may differ in different situations.[4] (Note that some economists also have included all three types of information in estimating expectations.)

The Contribution of Psychology to the Explanation of Financial and Economic Expectations

The surveys and models of psychologists catch more of the changes in expectations than do those of economists, but they, too, tend to underestimate changes. The best predictor of psychologists, one that economists tend to rely on, is the Index of Consumer Sentiment, but after 50 years, that concept still cannot claim to have a solid theoretical justification. Psychologists offer interesting material, but several factors are cited as helping to explain expectations that are not yet well specified or that are at least partially conflicting. As a consequence, this has not been an area in which psychology has had nearly as significant a conceptual impact on economics as in the recent work on preferences (especially the literature concerning preference reversal/construction of preferences), judgment (especially the recognition of judgmental heuristics) and utility theory generally (beginning with "prospect theory," which deals with how to evaluate alternative categories of prospects and the inconsistent but predictable attitude toward risk). It is not easy to understand why experimental cognitive psychology and experimental economics have not yet dealt much with the expectations component of decision making.

NOTES

1. For a review of the literature on expectations formation, especially the rationality of price expectations, see Kagel and Roth 1995, 609–12 (discussed in the Conclusion of ch. 4). Sunder observes, "Given the key role of assumptions about belief formation in economics, surprisingly little work has been done in modeling and testing the theories

of belief formation within environments where market discipline prevails (Kagel and Roth 1995, 468).

2. A rival theory, the theory of rational belief equilibrium, has been proposed by Kurz. This is outlined in Kurz, "Endogenous Uncertainty: A Unified View of Market Volatility" (unpublished manuscript, Department of Economics, Stanford University, Stanford, CA, September 9, 1997), summarizing work published since 1994, which was brought together in a volume released in 1997. While it would not be appropriate to attempt to evaluate that theory in this presentation, let me note the following comments on TRE which Kurz offers:

> The rational expectations equilibrium (REE) theory is based on several assumptions, but three of them are fundamental to my discussion here. These are;
>
> (A.1) The true probability law of the economy is stationary. In a *stationary* economy all the joint probabilities of economic variables remain the same as we move the time scale.
>
> (A.2) Economic agents know the true probability law underlying the equilibrium variables of the economy. This is the first component of "structural knowledge" which the agents are *assumed* to possess.
>
> (A.3) Agents know the demand and supply functions of all other agents. They can compute equilibrium prices of commodities and assets in the present and in the future for all possible exogenous fundamental information (i.e., news) in the future. This is the second component of structural knowledge which they possess.

In equilibrium all economic magnitudes depend upon the realization of the exogenous state but according to (A.3) all agents know precisely the functional relations, or the map between equilibrium magnitudes (e.g. production decisions of firms, prices, dividend payments, returns, etc.) and the state. Consequently, all economic magnitudes vary only with the variability of the exogenous state over time. Moreover, it is then *an* assumption that given any observed information, all agents agree on the *meaning* or *interpretation* of such information. That is, all agents agree as to the "state" of the economy that gave rise to the observed information.

The implication of these assumptions is that all financial risks and observed volatility arise from causes which are *external to the economy* and I call such uncertainty "Exogenous Uncertainty." Under the above theory, no risk can be propagated from within the economic system via human beliefs or actions. This means that the volatility of equilibrium variables is exactly equal to the level that would be justified by the variability of the exogenous conditions.

The above discussion enables me to offer a simple summary of the conclusions of the theory of rational expectations with respect to the nature of market volatility:

1. For each state of the exogenous fundamentals there is a *correct* equilibrium price of all securities in the market.

2. If you possess all exogenous fundamental information, you are able to compute the correct prices of securities and hence all uncertainty about prices will be resolved. By implication, hedging against the risks of all exogenous fundamentals is possible, in principle, and can control all risk associated with market volatility.

3. Active asset management has no function to play since the only investment management needed is the services of diversification and information gathering.

These conclusions of the theory have been at the foundation of contemporary research into the structure of market volatility. Unfortunately, they are in conflict with many theoretical and empirical observations and with the common experience of market participants. " . . . [T]here are several outstanding problems or paradoxes (sometimes called 'anomalies') related to the functioning of financial markets which this theory has failed to resolve and current academic research has attempted to develop special theories to explain each one of these paradoxes" (Kurz, "Endogenous Uncertainty," 2–4).

3. The following comments are drawn primarily from Kunreuther and Slovic 1996.

4. See the comments of Arrow et al. 1996.

Chapter 7

Behavioral Finance

Before turning to some guidelines for behavioral decision making, consider at least one of the major applications of the behavioral approach. Topics with a major social content, long ignored by mainstream economics, might have been selected, all the more so because, in recent years, they have begun to receive so much attention from the most traditional analytical framework. While important behavioral work is underway in that area, particularly with respect to marriage and the family, perhaps the greatest concentration of behavioral analyses and the most successful application of the behavioral approach has been in the area of financial economics. These studies, many of which could not be termed macroeconomic, are, nonetheless, at a more aggregate level than those discussed up to this point. Their findings have revealed that financial markets often reflect less efficiency than prominent academics had confidently assured us was the case. This has reinforced interest in the kind of micro analyses considered in the previous chapters, in part in the hope of helping to resolve the long, illusive search for the microfoundations of more macroeconomic phenomena. These studies also suggest that deviations from rationality at the level of individuals and enterprises often may not be overcome by market interaction.

This outline of behavioral finance considers eight topics:

1. The background: What are the basic elements of financial and economic rationality, and to what extent have studies undertaken within the traditional framework of economics been uncovering behavior with respect to money and income that is not consistent with financial and economic rationality?

2. Are there some psychological considerations influencing financial and economic decision making that ought to be incorporated into the models? (Are there some psy-

chological relationships where the evidence is so strong that we sacrifice some ability to predict if we ignore them?)

3. The data on financial transactions are perhaps the best available for any category of analysis, but how should the information used to make financial decisions be characterized?

4. To what extent can the volatility of financial markets be explained by financial and economic news, and by the rational expectations to which they presumably contribute?

5. Do financial markets overreact, and, if so does that overreaction extend beyond a few minutes or a few hours? (Doesn't arbitrage correct it rather quickly?)

6. How can certain seemingly nonoptimizing, nonmaximizing behavior by successful corporations be explained?

7. What explains the financial behavior of individuals insofar as it does not correspond to financial and economic rationality?

8. Given the mobility of international markets, and the velocity and low cost of information flows, is it possible that there are major inefficiencies in those markets. and, if so how can that be explained?

THE BACKGROUND: BASIC ELEMENTS OF FINANCIAL RATIONALITY

1. The basic definition of financial rationality is that decisions are consistent and that they seek to advance financial well-being.

2. Money now is preferred to the same quantity of money later; any preference for money later can only be explained by a supplementary compensation that is at least as high, in terms of the rate of return, as an individual could obtain for those funds in the financial markets. The same rate of return should apply to compensation for delayed payments between all periods in the future.

3. In making a purchase, any implicit rate of interest should not exceed the explicit rate at which the individual could borrow money. The implicit rates of interest should be the same on purchases of all goods and services.

4. The rate of additional compensation necessary to lead to a preference for money in the future rather than at present should be the same regardless of the amount of money involved.

5. Money seeks the highest rate of return available and is fully interchangeable: money is fungible.

6. An individual should determine his or her level of consumption on the basis of the income expected over the course of a lifetime, in relation to anticipated needs and wants over the same period of time. If unanticipated income is received in any given year, consumption from that windfall during that year should not increase by more than the marginal propensity to consume (MPC) of the portion of the additional income that would be allocated to that first year, not by the entire amount of the un-

expected addition or by the MPC of the entire amount. The unanticipated income represents an addition to lifetime income, most of which would raise consumption only in subsequent years. This would be modified only if receipt of that unexpected income led to the expectation of other similar additional income flows in the future, or if the receipt led to a change in the individual's rate of discount between consumption and saving.

BEHAVIOR WITH RESPECT TO MONEY AND INCOME APPARENTLY INCONSISTENT WITH FINANCIAL AND ECONOMIC RATIONALITY

Behavioral analyses questioning the first five elements of financial rationality have already been mentioned. Moreover, a number of traditionally oriented studies have led to the establishment of certain institutions to overcome difficulties that are often in part a recognition of less-than-fully rational behavior. For example, the "impatience" reflected in the inclination of many individuals to behave in a manner that leads them to sustain implicit interest rates higher than those they would have to pay in the market has been treated in part as a problem of self control, and has been alleviated in a second-best manner by (1) life insurance; (2) social security; (3) enterprise pension systems with required employee contributions; and (4) the use of simple rules of behavior in personal finance. Among these rules are the following: always keep at least x months of income in a savings account; maintain a special rainy day fund; don't borrow except to purchase a house or durable goods, and so on.

Extending the findings about violations of the principle of the fungibility of money, we see that if an individual had more than a single financial account, say, a checking account, a savings account, and an investment account, he or she should be equally inclined to withdraw money from any one; the marginal propensity to consume from each account should be the same. Efforts to verify the rationally appealing permanent income hypothesis have not been especially successful. Unanticipated income is not always treated simply as an addition to lifetime income. Consumption has proven quite sensitive to current income, and savings vary according to the source of unanticipated current income; relatively stable salaries, income from commissions, bonuses and strictly windfall income are all treated differently and lead to savings patterns that are not easy to explain in terms of financial rationality. Some of those additional funds are placed in checking accounts, which have a marginal propensity to consume near 1; another portion is placed in savings accounts with an MPC between 0 and 1; and a portion, ordinarily much less than might be assumed from the permanent income hypothesis, is placed in a longer term investment account, from which the MPC is very low, indeed near zero.

The composition of wealth matters, which has long been recognized in popular terminology. Witness the historical expression "land poor," and consider the phenomenon of retirees with large home equities who feel financially strapped and live much more frugally than others with comparable levels of wealth who rent and have more of their wealth in the form of stocks, bonds and particularly Certificates of Deposit and fully liquid savings accounts. Note, too, the change in consumption habits of retirees who finally sell their home or take out a "reverse mortgage." There is also a great aversion to incurring debt on life insurance even when the interest rates for doing so are much lower than those that consumers pay for other forms of borrowing. Analyses have shown that participation in IRA savings accounts and private pension plans tends to lead to higher overall saving rates, and not simply the replacement of one form of saving by another as many economists maintained would occur, following the rational tenets of the discipline, or at least this was true in certain years. Most of these initially surprising results were known before the recent flurry of interest in behavioral finance. They provided a more receptive background for the current studies, showing that much in financial analysis simply is not explained by traditional rationality calculations.

PSYCHOLOGICAL CONSIDERATIONS THAT MIGHT BE INCLUDED IN THE MODELS OF ECONOMICS AND FINANCE

Most of those who trade in financial markets have long been convinced that psychological factors affect transactions, at least in the short run. Some believed that although certain psychological phenomena were recurring, their force and frequency were largely unpredictable. Others in the field, being more confident, worked out rough rules of thumb. These developments notwithstanding, during the past several decades, financial theory moved in the opposite direction and became more rigorously rational than ever before. Even at the beginnings of the explorations into behavioral finance, leading figures such as Fisher Black hesitated to incorporate psychological variables into their models, concerned that while they were important, they were extremely difficult to quantify. There also was a fear of opening up a Pandora's Box and unduly complicating the analysis.

The pendulum has finally begun to swing the other way. While relatively few financial models incorporate variables from psychology, there is more of an inclination in reflecting on anomalous results to speculate about the possible applicability of various findings from the area of decision making. A few authors have endeavored to explain such results in terms of the quasi-rational patterns being documented by psychologists. Their work has been accompanied in recent years by experimental studies in economics and business administration. Several of these studies will be outlined in the sections that follow.

THE INFORMATION UNDERLYING FINANCIAL DECISIONS: THE NEWFOUND INTEREST IN "NOISE"

The Background: The Apparent Role of Ordinary Opinions in Influencing Stock Prices

Several studies have suggested that the prices of stocks at any given moment of time probably are attributable to the opinions of ordinary stock market participants and stock market analysts as much as to the hard economic and financial data underlying fundamental values. Those "hard data" also appear to reflect a measure of opinion. Perhaps the first relatively comprehensive study along those lines appeared in 1985, authored by Stanley Schachter and four associates.[1]

Schachter et al. maintained that the aggregate opinions of the community of investors influence stock prices just as opinions, social pressures and cultural factors influence a wide variety of evaluations in society. In affirming this hypothesis, they recalled a statement in the same vein by John Maynard Keynes, an economist who was as successful in investing in the stock markets as he was in developing academic ideas. Schachter and his colleagues contend that even such presumably objective data as price/earnings ratios depend on a variety of much less objective elements.[2]

Schachter et al. referred to a psychological dimension they called *dependence*, the degree to which an individual confides in external sources such as the opinions and actions of others, and events external to the decisions at hand. They then considered indexes of the prices of common stocks on the New York Stock Exchange during two periods, the first from the middle of 1949 through January 1966, when there was a rise of approximately 600 percent, and the second from February 1966 through January 1980, when the indexes fluctuated a great deal but wound up at a level somewhat below that at which they began.

The contrasting trend had very different effects on those who bought and sold stocks, they maintain. In the first period, when prices were rising almost steadily, few sought out the opinions of advisers on how to manage their investments, but this approach changed a great deal in the second period. To obtain a preliminary notion of the plausibility of their susceptibility/dependence hypothesis, they considered the effect of certain major events on the volume of transactions in the two periods mentioned. Specifically, they examined changes in the volume of stock market transactions following national elections and airline crashes. They found that the changes in the volume of transactions were five to six times greater during the second period than during the first, following both the elections and the airline crashes. They also ascertained the direction of price changes and the reactions to bull and bear market tendencies within the two major periods.

Overall, the authors concluded that there is sufficient evidence to warrant the following hypothesis: at times stock market prices are determined by elements other than classic financial and economic considerations. When markets are relatively bullish and most investors are relatively successful, there is a lack of sensitivity not only to elections and airline crashes but also to outside events in general. On the other hand, they concluded, when investors are relatively unsuccessful, there is an increase both in the sensitivity to such outside events and in the tendency to turn to the advice of others and to trade in response to that advice.

The Recognition of "Noise"

Most models of finance gave little attention to anything other than "hard data" until Fisher Black's 1985 Presidential Address to the American Finance Association. In that presentation, entitled simply, "Noise,"[3] Black made the following points:

a. Many participants in financial markets trade on the basis of noise (nonobjective elements that Black did not define precisely) as if it were news (objective information).

b. Noise is essential to the existence of market liquidity, but as much as it facilitates financial markets, it also makes them imperfect. Thus, while it is feasible to have models of equilibria for real financial markets, we cannot really speak of *rational* models of equilibria.

c. Without noise there would be relatively little incentive to buy and sell stocks; transaction levels would be low. Noise increases the incentives to trade, especially for those acting on the basis of information (markets with noise have more profit opportunities), but the presence of such noise also makes it more difficult to determine which are the truly profitable opportunities.

d. Arbitrage cannot always correct erroneous market prices because the positions taken often are not large enough due to the greater risk involved.

e. Many people are not conscious that their participation in the market is based on noise.

f. Some market participation is based on particular tastes that, like a preference for dividends (which is of questionable rationality), probably ought to be included in the utility function of a model that deals with real markets.

g. Numerous problems are involved in estimating expected returns, to which the presence of noise contributes. The presence of such noise probably is the principal reason for the use of simple rules that seem to violate the normal axioms of expected utility. Black claimed that these rules tend to become more sophisticated, presumably because of frequent and high-quality information feedback. However, he never published a paper supporting this assertion, perhaps because the supporting evidence was regarded as the proprietary information of his firm. This is particularly unfortunate because the psychologists Tversky and Kahneman insisted that it is very difficult to teach improved heuristics so that they more nearly approximate the models of rational decision making. That conclusion reflected what they had learned from the decisions they had studied in laboratory experiments, which, though significant in number, generally involved much less in the way of feedback than that available in financial markets.

h. Noise can change the rate of inflation, obscure the results that policies appear to produce and thus impede the effectiveness of traditional monetary and fiscal policy.

Followup analyses by various authors have made the following extensions and observations:

a. Arbitrage involves two types of risk: fundamental risk regarding the degree to which something is or is not correctly priced; and a risk involving the time horizon. If the market period is well defined and is short enough (a three-month option, for example), the arbitrageur who is correct runs little risk. If the time period is long, possibly even indefinite, then the presence of noise traders could so delay the return of prices to their fundamental or intrinsic values that an arbitrageur might not be willing to enter the market or to enter it with a sufficient amount of funds. The arbitrageur's fear would be that he or she would not be able to get out without a loss until a much later date than is regarded as reasonable. The eventual "reversion to the mean" of the incorrectly priced securities might take longer than a prospective arbitrageur is able or willing to wait. Prolonged undervaluation of prices could even bring on a bankruptcy that could ultimately preclude the correct revaluation of prices for those securities.

b. If market participants include both sophisticated traders acting on the basis of information and noise traders, then there could be some effects that raise the rates of return and other effects that lower those rates, with neither necessarily dominating. Noise traders may earn more than those who base their transactions solely on information, but their trades undoubtedly would be accompanied by higher levels of risk. In that case, the noise traders probably would enjoy a lower level of utility despite the higher rates of return.

c. If those who are obviously noise traders are able to obtain higher rates of return, what is likely to be the result in the marketplace? First, those who had been acting on the basis of information may decide to imitate the noise traders, perhaps attributing the noise traders' higher rates of return to correct market timing more than to the presence of higher rates of risk. If so, the level and effects of the noise trading will not tend to diminish. Alternatively, the information traders may continue to act on the basis of information alone, taking appropriate account of the higher risk that accompanied the higher returns and allowing themselves to be guided in their investment strategy by expected utility. In that case, the effects of the noise trading would tend to diminish—unless new noise traders enter the market (a distinct possibility, of course).

d. Alternatives to a traditional arbitrage strategy might exist; it might be possible to collect information on the apparent behavior of the noise traders and then buy or sell in advance of the anticipated trading patterns of the noise traders. That might overcome the effects of the noise trading where the noise was of a predictable pattern—but not if the nature of some of the noise varied.

e. Closed mutual funds such as the German Fund, the Mexico Fund, the Brazil Fund, the Korea Fund and others are quoted on the New York Stock Exchange. Such funds differ from open mutual funds such as Fidelity Magellan, Templeton Global and Vanguard Index 500 in that their values are not determined by the weighted average of their component shares. The prices of the closed funds ordinarily are either higher or lower than the weighted values of the shares in the companies that they have invested in, leading to what are referred to as premia and discounts. The premia sometimes reach 50 percent and 100 percent of the actual market values they represent. Transactions costs, administrative regulations and tax considerations explain relatively little of the sometimes large gap between the market value of the closed funds and the market value of the stocks they represent. The key in understanding the ongoing disequilibria appears to rest with sentiment responses of individual investors, and not anything related to financial rationality.

THE VOLATILITY OF FINANCIAL MARKETS

The seminal study on volatility was undertaken in 1981 by Shiller.[4] Up to that time, accepted financial models indicated that the real price of stock shares was equal to the present value of future dividends, rationally expected, adjusted by a constant rate of discount. Shiller showed that from 1870 through 1970, the volatility of stock prices was vastly greater than that of dividends—five to thirteen times as great as that of the present value of subsequent dividends. Three years later, Shiller attempted to explain the results in terms of social psychology and fads, and he proposed an alternative model featuring sophisticated and unsophisticated investors. In his 1989 volume, *Market Volatility*, he contended that it is possible to learn more about the dynamics of speculative markets than about ultimate causes. Here he may have been thinking about phenomena such as the so-called January Effect whereby small firms usually do much better than the rest of the market during the first month of the year; certainly, an understanding of causes has been more difficult to come by.

Comments by other economists and financial analysts during the last half of the 1980s (Thaler 1993, ch. 5, 6 and 8, along with ch. 7, also by Shiller) were along the following lines:

1. Many companies smooth out their dividends so that they do not necessarily reflect earnings in any given year. While true, this does not even remotely offset the disparity in the observed volatility.

2. The notion that fads can influence decisions about stock purchases and sales is consistent with the emerging information from psychology concerning the way people recognize and act on information. Moreover, deviations in stock prices often cannot be explained in traditionally rational terms. One study, by David Cutler, James Poterba and Lawrence Summers (Thaler 1993, ch. 5), shows that macroeconomic performance fails to explain even half of the variance in aggregate stock prices, nor does the inclusion of major political events seem to help much. As Summers observed, this suggests the need to examine the evolving literature of psychologists and economists on individual decision making under uncertainty (Thaler 1993, ch. 6, 164–65). It may be useful to develop models, he, Cutler and Poterba added, that explain (a) why shocks with small effects on the discount rate or cash flows can have large effects on prices; and (b) why, and, if so, the degree to which price movements are a function of the

consensus of opinions about the implications of certain information (Thaler 1993, ch. 5, 149).

3. The volatility of stock prices subject to hostile takeovers also is contrary to what one would expect from efficient markets.

4. According to Christopher Sims, the extraordinary stock/dividend data presented by Shiller have three possible explanations (Thaler 1993 ch. 7, 216–217):

a. People have mistaken expectations about the economy and future rates of return—which may have implications for resource allocation and government intervention to modify that allocation of resources.

b. The fads referred to by Shiller represent real fluctuations in people's present and future consumption levels and are reflected in the discount rate.

c. Arbitrage does not function very well.

DO FINANCIAL MARKETS OVERREACT?

The articles on volatility apparently prompted more economists to examine whether markets seriously overreact—although a general interest in that phenomenon dates at least to the studies of the Cobweb Theorem in the period just after World War II. "Does the Stock Market Overreact?" asked De Bondt and Thaler,[5] building on earlier work by other investigators, especially Basu and Dreman. Thus began a debate that has overturned a great deal of traditional thinking in financial economics.

In the earlier, less rigorous days of financial analysis, there had always been a certain amount of discussion about stock prices possibly diverging from fundamental values. Then, in the 1960s and 1970s, came the work of Malkiel, Fama and Jensen, among others, which seemed to show that financial markets were efficient and that stock market prices reflected intrinsic values, with any fluctuations from that reflecting a "random walk." Presumably, future changes in prices were not predictable, and this conclusion was firmly maintained.

There was, of course, anecdotal recall of Keynes's views about the importance of psychological factors in financial markets, and there were the more recent writings on noise, fads and sentiment. While some traders based their decisions on solid information, there also were noise traders, who, as already noted, sometimes earned more than those who dealt with hard data alone (or primarily). Cutting both ways was the work of psychologists (and, increasingly, economists) concerning the reversion to the mean thesis. Whether or not prices reflected their intrinsic values at a given point in time, they tended to gravitate toward their mean values in the long run. All of this helped to undermine the strong form of the efficient market hypothesis and to substitute for it a modified, longer run version, but one indicating that perhaps some predictions could be made about prices in the stock market after all.

In 1979, an important finding of financial irrationality by Modigliani and Cohn concluded that equities on the New York Stock Exchange had been undervalued since the 1960s and that the extent of that undervaluation by the late 1970s was of the order of 50 percent. This finding was attributed principally to the fact that investors capitalized equity earnings at the nominal interest rate rather than the economically correct rate (a dramatic and continuing example of the type of money illusion discussed by Shafir, Diamond and Tversky in 1997). The article might have been completed even earlier, but the senior author indicated that he had been "preaching the gospel of efficient markets" and the hypothesis of such extreme financial irrationality "was lightly dismissed as too preposterous to be entertained seriously" (Modigliani and Cohn 1979, 35).

In the late 1970s, both Dreman and Basu found that the purchase of stocks with low price/earnings ratios yielded abnormally high returns, more than compensating for the risk. The explanation, Basu speculated, might be that the low prices had reflected temporary pessimism. Other investigators found similar results from other indicators; high dividend rates suggested that the prices of those stocks were too low, as did stock prices that were low in relation to book values. But the real breakthrough for financial economists in grasping the significance of the undervaluation phenomenon seems to have come with publication of De Bondt and Thaler's article in 1985, and their followup work of 1987 and 1991, in response to rebuttals from the defenders of the traditional efficient market hypothesis.

De Bondt and Thaler noted that if stock prices systematically overshoot (to both good news and bad), their reversal should be predictable from the price/earnings data of the past. They showed a reversion to the mean of stocks with differentially high or low P/E ratios in the preceding three to five years. A strategy of selling the "winners" and buying the "losers" generated a rate of return well above the market average, sufficiently so as to more than compensate for the probably added risk of purchasing losers. The reversals or reversions to the mean were much greater for the losers, which gained about 20 percent more than the market average, than for the winners, which did about 10 percent less well than the market average.

Two doubts remained. First, how much of the differential between the subsequent fortunes of the winners and the losers was a compensation for added risk? Second, inasmuch as De Bondt and Thaler's results revealed that much of the "excess returns" occurred during the month of January, was this just another revelation of the incompletely understood but already relatively well-documented January Effect?

The first question received a great deal of attention. Two leading authorities in the field published a study maintaining that most of the differential return was just compensation for added risk. However, many other studies, using alternative econometric approaches, cast doubt on the risk compensation argument. Estimates of the rate of return differential that was not attributable to risk compensation tended to be of the order of 10–15 percent in the United States. Comparable results were found in Canada, Great Britain and fifteen other countries, with an even more pronounced payoff to the strategy of selling winners and buying losers in emerging country stock exchanges that are not as broad based or sophisticated. De Bondt and Thaler's later work provided new evidence showing, first, that little of the augmented rate of return was due to risk compensation, and, second, that the winner/loser phenomenon was separate from the January/small-firm anomaly. Some studies have shown that there is a reversion to the mean and thus, stock market predictability for groups of stocks, even in the short run, though the shift is not as great as in the long run. Several financial economists who have been active in this research are advising an asset management firm in investment selections for pension plans, and Dreman has been engaged in contrarian investment since the late 1970s.

All of these studies have had major repercussions on the earlier conclusions about the efficiency of the financial markets, as can be seen in 1992 and 1996 articles by Fama and French. The 1992 article acknowledges the ability to predict trends in the prices of groups of stocks with different price earnings ratios. Although the article maintains that ability to predict may reflect in part a rational response to changing macroeconomic variables, it concedes that some of the phenomenon may be due to market inefficiencies. The overreaction effect also has been supported by Chopra, Lakonishok and Ritter (Thaler 1993, ch. 10), who estimated that extreme prior losers outperform extreme prior winners by 5 to 10 percent a year, after adjusting for risk and enterprise size. Note that overreaction is not common in very short-term options markets, presumably because of the effectiveness of arbitrage operations within the confines of 60- and 90-day periods, yet options markets analysts were not yet willing to comment on the possible role of overreaction and price predictability once the options periods were lengthened.

Finally, what should be the reaction of stock prices to unexpected earnings announcements? If markets are truly efficient, any surprises in the specific figures should be minor because the markets would have been aware of the underlying favorable or unfavorable developments. There have been unexpected earnings announcements, of course. Those of unexpectedly higher profits have led to increases in the prices of those stocks, while those of unexpectedly lower profits have led to decreases in share prices. Much more disconcerting is the fact that the price changes do not take place only on the day of the announcement. Rather, in the case of increases, for example, the changes take place over the course of a number of days and are repeated, albeit in lesser proportion, at each of the next three quarterly profits announcements. One study revealed that a strategy of selling stocks with unexpected declines in profits and buying those with unexpected increases led to a return of 4.2 percent in 60 days (not counting transaction costs). The phenomenon may reflect a reversion to the mean from an earlier state of incorrect valuation and is not necessarily a reaction to the earnings announcements as such. It is noteworthy that the underreaction to profits announcements as a predictor of future stock prices has come from professional stock analysts as well as from the general public.[6] A recent presentation on earnings surprises, and the reaction to them, together with a general discussion of contrarian investment themes, can be found in Dreman and Berry 1995.

All of this is leading to reformulations of the efficient market hypothesis and should help foster interest in a more truly behavioral theory of markets.

CORPORATE FINANCE

Advances in Behavioral Finance deals with four topics in the area of corporate finance—the search for stocks paying high dividends versus the inclination toward "growth" stocks that have a greater tendency to reinvest profits and register high capital gains; the short- versus long-term orientation of profits; the hostile takeover phenomenon; and the initial public offerings (IPOs)

Dividends and Capital Gains

Dividends and capital gains ought to be perfect substitutes in the absence of taxes and transaction costs, and stocks offering principally capital gains ought to be preferred in countries such as the United States where dividends usually have been taxed at higher rates. The preference of many people for stocks with high dividends over those that offer the promise of more substantial capital gains (except perhaps in periods of stock market boom) may perhaps be explained by two contributions from psychology. One is prospect theory—the theory of cognitive psychologists that explains risk aversion/loss aversion tendencies and the greater valuation that most people assign to losses than to the same dollar amount of gains—and the other is the need of many people for self-control devices. With respect to prospect theory, the explanation is in part that realizing income through the sale of a stock involves a sense of loss, a sense of regret, and most people seek to avert losses. On the other hand, no sense of loss accompanies the receipt of dividends, which, moreover, represent a relatively more certain income (certainty being preferred to an even somewhat larger expected value of income).[7] The desire for stocks that pay relatively high dividends is also said to reflect a self-control device, especially among older people—the desire to avoid spending one's capital. While the use of investment counselors also could provide a means of limiting capital sales, that involves a cost that might be as large as the frequent differential between earnings through dividends and earnings through higher capital gains.

Short- Versus Long-Term Profits

U.S. enterprises have been criticized as being oriented more toward short-than long-term maximization. Findings from psychology as well as facts of the institutional environment help explain this seeming irrationality. Arbitrage in long-term assets is more expensive than arbitrage in short-term assets (and riskier because of noise trading). Thus, long-term assets tend to reflect, to a relatively greater degree, pricing that is incorrect at any given moment. Long-term projects may involve a delay in recognizing pricing errors compared to short-term projects. Compensation to management tends to be based on annual and even quarterly results, but in the short run compensation tends to be less pronounced for the favorable behavior of market shares than for unfavorable market behavior, this, without regard to whether the unfavorable market showing is only a short-term phenomenon. It is sometimes said that the same orientation toward the short term does not appear to prevail in Japan. Nonetheless, the slowdown in Japan's economic growth in the 1990s and the reticence to undertake certain policy changes, may indicate that some of the same applies there as well. That is, not all of the Japanese economy is as long-term oriented vis-à-vis their U.S. counterparts, as suggested in David Halberstam's fascinating account of the automobile industry, *The Reckoning*.

Hostile Corporate Takeovers

Hostile corporate takeovers were strongly defended by business school analysts such as Jensen who maintained that they contributed to greater efficiency. Following that came empirical studies by Scherer and others indicating that the principal beneficiaries of such takeovers were the shareholders of the companies taken over, along with the merger and acquisition specialists who organized the takeovers, and not the newly merged enterprises.[8] Then, in the midst of the evidence casting doubt on the efficiency of financial markets came the analysis of Richard Roll (Thaler 1993 ch. 17) suggesting that the main motive behind many hostile takeovers has been the "chutzpah" and personal ego of those initiating the bids. This analysis raised the question of whether this nonfinancially maximizing motive might explain why so many mergers have not been financially successful. This stands the original, efficiency argument for hostile takeovers on its head. At the same time, it provides a caution to those who insist that prevailing market prices are often far from those that reflect fundamental values.

Initial Public Offerings of Stock Shares

Some studies have provided evidence that IPOs are priced low relative to the initial demand for them, while others have implied that the initial prices were high relative to their "long run" demand (actually, the demand for the shares three years later). Can both possibly be correct?

INDIVIDUAL BEHAVIOR

This section deals principally with (1) the rationality of investors, (2) the disposition to sell winners too early and to hold on to losers too long, and (3) the credit card market.

Investor Rationality

Efforts have been made to distinguish between the rationality of sophisticated investors, who presumably base their decisions on information and use careful methods of calculation, and unsophisticated investors, who presumably are more inclined to trade on the basis of "noise," behaving less rationally. While this distinction seems to be useful as a first approximation, we need to take note of some special factors. First, an article by Shiller on "Speculative Prices and Popular Models" (Thaler 1993, ch. 19) shows that psychological factors are more important in explaining the ups and downs of sophisticated financial markets that offer frequent, reliable feedback data than in explaining much less sophisticated, once or twice in a lifetime, real estate markets. Second, while various studies have shown that financial analysts tend to pay more attention to the reasoning and particularly, the conclusions of their colleagues instead of calculating strictly on their own, such behavior often may reflect the use of heuristics with relatively known and ascertainable biases. It does not necessarily reflect a dependence on rumors, unstructured or random noise, and so on, which probably are more common among unsophisticated investors. Indeed, the sophisticated investors' failure to use all of the optimization techniques that they have learned and to act in what economics and finance term a rational manner, as well as their inclination to incorporate some psychological factors into their reasoning, may reflect their sophistication and reasonability, if not traditional rationality.

The financial investment community may do that to a degree, but it also seems to incorporate some rather biased noise. There are variations between individuals and according to types of situation, however, and although some studies offer overall conclusions about the "rationality" of such financial agents, little effort is made to disaggregate the findings as much as would be useful. It is striking, however, that some very successful stock brokers and investment bankers in the United States and in Mexico who are keenly aware of traditional optimizing theory (sometimes even teaching it part time in universities) hold that that theory cannot explain many of the actions they undertake in the financial markets. Moreover, financial economists have been among those who have most seriously applied the findings on decision making that are being generated by cognitive psychology.

The Disposition to Sell Winners Too Early and Ride Losers Too Long

Shefrin and Statman set the tone for chapter 20 of *Advances in Behavioral Finance* (Thaler 1993) by first endorsing a comment by Kahneman and Tversky (1979) to the effect that a person who has not made peace with his losses is likely to accept gambles that would be unacceptable to him otherwise. This suggests the possibility of considerably more potential for change in the risk/

return tradeoff than economists and financial analysts are inclined to assume, even allowing for the passage of time. Presumably the tendency to value incremental gains ever less as they increase helps explain a tendency to sell winners too early, which may be particularly inadvisable if tax laws favor long-term gains, though as the authors note a tendency toward loss aversion could limit the tendency to sell winners too early. (With respect to the loss of the asset, see also their comments on dividends and capital gains in Thaler 1993, ch. 15.) Shefrin and Statman maintain that loss aversion figures to a greater degree in explaining the reticence to sell losers. Indeed, many individuals find it necessary to rely on special self-control measures, or special rules of thumb, to finally realize the sale of losers. Rather than firmly establishing any definitive new explanations, the study's principal contribution is its ability to stimulate the reader to question and rethink traditional positions, recognizing that the traditional positions may not always involve the relevant assumptions.

The Credit Card Market

Ausubel attributes the failure of competition in the credit card market to consumer irrationality, or, more accurately, consumer delusion (Thaler 1993, ch. 21). Four thousand enterprises sell an essentially homogeneous service. The ten largest credit card distributors account for two-fifths of the market. This figure is more than might be expected for a homogeneous service, but it is hardly the kind of concentration that will give the market the power necessary to restrict competition. Nonetheless, competition is minimal with respect to the most important variable, the rate of interest charged on outstanding balances. Various explanations are considered, but the evidence points most strongly to consumer irrationality. Most of those who obtain credit cards do not seek out banks or other distributors that offer the lowest interest rates, though somewhat more search is made to find the much less important annual fee. The reason is that consumers are convinced that they will pay their bills in full each month and that they will not use this expensive form of credit. Even after the fact, two-thirds of those with credit cards maintain that they have not borrowed during, say, a two-year period—that they have always paid off their outstanding balances in full. On the contrary, data from the banks reveal that two-thirds have failed to do so at least once, and a substantial minority of others, many times.

INTERNATIONAL MARKETS

The Thaler volume (1993) addresses two groups of studies that question the efficient markets hypothesis at the international level. One deals with the lack of international diversification of portfolio investment, and the other with foreign exchange. Beyond these, there is anecdotal evidence of quasi-rationality in other sources as well.

Portfolio Diversification

One of the first concepts that is taught in finance and financial economics is the importance of diversifying investment in order to reduce risk. Studies show that the correlation between the rates of return on portfolio investment in each of the leading industrial countries and the group of other such nations averages approximately 0.5. Obviously, international diversification would be advantageous. Nonetheless, in the late 1980s, more than 98 percent of Japanese portfolio investment was in Japan, 94 percent of U.S. portfolio investment was in the United States, and 82 percent of British portfolio investment was in Britain (as much as 94 percent in 1979). In order for such concentration to make sense, the investor in each of those countries would have had to believe that rates of return were substantially higher in his or her country than in the others. Even if the only option available had been the U.S. market, in order to justify not placing relatively more funds abroad, an average British investor would have had to believe that UK investments offered returns of the order of 5 percent higher than those in the U.S., something that was not true, and that there would have been little reason to expect for the period ahead.

How can this lack of portfolio diversification be explained? Institutional restrictions have played a role, though a very small one, except for a few countries such as Korea. Transaction costs also are not a major factor. The key part of the explanation revolves around idiosyncrasies of investment behavior. For example, although most U.S. and Japanese investors had access to largely the same information, in 1990 American investors expected the Dow Jones average to decline 0.3 percent, while Japanese investors anticipated a rise of 12.6 percent (which still did not entice many Japanese into the U.S. stock markets). On the other hand, U.S. investors expected a decline of 9.1 percent in the Nikkei, approximately 20 percent less than the Japanese expected. It seems particularly difficult to estimate differences in expected returns between countries. And it seems even more difficult to estimate the risk differences between countries— apparently even for countries with as much affinity and mutual exchange of all types of information as Great Britain and the United States. Finally, the risk differences between countries seem to have increased recently, even as (because?) the international mobility of portfolio investment has risen. This led, in late 1997, to an at least temporary reversal of the increase in portfolio diversification that had begun to take place.

Much of the same lack of portfolio diversification operates within each country, moreover. The majority of people who own their home live relatively close to where they work; they have not diversified geographically, so there is a relatively high correlation between their returns on human and physical capital.

Foreign Exchange

The foreign exchange phenomenon is even less clear cut. Interest rates higher in one country than in another or a need to offer a larger amount of the first country's currency for future purchases of the other country's currency than is required in the spot market both suggest that the first of the two countries is headed for a devaluation. That is not what most of the statistical evidence reveals, however, and puzzled statements about this surprising result have been made by Paul Krugman and other leading international trade economists. Errors in expectations or errors in estimating risks may explain the apparent anomaly. Or it may be that the markets are indeed very efficient, with the differences in interest rates and forward exchange rates providing market signals that lead quickly to corrections in the underlying fundamentals. It does not seem likely, however, that this second factor could explain more than a handful of such cases.

NOTES

1. Schachter et al., "Some Causes and Consequences of Dependence and Independence in the Stock Market," ch. 22 in Maital and Maital 1993. Most of the rest of this chapter is taken from Thaler 1993.

2. Undoubtedly this helps explain why earnings estimates of Wall Street analysts have differed so much from actual earnings. On the overoptimism and relatively poor record of those analysts, see the work of Dreman cited in the Bibliography, particularly Dreman and Berry May–June 1995. The conclusions about overoptimism are consistent with those of Olsen 1997 who found a "desirability" bias among professional investment managers—a tendency to overpredict desirable outcomes.

3. Ch. 1 in Thaler 1993.

4. Shiller, "Do Stock Prices Move Too Much to Be Justified by Subsequent Changes in Dividends?" ch. 4 in Thaler 1993. See also Shiller 1989.

5. De Bondt and Thaler, ch. 9 in Thaler 1993.

6. The profits announcement/price predictor phenomenon need not conflict with the price/earnings (P/E) winner/loser anomaly; selection of P/E winners and losers would be based on averages over a three- to five-year period of time, not that immediately preceding or following earnings announcements.

7. However, it is not clear whether this loss aversion explanation holds as strongly for the most successful stock market investors. That said, renowned investor Warren Buffet is supposed to rarely sell on or in the process of declines in the prices of shares, though, in his case, that refers to declines after substantial previous share appreciations, and the rationale is to avoid capital gains taxes.

8. For the views of Jensen, Scherer and others on the efficiency of corporate takeovers, see "Symposium: Takeovers," *Journal of Economic Perpectives*, Vol. 2, No. 1 (Winter 1988): 3–82.

Chapter 8

Guidelines for Decision Making

In the final chapter of *Judgment in Managerial Decision Making*, "Improving Decision Making," Bazerman offers four strategies that he terms alternative and complementary. They are:

1. Acquiring experience and expertise
2. Debiasing judgments
3. Using linear models based on expert judgment
4. Adjusting intuitive predictions

It would be hard to disagree with the first, acquiring experience and expertise. The second, in Bazerman's words, involves "unfreezing, change and refreezing"—basically reducing or eliminating questionable cognitive strategies or decision-making practices from the past, incorporating changes that reflect the recent lessons of decision theory and then "freezing" a new approach to decision making. Such a "refreezing" may be open to question, given the still unsettled nature of certain points and the lack of a clear behavioral paradigm for decision making. It seems to invite a new and not-yet-warranted orthodoxy.

Bazerman's third strategy, using linear models based on expert judgment, draws on findings by several prominent investigators that such models predict better than the experts themselves. That strategy is one for serious consideration, but what follows in this chapter is nonetheless somewhat at odds with the approach.

The fourth strategy for improving decision making, adjusting intuitive predictions, is drawn from the work of Kahneman and Tversky and involves five components:

1. Selecting a comparison group
2. Assessing the distribution of the comparison group
3. Incorporating intuitive estimations
4. Assessing the predictability of the analyst's forecast
5. Adjusting the intuitive estimate

What follows has most in common with the titles of the first and the last of Bazerman's four strategies but differs somewhat in conception.

Decision making is carried out by individuals, families, business enterprises, cooperatives and other nonprofit institutions, governments and multigovernmental international organizations. The nature of the decision-making process may differ somewhat from entity to entity, not only insofar as the objectives are concerned, but also with respect to the capacity and likelihood of realizing those objectives. Whether or not the objective ordinarily is framed in terms of profits or the welfare of the relevant entity, the tradition of the experts has been to view the goal of decision making as an attempt to do the best possible, that is, to optimize. But if individuals and enterprises sometimes have more than a single consideration in mind (particularly important in the case of nonprofit groups) and if implementing optimization is not always feasible in any event, then perhaps any general guidelines for decision making should refer to a process that would *allow for*, but not necessarily lionize optimization as not only a desirable but also ordinarily a feasible objective.

In considering a set of guidelines, it is useful to take note of some of the important characteristics of decision making, including the following:

1. *The objective(s) of individuals and enterprises (and the tradeoffs between objectives if there is more than one, or the range for which one or another is dominant and the others are of secondary, even negligible significance).* At least two issues are involved here. First, in most economic and financial decisions, is there but a single objective, or is there more than one? If there is more than one, are there means to resolve the problem, such as taking cognitive dissonance into account and finding ways to overcome the dissonance of multiple concerns? Second, if there is more than a single concern or objective, what are the tradeoffs between them—what are the marginal rates of substitution? If the multiplicity of objectives holds only beyond some range, what then is the range for which such tradeoffs need to be taken into account (and what are the tradeoffs)? Perhaps many economic and financial decisions fall into this last category, in which case there is no general need to take account of multiple objectives and their tradeoffs. However, it is necessary to have rough estimates of the point at which (or the circumstances in which) multiple considerations become significant and to discern the tradeoffs that are then relevant (as well as any major fluctuations in the tradeoffs at any further points or under any other circumstances). The gist of this is probably a manageable task, except perhaps for the last aspect on

fluctuations, where the costs of preparing the estimates would likely exceed the benefit of such refinement.

2. *The nature of the "horizon scanning" that is employed to identify (a) problems that are among those that most warrant attention and (b) alternatives that are among those that most warrant being considered to resolve those problems.* Herbert Simon has observed that standard decision theory has completely ignored this early stage of the decision process. It is therefore the point at which there is the greatest danger of following procedures that do not even lead to satisficing, not to mention maximizing. Write-ups of the way successful survivors have proceeded and analysis of those accounts might prove valuable in recognizing heuristics and in capturing the biases of those heuristics. Both should be done as soon after the horizon scanning and alternative identification as possible in order to avoid the dual dangers of recall difficulty, on the one hand, and intentional or unintentional modification of recall, on the other.

3. *The relative importance of the decision at hand. For business enterprises, for example, considerations might include such factors as the proportion of the firm's assets employed, the magnitude of the operation relative to the firm's overall level, and, in particular, the long-run profit/risk potential of the decision (the short-run potential, too, if the firm has outstanding financial obligations and capital markets are imperfect).* The relatively less important the decision, the greater the cost-benefit justification of employing quasi-rational heuristics. It should be possible to draw up guidelines indicating which types of decisions of a given type of enterprise are probably best handled by informal judgmental heuristics, which justify a more formal approach—perhaps even efforts to upgrade the heuristics over the course of time—and which categories of decisions appear to be of sufficient importance to justify an effort at an optimizing technique if the data and tools are adequate. Perhaps just as important, an effort should be made to gauge any tendencies toward reliance on quasi-rational heuristics that extend beyond what can be justified in cost-benefit terms, by those with whom decision makers have to deal. This should lead to a potentially better outcome for decision makers than would use of the traditional assumption of economics and finance that competitors always will select the alternative that is optimal for them.

4. *The time frame in which the decision must be made.* Even in the case of complex decisions of major import, it is sometimes necessary to resolve matters relatively quickly. Failure to consider such possibilities in advance and to have several well-conceived heuristics to fall back on as second best approaches for various types of situations may lead to postponing decisions that need to be made, or to making true "seat of the pants" decisions that reflect much less than satisficing or quasi-rationality.

5. *The nature and quantity of information available to an individual or an entity, relative to what is likely to be necessary in order to make an optimal decision.* For various types of situations in which one or both are lacking, there is a need for well-conceived contingency planning in terms of heuristic alter-

natives. The problem may not be a time constraint so much as the inability to obtain the type or quantity of information necessary.

6. *The relative novelty of the type of decision—the frequency with which an individual or an entity has made similar decisions in the past (or is aware of the experience of others in similar kinds of decisions) and the likelihood that similar types of decisions will have to be made in the future.* Situations of relatively greater frequency, including the anticipation that the same general type of phenomena will be repeated, provide a learning basis for systematic, though still imperfect adjustments to any reasoning by analogy heuristic. Such adapted reasoning by analogy heuristics would be most justified when decisions must be made in a particularly short time frame or when important elements of the information for optimizing are missing.

7. *Any indicators of the accuracy with which the decision maker perceives (a) the information that it already possesses and (b) such additional information as it does not yet possess but that it has to decide about obtaining in order to achieve its objective(s).* In addition to being aware of the informational demands to optimize and even to employ various heuristics, as well as of the costs of obtaining such information, a good guideline for decision making also should estimate the errors in data perception (or the lags in perceiving data accurately) that are likely to accompany the various categories of data, based on past experience and any other indicators that may be available. (If information is not perceived accurately at the time a decision is made, then even "maximization" amounts to maximization of an alternative different than the one actually at hand. Related to this is uncertainty about the logical implications of information that one actually possesses, as expressed in Radner 1996.)

8. *The range of alternative techniques for decision making that are available to the individual or organization, and the cost of time required for each, along with any known biases involved with each, as well as the revealed tendency of the decision maker in question to avoid or reduce those biases.* The emphasis is on the need to take account of biases (and any tendency to reduce those biases) in selecting a second best means of judgment.

9. *The efficiency of the information search process(es) used by the decision maker, or the consistency of those search process(es) with the objective(s) of the entity and the optimization techniques or heuristics chosen to realize the objective(s).* The point here is to take note in advance of any likely difficulties in implementing judgmental heuristics as well as optimization techniques.

10. *The procedure for reviewing and revising both the decisions taken and the decision-making procedure(s) employed.* This is to ensure that there are checks on even the most accurately anticipated biases and to take account of situations in which it is not possible to gauge likely results well in advance.

11. *The degree to which the anomalies of financial and economic behavior, and the biases involved in using rules of thumb, are affected by prevailing institutions, both public and private.* Frey has opened the exploration of this topic.[1] He notes the circumstances under which anomalous behavior at the in-

dividual and more aggregate level is either reduced or magnified by the market, the prevailing political system (with attention to democracy), administrative decision making, and the nature of the bargaining system between individuals and groups. Some anomalies from rationality are not inevitable, nor are they equally likely under all institutional arrangements. It appears to be possible to influence, if not totally eliminate, anomalous behavior and decision-making biases—though usually only at cost. Frey points out several interesting possibilities.[2] A serious guideline for decision making should involve a systematic examination of how alternative institutional arrangements affect the kind of anomalous behavior that deviates from what we think of as financial and economic rationality and that has been increasingly documented. In any event, more active consideration of the consequences of institutional alternatives is warranted.

One of the keys to improving decision making is the ongoing collection of data on these eleven factors and the analysis of that data in order to monitor the learning process and to revise hypotheses about what is effective for the decision unit.[3] A few suggestions on how to approach this process of learning and hypothesis revision may be gleaned from experimental economics and the related field experiments. However, most actual situations are likely to differ quite a bit from carefully controlled laboratory exercises. Ongoing real-world observations may suffer in precision, but what may be gained in comparison with the laboratory experiments is a better understanding of the reasoning processes of the individuals and enterprises involved. Moreover, determining whether certain types of answers were feigned might be less of a problem and whether those involved in an experiment were *behaving* as they would in a real-life situation would not be a concern. In addition, it would be possible to isolate the decision making of those who are highly successful in economic or financial terms, which has not yet been feasible in laboratory experiments.

Use of optimization techniques does not always lead to the best results, as already mentioned. Among the most important reasons for this are the difficulties in implementing the rational decision making of optimization techniques. We know that even the most successful people and organizations rely on routines and rules of thumb for at least some aspects of their decision making. It has been well documented that rules such as availability, anchoring and representativeness are employed. Unfortunately, many types of decisions seem to call forth routines, strategies and rules of thumb that, while usually simpler than optimization techniques, are more complicated than the simple use of one or another of the small number of heuristics that have been substantiated in experiments. Some such rules of thumb may vary from individual to individual and enterprise to enterprise, or at least they may vary according to the type of situation and to the framing of the options. Moreover, many of the rules tend to evolve; there is a sometimes slow, though recognizable process of adaptation. Thus, in order to develop guidelines for decision making for the individual or other entity, there is no substitute for observation at the individual and organizational level—and observation at the time that the decisions are made or very shortly thereafter. The generalizations that will be required to advance behavioral economics and behavioral finance are likely to require many such case studies to develop the hypotheses that are then tested—to develop hypotheses that are manageable and at the same time reflect actual behavior.

Perhaps the main difference between this approach and that of the two last strategies noted by Bazerman is that while the expert is the starting point of the strategies recommended by Bazerman, the revealed expertise of the most successful would be the starting point in what is recommended here.[4] To help the would-be survivor, instead of making adjustments to the expert analyst's intuitive estimates, as in the recommendations of Bazerman, Kahneman and Tversky, the final adjustments, leading to the specific decision-making guidelines, would be derived from differences between the rule of thumb experience of the would-be-survivor and that of the most successful survivors, trying to take into account the differences between the entities and the circumstances. Only after gathering a good deal of this type of evidence might it be possible to speak of truly generalizable rules of thumb for successful decision making. Such rules of thumb, if they are discovered, may prove to be relatively simple, but they are likely to be more numerous and more complicated than availability, representativeness and anchoring or the matching and melioration that were also referred to earlier.

The accumulating evidence on anomalies shows that it would be irrational to systematically use available, normative economic and financial models to predict what is likely to happen in all types of natural economic settings; all too often, the predictions would be mistaken. Moreover, we have the beginnings of a basis for gauging the areas in which they would be mistaken. Why, then, as Roth has written, "hasn't utility theory been swept away?"[5] The answer is not that that normative theory sometimes predicts quite well, but rather that alternative theories often predict just as poorly.[6] A comprehensive behavioral theory simply is not yet available. There is a way out of this conundrum, however.

In the absence of a comprehensive behavioral theory of decision making (i.e., in the absence of a formal decision theoretic structure), a three-step approach might be pursued. As a first stage approximation, note should be taken of the predictions concerning decision-making behavior that would be expected, using normative economic or financial theory with its optimization techniques. Second, indications might be made, even if only in approximate terms, of the order of the deviations from optimal results that could be expected, as estimated from the accumulating evidence on the heuristics used by individuals and organizations (the successful, but also the less successful, whose actions influence what happens during the process of reaction to changes as well), and on the direction and magnitude of the biases from optimal behavior that those rules of thumb involve. The third step, to improve the estimates of the anticipated deviations from optimality over the course of time, would be to conduct research, or better still, to gather evidence on decision making from specialized consulting firms and directly from individual enterprises; on the heuristics used by enterprises, particularly successful enterprises, in making choices; and on the deviations from optimization attributable to the use of such simpler guidelines. Little research of this type has been undertaken, and some form of special tax treatment or other subsidization is likely to be required to induce organizations to reveal such information. But it is necessary to supplement the results of experimental economics with findings from natural economic settings, in part to provide a check on the results of experiments, but particularly to ascertain the types of situation (simple as well as complex) for which experimental evidence does not provide an adequate guide.

Much of this presentation may seem rather heterodox, but the reader should consider that a number of prominent economists who once assumed that the impressive construct of normative economic analysis also served reasonably well to describe the way in which survivors actually behaved have come to conclude otherwise. Some have modified their models so as to require a less extreme form of rationality, in an effort to have the same theory apply to the descriptive as well as prescriptive domain. A few are attempting to redefine economic and financial rationality, joining others who look to the creation of a truly behavioral theory that would explain *actual* decision making (at least that of successful survivors). Finally, an increasing number of economists and financial analysts have come to include the type of material presented in this volume in their reading assignments, even some who once denied the existence of cognitive imperfections by survivors or in markets, and who, though they have come to acknowledge them, now contend that such cognitive limitations have been receiving too much attention in recent years. Whether or not the data gathering and the followup course of action recommended here help facilitate the development of a behavioral theory of decision making with fewer anomalies than neoclassical normative theory, it should help improve predictions about economic and financial behavior, and the success of policies, public and private, that depend on the accuracy of those behavioral predictions.

NOTES

1. See ch. 11 in Frey 1992.
2. This theme is developed further in Frey and Eichenberger 1994.
3. In addition, perhaps even before undertaking this, the reader is encouraged to consult March 1994, especially ch. 1, "Limited Rationality," and ch. 2, "Rule Following."
4. Another alternative, as Kurz notes, is to use simple decision rules such as those from game theory that are not *entirely* rational but lead to equilibrium solutions, and "may possess interesting properties" (Kurz, personal communication, November 1, 1997). Since one such irrationality often involves the assumption of a lack of memory, my reaction to this alternative is that it is not likely to predict well on a regular basis until more game theory becomes, in Camerer's terminology, behavioral game theory. The kind of empirical work recommended in this chapter could contribute to that.

5. Roth 1995, 76–79 and the comments of Roth in Arrow et al. 1996, 198–202.

6. Moreover, Machina and others have constructed alternative theories of utility (sometimes referred to as nonexpected utility theories) that overcome some of the most striking anomalies of expected utility theories. (See, e.g., Machina 1987.) For Camerer, Machina's theory "has shown that some basic results in economics can be derived without expected utility maximization" (Kagel and Roth 1995, 676; also 626, but note the qualification at 680, note 40). Kurz states,

The very large literature on non-expected utility theory has shown that you can construct a perfectly reasonable theory of utility under uncertainty which will be compatible with the Allais and Ellsberg paradoxes. The names of Mark Machina, Larry Epstein, Menahem Yaari and many, many others may be mentioned here. The essential fact is that economic agents do not seem to assess probabilities in the same way as the mathematical model of expected utility does and this is particularly the case around probabilities of 0 and 1. Models of non-expected utility allow a non-linear transformation of the probabilities so that relative to the transformed probabilities the economic agents are perfectly rational and do not violate the axioms. (Personal communication, November 1, 1997). Kurz goes on to say, ". . . the main aim of the theory of utility under uncertainty is to explain market behavior such as risk aversion, the purchase of insurance, optimal portfolio choices, portfolio diversification etc. What has been shown by Mark Machina . . . is that when it comes to these basic activities the models of expected utility and non-expected utility make virtually identical predictions. So, *broadly speaking* we can say that the failure of the expected utility theory does not imply that the predictions of the theory relative to behavior under uncertainty are wrong. To put it differently, you can reformulate the utility model under the axioms which allow the transformation of the probabilities and then proceed to develop the optimal consumer demand for securities, insurance etc. The model with non-expected utility will be compatible with the usual observations about risk aversion, portfolio diversification etc. except that these propositions will be derived from a non-expected utility theory which is compatible with the Allais and Ellsberg examples.

The next-to-last sentence should be noted, in particular, but some of the empirical evidence cited here indicates that the equivalency of the results derived from models of expected and nonexpected utility has not yet been established for *complex* economic and financial activities. Even if it is possible to claim that the new theories of utility have saved normative, prescriptive economic and financial theory, there would still seem to be a need for a descriptive theory that predicts better, once we leave the confines of laboratory testing, with its clear, limited and relatively simple options.

Chapter 9

Postscript

Several publications which should be noted in the text came to my attention during the last two months of 1997, after the manuscript had been submitted to the publishers. These have been noted briefly in the body of the main text.

Decision Sciences: An Integrative Perspective (Kleindorfer, Kunreuther and Schoemaker 1993, referred to hereafter as KKS 1993), had been overlooked and requires a more extended comment. This volume, a text for advanced undergraduates and graduate students in courses in decision sciences, draws on philosophy, economics, sociology, psychology and management science. It takes aim at the broad range of decision making, not just economics and finance. *Decision Sciences* considers decision making on the part of the individual, groups and at the societal level, and maintains that decision making at each of these levels depends importantly on the characteristics of the other levels and the nature of decisions that are made at those other levels (the quality of "nestedness").

The book calls for careful descriptive analyses of the institutional arrangements associated with specific problems as well as with the actual decision process. "Only by understanding the context in detail can one suggest meaningful ways of improving decision making" (KKS 1993, vii). This descriptive/prescriptive linkage is perhaps the central theme of the book.

Chapter 1, "The Scope of Decision Sciences," outlines interrelationships between what are characterized as the Problem Context, Problem Finding, the Legitimization Process and Problem Solving. The Problem Context is defined to include the social context, institutional constraints and available information. Problem Finding involves identification, acceptance and representation. The Legitimization Process includes determining the impact on stakeholders, rationalizing the choices to them and implementing those choices. Problem Solving incorporates clarifying values, searching for and evaluating alternatives and the actual process of choice. The fundamental issues are listed as linking descriptive and prescriptive analyses, recognizing abilities and limitations and linking nested decision structures.

The text elaborates on these concepts and interrelationships, presenting a valuable framework for thinking about decisions and providing applications of the multiobjective, multidisciplinary approach which reveal that the relative importance of each of the factors varies from problem to problem. That is at once both the strength and weakness of the approach—weakness, as well, because no unequivocal guidelines are presented to indicate the manner in which to determine the relative importance of the many factors.

Chapter 2 deals with the identification of the problems to be solved and demonstrates the relationship between problem finding and problem solving. This is often overlooked in discussions of decision making, though even here there is no explicit reference to horizon scanning (particularly important for decisions involving technological change).

Chapters 3–5 cover individual decision making. Chapter 3 deals with prediction and inference, and with judgment and uncertainty. It most nearly corresponds to Chapter 4 of *Rationality Gone Awry?* (on valuation and choice), and the supporting appendices cover the ground of Chapter 5 in this volume, but in greater detail and more technically. The chapter concludes, in part,

no *simple* and *general* model exists for describing how preferences of individuals are determined and how choices are or indeed should be arrived at. Process models can capture the sequence of steps that individuals may follow in dealing with a particular problem, but these models pay little attention to why one alternative or attribute is intrinsically valued more than another. Outcome-based models assume that individuals are guided by personal utilities in valuing choice, but, as we have seen, people systematically violate axioms that appear to be quite reasonable on the surface. (KKS, 175)

And alternative approaches are said to be only partly successful. The authors explain:

- "Each problem has a unique set of characteristics and associated institutional arrangements and constraints. *Complexity matters.*"
- "Each individual has his or her own set of constraints and perceived links with other problems. *Nestedness matters.*"
- "Small changes in a problem's wording may lead to different reference points, different information processing strategies, and different allocations of attention to specific dimensions of the problem. *Context matters.*" (KKS, 176)

Chapter 5, "Evaluating Prescriptive Approaches," begins by defining descriptive, normative and prescriptive theories. Normative theories are characterized as "theoretical benchmarks for how decision makers *should ideally perform,*" while prescriptive theories are concerned with *"helping decision makers improve* their performance in problem finding and problem solving, given the complexities and constraints of real life." While *Rationality Gone Awry?* takes note of normative theories, it refers to descriptive analyses, not theories. It endeavors to help decision makers improve performance, but only expresses a hope that the evidence on successful problem solving will contribute toward a prescriptive approach (which is referred to as a behavioral theory of decision making) sometime in the future.

The chapter evaluates five "holistic" approaches for coping with the problem-solving phases, namely: (1) an intuitive approach; (2) the use of linear rules with "bootstrapping" applications; (3) decision support systems, beginning with such constructs as portfolio theory; (4) mathematical programming; and (5) a decision analysis approach. Which of these (or others) are employed would depend on the structure of the problem, the context and the decision maker's criteria for solving the problem in question and legitimizing the decision. This involves consideration of the decision maker (his experience/skills, values, goals and cognitive style), the type of problem (its structure and complexity, the values it evokes and the data requirements) and the "legitimation" criteria (optimality, understandability, defendability, accuracy), along with the solution approaches (intuitive, formal, computer based). Two figures provide the reader with a useful framework for contemplating the extensive range of relevant elements and interrelationships, and the suitability of each of the holistic approaches for five different problems is discussed (some of which do not have to do with economics and finance). Unfortunately, all this does not quite come to grips with the critical matter of how, precisely, to gauge the tradeoffs.

Chapters 6–9 deal with multipersonal decision making. Chapter 6, on group decision making, discusses theoretical and experimental work in social and industrial psychology and various aspects of decision processes in groups (Groupthink, group decision support systems, conflict resolution, social judgment theory, group estimation of probabilities and learning). The applicability of the cognitive concepts discussed at the individual level is implicit, but is not always made explicit.

Chapter 7 deals with formal models of group decision making, such as game theory, auctions and the analysis of the relations between principals and agents. Chapter 8, on organizational decision making, discusses the rational unitary model, organizational and political models. It maintains that concepts are required that go beyond the traditional rational models and the literature of individual decision making. Chapter 9, "Societal Decision Making," emphasizes low-probability, high-consequence events such as natural (or man-made) disasters. It emphasizes that individuals are often imperfectly informed about risks so that their behavior is not consistent with normative theories of choice, such as expected utility theory and Bayesian analysis, and this is compounded by the fact that experts frequently disagree on the nature of societal risks.

The Epilogue characterizes problem solving as an art as much as a science,

and lists five guiding principles: (1) the critical nature of context, (2) the need
for a process approach involving procedural rationality ("Good decisions result
from sound processes, in much the same way that great golf or tennis shots
result from great swings,"), (3) the need to take account of bounded rationality,
(4) nestedness and (5) legitimization.

Rationality Gone Awry? documents the economic and financial anomalies that
are crucial for an argument such as that presented in *Decision Sciences*, although
the argument of the latter goes further than that of the former and may be more
controversial. *Rationality Gone Awry?* attempts to indicate which of the anomalies are particularly important and cry out for major variations from normative
theory in order to contribute to actual problem solving and how one might go
about ascertaining this critical matter further. It does not assume that a significantly different "prescriptive theory" is needed in *all* types of decision-making
situations in the financial and economic area. Moreover, this book is even more
inductively oriented, and less inclined to characterize the emerging findings and
resulting decision-making aids as theoretical just yet, though it is equally as
concerned with the long-run need to build toward a multidisciplinary behavioral
theory to cope with the resolution of problems in natural financial and economic
settings (i.e., in real life).

Appendixes

Appendix A

Rules of Thumb (Heuristics)

Decisions are often made quickly, or at any rate, without any elaborate calculations. Indeed, it is often quite efficient to do so, especially for routine matters. Even when more care and consideration are involved, resort is often made to simplifying rules of thumb or heuristics. Decision makers use heuristics or rules of thumb for many reasons, some quite laudable and others perhaps regrettable.

To begin with, decision makers may be unaware of the best ways to solve their problems, and, in addition optimization techniques have not yet been devised for some types of problems. (Some problems may never lend themselves to unique and truly optimal solutions.)

Second, a decision may be required before perhaps extended optimization calculations can be made—though this is less of a problem at present than before the advances in computer technology.

Third, use of a quick rule of thumb may better enable the decision maker to keep certain decisions secret until he or she chooses to make the decision known. (This reason for the use of heuristics may have gained force as a result of certain recent invasions of electronic privacy.

Fourth, the decision maker may be unable to obtain all the information necessary for an optimizing solution; or, if the information is available, the cost of the full search process may exceed the benefits of the added gain; or—and this may be of particular importance in limiting the search process—it simply may not be possible to gauge the benefits.

Fifth, the problem may not be in obtaining the information but in perceiving it accurately by the time the decision has to be made. Recall of past experiences may help remind decision makers that on occasions some information that was costly or time consuming to obtain, proved of limited value or was even misleading because it was not perceived correctly at the time of decision making.

Sixth, an extraordinarily large amount of information may overwhelm the decision maker, not only because of a lack of programs to handle the data, but even in cases where such programs exist, because of the emotional character of the particular decision or the decision maker.

Seventh, decision makers who ordinarily make optimization calculations may be tempted to stray from that course by what appear to be "winning formulas" of others. They may imitate those "winning formulas" without recognizing adequately that they involved more than offsetting higher risks, or in some cases without recognizing that publicity about the "winning formulas" involved a good deal of puffing and only *seemed* to lead to higher earnings.

Eighth, heuristics may be used to help determine decisions by those individuals and enterprises that have multiple objectives (even if only momentarily), or for whatever reason, do not seek to optimize (even if only temporarily).

Ninth, even where there is just a single objective and that objective is to optimize, heuristics may be used if implementation of that objective presents serious difficulties for any reason, and even if only temporarily.

Many, if not most, organizations have standard operating procedures. These are basically rules of thumb or heuristics used to handle everyday situations, and perhaps a few more major types of decisions that are specific to the industry or firm. Some are written and posted; others are simply implicit. At times, the heuristics exist and are pursued, but those who employ them have difficulty in verbalizing what they are. Sometimes they state that they reason "by the seat of their pants," which makes many decisions appear to be more ad hoc than they really are. A substantial minority of economists have considered the possibility of generalized decision-making alternatives to maximization, at least since the late 1930s, when Hall and Hitch wrote of the markup pricing that characterized the business firms that they interviewed. Psychologists and marketing specialists have devoted a great deal of effort to explaining alternative approaches to decision making by consumers. These efforts were touched on in the text. The full list of decision rule categories includes what the psychologists term affect referral, linear compensatory decision rules, nonlinear compensatory decision rules, conjunctive decision rules, disjunctive decision rules, lexicographic decision rules, sequential elimination, the lexicographic semiorder decision rule and the additive-difference decision rule.[1] Added to these categories are the special considerations that psychologists posit for the decision making of families and other special affinity groups.

Early on, Simon, drawing on the work of others, outlined a heuristic program for locating warehouses. His program included eight steps but nonetheless involved a simplified procedure. This exemplified what has been characterized as specific heuristics or rules of thumb, but he has devoted a great deal of effort to developing more generalizable heuristics. Simon characterized much of what economic actors did as satisficing, not only because of motivational considerations (indeed, not primarily for that reason), but because of limitations in the access to information and in calculation capabilities already referred to. Simon and his colleagues introduced "heuristic programming," computer programs that simulated some nonquantitative, nonformal procedures that people use to solve problems. These programs emphasized experience and allowed for computer-modified performance. Earl characterizes Simon's work in this area as follows:

[Simon] has been at the forefront of work on artificial intelligence, trying to see whether mental processes can be represented in terms of computer programs. . . . Lying behind all this work seems to be the notion that it is useful to imagine minds as if they function very much like sets of computer programs, which operate according to particular grammatical codes. Life may therefore be seen as the processing of information followed by actions that entail the working through of *procedures* selected from *menus* of possible procedures by the *rules* according to which the information processing has been done. Decision makers either completely implement their chosen procedures and then bring into play further procedures for deciding what to do next or, if problems are encountered, they switch to other procedures that their information-processing rules deem more suitable for handling the situation. (Earl 1995, 67)

This reflects Simon's dedication to improving the nature of heuristics, but it also may help explain why some social scientists—some sociologists, for example—regard Simon as reductionist.

The psychologists Tversky, Kahneman, Slovic and their colleagues advanced the discussion a step further. On the basis of their understanding of human behavior, they posited that individuals used certain generalized rules of thumb or heuristics and they conducted numerous laboratory experiments to verify their hypotheses. Those experiments also revealed the nature of the biases associated with the heuristics, biases that most psychologists did not think were easy to reduce, much less eliminate. Some of the behavioral results they obtained seemed to undermine basic axioms of economics, which led economists and business administration specialists to run their own experiments, paying more attention to incentives than the psychologists had. To their surprise, initially, at least, most found support for the notion that even those with incentives to optimize tended to use quasi-rational short cuts. Some experiments, however, revealed that it was possible to reduce the biases for similar, repeated decisions. The emphasis, particularly by the psychologists, was on three heuristics in particular: representativeness, availability and anchoring. The case for the generalized heuristics rests on these three and, to a lesser extent, on the matching law and melioration. Other candidates for generalized heuristics have been proposed, including concreteness, event matching, imitation, simulation and satisficing (where satisficing is combined with the phenomenon referred to as aspiration levels). Concreteness draws on the fact that people tend to remember information in exactly the same form as it was given to them. Event matching is a procedure whereby people match their behavior to the properties of rewarded trials. (An example offered by Antonides concerns the approach of riders to catching a bus.

If the bus arrives late one-third of the time, then while it might seem rational to always be at the bus stop on time, an event matching strategy would be to do so only two-thirds of the time.) Imitation has something in common with the reasoning by analogy to which the text refers. The heuristic of simulation uses as a basis for judgment the ease with which examples or scenarios can be reconstructed. It differs somewhat from what economists generally mean when they refer to the term.

There are a number of problems, however. While these heuristics have been informed by the findings of psychology and it has been possible to ascertain the kinds of behavior exemplified by such heuristics as representativeness, availability, anchoring, matching and melioration, there is no theory of heuristics, as is reflected in the variation in the degree to which representativeness et al. are manifest. Some of the psychologists involved have indicated (orally at least) that perhaps other heuristics might be uncovered by careful questioning and observation in real-life situations. Moreover, the applicability of the various heuristics and the seriousness of the biases seem to vary. Some problems apparently draw on more than one heuristic, but as yet no guideline has been established for anticipating the mix of heuristics that may apply to different types of problems or the degree to which the biases detected for the three major heuristics may be altered when they are combined (or when they are used simultaneously, or the sequence with which they are employed is altered), or when still other heuristics enter, or if they also vary according to external circumstances or the emotional state of the decision maker. The framing of problems seems to influence the heuristics that are relevant and the seriousness of the biases—and as already observed, there is not yet any theory of framing.

Clearly, decision makers use heuristics or rules of thumb, and now we know more about them than before, but do we know enough to apply them to other than very simple situations? How many heuristics with which types and degrees of bias may be at work in resolving the often complex problems of business and government? And how do the presumably only quasi-rational heuristics of highly successful survivors (and the way in which those heuristics tend to be improved) differ from those of the businesses that barely get by and from the consumers who don't seem to have as high a standard of living as others with lower levels of income? Even assuming that the best analyses of financial and economic phenomena should take account of heuristics, do we dare use this approach in analyzing complicated problems until we know much more about heuristics? Careful case studies of at least moderately complicated field situations would seem to be of the highest priority—and such inductive efforts might be vital to uncovering a theory of survivor-oriented heuristics.

NOTE

1. See, for example, W. Fred van Raaij, "Information Processing and Decision Making. Cognitive Aspects of Economic Behavior," in van Raaij, van Veldhoven and Wär-

neryd 1988, 93–96. A version of the discussion presented by van Raaij that is more accessible to economists, along with an explanation of the position that some consumer purchases are made essentially without a conscious decision process, being influenced (even imposed) by group norms, can be found in Earl 1995, 67–76. Actually, the last of these, decisions heavily influenced by societal norms, may be more common for social and political decisions than for those of consumers. Note, in any event, that some authors have claimed that many choices reflect a kind of experimental activity more than a conscious decision process. Tversky took this position, explaining preferences as the result of choice, rather than the reverse, as stated in the text. In the area of business decisions, March also maintained that many choices reflected a kind of experimental activity, as Earl notes.

Appendix B

A Case Study: Entrepreneurial Response to Economic Liberalization and Integration: An Application of the Behavioral Approach to Financial and Economic Decision Making

Do the anomalies being uncovered by Behavioral Finance and Behavioral Economics amount to more than curiosities? Are they more than merely exceptions to the well established general rules? Or do they reveal the need for and help point the way to a new paradigm, or at the very least, a significantly revised one? This appendix suggests how great the potential for further inquiry along these lines may be. It deals with Uruguay, a developing country that enjoyed a standard of living comparable to that of Canada and Australia from the 1920s through the mid-1950s, and perhaps somewhat higher than that of better-known Argentina. It is a country in which the most celebrated individuals have rarely been entrepreneurs. Uruguay's economy was relatively closed for several decades (highly unusual for a country with a population of only 3 million), and has only recently become subject to strong competitive pressures from abroad. The results of the study are tentative, and the relevance of what might be characterized as behavioral anomalies probably is greater than in a larger and long, more open economy such as the United States, or in Japan, the European Union and even Mexico, Argentina or Brazil. Still, the findings would seem to establish a case for proceeding with other such behavioral analyses and for efforts to verify the hypotheses that emerge regarding economic behavior, for other developing countries as well as for Uruguay, and to see if some of them do not hold for advanced economies, too.

After reading Section I, the reader might skip to Sections IV-D and E, and Section V, and decide at that point whether to examine the supporting Sections II, III and IV-A through C.

I. INTRODUCTION

The project under consideration provides a preliminary verification and somewhat fuller specification of behavioral hypotheses that could be used to design policies capable of promoting a more efficient response of enterprises to the changing incentives of increased economic liberalization and integration. The analysis is based on in-depth interviews of Uruguayan manufacturing enterprises at a time when they were experiencing a greatly increased opening of their economy to the world at large, and as the date of further integration with Argentina, Brazil and Paraguay approached.

Since 1990, the process of Uruguayan liberalization and the perspectives for increased integration have accelerated, and overall economic growth has been somewhat higher than in the years immediately preceding. The growth of the industrial sector has lagged behind the economy as a whole, however, even declining in absolute terms during two of the years, though finally showing renewed strength and a notable rate of increase in 1996. Employment in manufacturing dropped significantly, reflecting the stagnation in part, but primarily the initiation of major efforts to increase productivity. The views of Uruguayan manufacturers about the anticipated evolution from the preexisting preferential trade agreements with Argentina and Brazil to a full-fledged Common Market by the announced 1995 date wavered between concern about the extraordinary challenge to conviction on the part of many that nothing so drastic would be realized. Only in August–September 1994 did virtually all industrialists come to conclude that a definite, even if somewhat gradual move to greater economic integration was virtually assured. Consolidating that, the electoral victory in November 1994 of the political party most closely associated with measures to promote Uruguayan industrialization and the nearly equivalent vote of the three major political parties, including the party drawing its strength from organized labor, eased concerns as to whether the new government would ignore any serious adversity that might follow the further steps of economic integration that were scheduled to begin in January 1995.

In the related work that preceded this project, in-depth interviews were conducted with Uruguayan industrialists, government officials, bankers, economists and labor union leaders. Although a structured outline was employed, the interviews were open-ended and emphasized the desirability of extensive explanations of decision making currently in process or recently undertaken and well-recalled, rather than perhaps perfunctory responses to each question. The objective was to attempt to gain an understanding of decision-making process, both those leading to successful and unsuccessful results. Many of the questions reflected recent work in cognitive psychology.[1] The study led to an initial report, presented in November 1992 in Uruguay and in August 1993 at the annual meeting of the Society for the Advancement of Behavioral Economics in the United States, and circulated in April 1994 as a Working Paper of the Kellogg Institute of the University of Notre Dame.[2]

There are fundamental considerations for seeking to understand the reasoning processes that underlie decision making, as indicated in the text. These may help explain some recent results in experimental economics that conflict with certain conclusions of game theory, an approach which assumes a high degree of what economists define as rationality. Then, too, consider research which shows that near (but not quite maximizing) behavior that may not penalize individuals much can lead to economy-wide losses of significant dimensions[3]—this juxtaposed with the substantially greater deviations from maximization that are found in economies (in East Asia, for example) which have sustained growth rates so high that it might seem counter to all sense to characterize that growth as reflecting major economic losses. What kinds of assumptions and reasoning processes underlie decision making if actual results can differ so, and can even improve upon those that the methodology of traditional economics indicates are likely?

This study uncovered further support for most of the findings of the earlier analysis cited in the second note to the appendix. Perhaps the most important result of the study is to specify a number of rules of thumb that businessmen, who clearly seek a high level of profits, appear to employ for decision making. As in the case of rules of thumb generally, these may not be consistent with the rational, maximizing guidelines that economists refer to, nor with the maximizing (or near maximizing) outcomes that many of the most successful businessmen probably aspire to. The findings help explain why Uruguayan manufacturers have seemed to lack a sense of urgency in addressing the threats and opportunities of increased economic integration with its neighbors. The in-depth questioning about decision-making processes also gives increased attention to alternatives that may be mutually acceptable for helping resolve an important policy conflict between manufacturers and exporters, on the one hand, and the government on the other; this dispute (over whether to sharply accelerate the devaluation of the country's currency) has threatened, at times, to undermine recent progress toward economic liberalization and integration.

II. THE OVERALL METHODOLOGY

Four basic considerations underlie the study.

First, the recent work by cognitive psychologists and economists referred to above and, in particular, in the text provides compelling reasons for understanding decision-making processes better.

Second, economists have begun to ask individual economic agents to *explain* phenomena. This is a new effort with one or another of the following objectives: (1) to supplement "hard data" on production, trade and financial transactions; (2) to help eliminate from further consideration at least a few of the sometimes embarrassingly large number of theoretically plausible explanations; or, (3) to uncover an hypothesis worthy of testing when the investigator is truly at a loss with respect to the relevant theoretical explanation. Despite the earlier insistence of many prominent economists that it was the business of other social sciences, not economics, to explain underlying factors, some of the new survey efforts are coming under attack for not turning up enough evidence on *why* economic agents behave as they do, and what the underlying reasoning processes of decision makers are. Even more serious, there are indications that some of the survey responses are misleading.[4]

Third, the New Institutional Economics has clarified the need to take careful account of transaction costs, agency considerations, informational asymmetries, optimal sequencing, institutional settings and even ideology in properly framing economic problems. All this underscores the danger of automatically applying the same detail of analysis (not to mention the same policies and implementation procedures) to superficially similar problems in different settings.

Fourth, also following on the work of the cognitive psychologists, the study has given a good deal of attention to the possible importance of the way in which questions about financial and economic matters are formulated (i.e., to what is referred to as framing). This can be seen especially in the framing of the question about the objectives of the enterprise, in the alternative efforts to draw out information on the guidelines employed for decision making and in the consideration given to the sequence of certain questions.

III. THE QUESTIONNAIRE

(Available from the author on request)

IV. THE RESULTS

A. General Considerations

(Available from the author on request)

B. The Characteristics of the Firms Interviewed

Tabulations for the 36 enterprises interviewed reveal that 12 were engaged in activities in which Uruguay could be said to enjoy a favorable international position (meatpacking, dairy products, woolen textiles and clothing and leather clothing), 15 were in an intermediate position (other foodstuffs, other clothing and chemicals) and 9 in an unfavorable position (cotton and synthetic textiles, metallurgy, metalworking and vehicles). Eighteen of the interviews were held with owners or directors, 7 with general managers, 8 with division managers and 3 with middle-level supervisors.

The years of enterprise initiation were as follows:

Before 1930	4 firms
1930–1973	20 firms

1974–1982	5 firms
1983–1984	3 firms
1985 and after	4 firms

That is to say, 13 firms were initiated in years of relatively free trade or trade liberalization, and 23 in years of significant protection. Relatively more of the industries categorized as favorable began operations in the freer trade periods.

All of the firms had plants in Montevideo and vicinity or were close enough to get critical supplies from Montevideo within four hours.

The great majority of the enterprises had no more than a small number of principal shareholders.

Twenty-four firms were 100 percent Uruguayan-owned or dominantly so, while 11 were foreign-owned or dominated (one was half and half).

Size: rather than use uniform definitions of the number of employees, the value of assets or the value of sales for such intrinsically different activities as clothing, meatpacking and steel, the firms were asked to gauge themselves in terms of the degree to which their production, distribution and R&D capacities were sufficient to enable them to approximate the minimum economies of scale needed to compete internationally (although, as several firms pointed out, even in international competition it is sometimes possible to succeed in niches and/ or due to special attention to marketing, even without having minimum economies of scale). In terms of the MERCOSUR market, 10 judged themselves large enough to compete with ease, and 16 as probably having of the dimensions necessary to compete, at least in niches (all 26 of which were categorized as medium-sized firms). The remaining 10 regarded themselves as too small to compete in the larger, more competitive market. In terms of the local market, 17 might be categorized as large, 14–15 as medium sized and 4–5 as small.

Eight firms estimated their profits to be at a rate higher than average in their branch of industry, and that group probably reached 10 firms, taking account of all of the statements made. Twenty to 21 firms concluded that their rates of profitability were about the same as the average for their group, and 4 to 5 below the average. Of those in the internationally competitive group, 11 of the 12 responding to this question placed themselves in the above average or average groups. (Until very recently it would have been very uncommon for Uruguayans to claim higher-than-average profits.)

Some respondents possessed only a secondary school education (sometimes augmented by subsequent special studies), but the great majority of enterprises had one or more university graduates among their key decision makers. In most firms, half or more of the decision makers had college degrees, and those with training in engineering and the applied sciences were almost as large a group as those with preparation in accounting and business administration. Only a few were lawyers.

Twenty-eight of the 32 that responded to the question on exports indicated that they did sell abroad, and 20 claimed to export more than 40 percent of output. There was almost an even division between those who stated that their exports had increased since 1993 and those who claimed stability or decreases.

C. The Consistency of Responses

(Available from the author on request)

D. Heuristics/Rules of Thumb When Maximizing Guidelines Do Not Appear to Have Been Followed

The first point is that greater pressures and adversities not only caused those enterprises with maximization goals to pursue them more effectively than before, as just noted (and as Cyert and March found 30 years ago[5]), but also appears to have helped shift enterprise objectives further toward profit maximization; 20 of the 36 firms indicated that their objective was to maximize profits (14 in the long run, 6 over a period of 3 to 5 years), and 3 of those firms indicated that it was recent trends—the new competitive pressures—that had led them to seek profit maximization. The interviews turned up a great deal of evidence of the use of rules of thumb that aimed at helping firms perform reasonably well, perhaps better than before, but were not strictly maximizing procedures. This subsection outlines those rules.[6]

1. Generalized Guidelines for Decision Making That May Not Be Maximizing

(a) Nine of the firms stated that they had an overall strategy or plan, and that that strategy or plan played a major role in their investment and other major decisions. Four of those firms were foreign subsidiaries, but maintained that their strategy was shaped and decisions regarding many important matters were determined locally. (This differed from the other 8 foreign enterprises, which acknowledged that most major decisions were made abroad.) Broader and longer-term considerations are involved in the formulation of such strategies and plans, but not all may have been dominated by maximization considerations. Moreover, they are redrafted only at intervals; pursuing a previously developed plan may not be nearly as effective in maximizing profits (or another firm goal) as when it was drawn up. Nonetheless, resorting to a well-developed strategy to determine particular decisions may often reflect a move toward maximization despite the possible biases entailed, especially if there is recognition of the direction (and the approximate magnitude) of the biases.

(b) In the face of the new competitive pressures of MERCOSUR and an increasingly open economy, 6 firms decided, apparently without much further calculation, to simply accelerate the initiation of previously planned investments (though the very same investments may no longer have been as optimal as before).

(c) A number of firms left important components of activity in the hands of outside consultants. In the case of 8 enterprises, this seems to have been primarily with respect to the collection and analysis of information, but 12 allowed consultants to intervene in some aspects of the basic decision-making processes of the firm (4 firms in the favorable category, 6 in the intermediate category and 2 in the unfavorable category). It is not clear whether the consultants always employed a maximizing calculation in arriving at their recommendations; they, too, may have resorted, on occasion, to rules of thumb.

(d) Five firms acknowledged that their use of careful cost/benefit analysis was restricted to a limited number of options, but it was not always clear how those options were selected and how the preliminary eliminations were made (what kinds of rules of thumb may have been employed in those key initial decisions). Moreover, there were indications that the standards for the preliminary selections and eliminations from consideration sometimes varied.

(e) Use of a cost/benefit mentality, but without precise calculations, *except for major decisions*, was the rule of thumb for 12 firms. That seems reasonably efficient insofar as it avoids costly calculations in those cases in which the benefits are small, but the approach probably leads to the kind of overconfidence in judgments that psychologists have documented, and thus to a tendency to forgo careful calculations even on some occasions in which it would be advantageous to use them.

(f) Nine firms seemed to carry the former approach one step further, using a cost/benefit mentality, but *as a general rule* avoiding careful calculations. Such an approach is likely to lead to major biases in those cases in which the number of relevant considerations is large or some of the considerations are complicated, or in which the interrelations are great or the time periods are long.

(g) Many enterprises emphasized the importance of certain "key" areas, and said that the policy of their companies was to strengthen those aspects. They seemed to be saying: if we pay close attention to quality and marketing (or to training and technological development, e.g.), our competitiveness and profitability will follow. The selection of the various "key" areas seemed to reflect reasonable considerations, but the measure and manner of implementation of these emphases often failed to involve any cost/benefit calculation even if, as was usually the case, use was made of a cost/benefit approach for some activities of the firm (such as major new investments). The firms that employed such guidelines usually mentioned two or three key areas which they sought to emphasize. Those most cited were: investment (in which case cost/benefit calculations ordinarily were used) (15 firms); training (15 firms); technological development (13 firms); marketing (13 firms); the quality of the product (12 firms, 8 in the unfavorable category); product differentiation and style (8 firms); increased employee motivation (8 firms); the quality of inputs (6 firms, 4 in the favorable category); and total quality control (3 firms).

(h) Along somewhat similar lines, many firms assign an initial priority to maintaining (or augmenting) areas of enterprise strength or alleviating areas of weakness. There is some overlap with the "key" categories just discussed. Eight firms indicated that they emphasized areas of enterprise strength, 4 of these involving technical assistance provided to primary sector producers of inputs they processed. On the other hand, 27 firms stated that they assigned high priority to the alleviation of areas of weakness. Eighteen mentioned efforts to improve the operational efficiency of existing processes, 7 (including several of the same firms) mentioned the need to increase product specialization and increase economies of scale, and 5, the need to increase training at one or another level. (Among the other areas of weakness cited by 2 or more firms were financial constraints, attitudes adverse to change, and problems in management decision making). As above, the emphasis on areas of strength or the efforts to alleviate weaknesses did not appear to be subject to careful calculation or periodic review.

(i) Some firms stated that (some of) their decisions are influenced to a significant degree by experiences. In effect, rather than rely solely (or principally) on new calculations, they reason by analogy with some experience in the past. Three firms emphasized the recent past, which has elements in common with the anchoring heuristic noted by psychologists, in which undue weight is given to the data of the immediately preceding period, or with the availability heuristic, in which undue weight is given to information because of its recent and/or attention-getting characteristics. Thirteen firms appear to draw not on a single, seemingly very similar experience, but on the accumulated experience of the past to make their analogy. Some of the firms look principally at their own experience, while others look at the experience of a broader range of firms (or at the experience of successful foreign firms in their field).

2. Guidelines for the Information Search

One of the most striking findings of this study is the informality of the guidelines used in the search for information, even among those firms that state that they seek to maximize profits, and even after the onset of new competitive pressures that lead to efforts to reduce costs and improve competitive position. Only 2 enterprises appeared to have used reasonably precise cost/benefit analyses in orienting their information search, and that only for a small number of their decisions. Three firms relied heavily on the advice of outside consultants (in one case, on a partner in a joint venture), but they were not always aware of the guidelines that underlie the outside advice. Five firms stated that they used a cost/benefit mentality but did not make calculations, 2 depended to a considerable extent on reasoning by analogy with information search experiences in the past, 2 collected information on what they regarded as key variables, 3 stated that they collected information until their leading doubts were resolved, and one firm conceded that its custom is simply to collect data as long as time permits. Three firms employed varying guidelines, only some of which reflected a cost/benefit mentality. *Twelve firms appeared to have no clear guidelines, certainly none that they could verbalize*; they simply mentioned the categories of information on which they regularly gather information, mentioned several different considerations or stated that they did not have any consistent guidelines for their information search. This far-from-maximizing search behavior is consistent with that identified in an earlier study of real world decision making, and is essentially at odds with the more nearly optimizing behavior of search rules of thumb observed in a laboratory experiment,[7] not to mention the entirely optimizing behavior of strategies from game theory.

E. Principal Findings from Tabulations of the Individual Questions

1. Reasoning by analogy from the past seems to be a fairly common practice that is used to supplement and sometimes replace careful calculation. When attention was drawn to a particular major adversity in Uruguay's past (such as the extreme financial difficulties and frequent bankruptcies associated with efforts to repay credits, following the 1982 devaluation), and it was asked whether that experience continued to affect contemporary decision making in the same area, just under half of the firms responded affirmatively, and when asked if there was some experience from the past that influenced their decision making, fully three-quarters responded affirmatively and most gave convincing examples. Of that group, some enterprises assigned only moderate significance to the experience of the past, but a larger number characterized such experience as important. While the specific experience of the early-to-mid-1980s credit adversities did not continue to affect contemporary decision making as much among enterprises in industries in which Uruguay had a favorable competitive position as among those in an intermediate or unfavorable position, those enterprises in favorable position industries were approximately as likely as those in intermediate position industries to maintain that, in general, experiences from the past had had and should have a significant impact on decision making. (However, the strongest affirmations along those lines came from firms in the industries in which the country's competitive position was estimated to be weakest.) It would be interesting to see whether these results would be altered if the more general question were to precede the reference to a specific favorable or unfavorable earlier decision. It does seem, though, that interviewing in this area requires a "warm up period" involving several questions before a decision maker is willing to acknowledge that he or she continues to allow the analogy with some past experience to influence a decision, and particularly to lead to one that might deviate from what would be indicated by a more rigorous analysis (especially for those with a degree in business administration for whom the question must seem like a query as to whether they use the rational guidelines they were taught or, if despite that instruction, they act in a manner that their instructors probably would regard as irrational).

2. The Endowment Effect. Major contributions from psychology and exper-

imental economics have established that people tend to value gains less than the same amount of losses. They are loss averse and seek to conserve their endowment.[8] While the most dramatic examples of this have come from the differences between the prices that people are willing to pay and those that they are willing to accept for goods not really intended for subsequent exchange, to put the phenomenon in proper perspective and relate it to business activity, gains are valued less than losses only at some reference point, although the empirical work on the subject might lead one to think that loss aversion relates to a gain or a loss from any given situation. The latter view would give support to the expectation of a conservative response from businessmen (especially Uruguayan businessmen, who have a particular reputation for conservatism), and has led some to conclude that businessmen require a higher return and/or lower risk on a new investment than that which they deemed adequate for their last undertaking (indeed, perhaps even a better risk and return combination than they actually obtained on their last investment if that was higher than what they originally anticipated).

Joshua Ronen, a leading writer on entrepreneurship, notes, however, that some entrepreneurs "seem to exhibit increasing appetite for wealth and accomplishment" and "have a marginal utility that increases with wealth."[9] For them, the wealth "is not just monetary wealth." It encompasses also "prestige, power, sense of independence, peer recognition, social status, and other attributes." Ronen then argues, not that there is no "reference point" at which gains are valued less than equivalent losses, but that this takes place only above a certain aspiration level, and that the aspiration level may be higher and more subject to rising further among innovative entrepreneurs than among others. The interviews undertaken for this study support this view and, indeed, extend this line of reasoning beyond true entrepreneurs (innovators) and into the business community generally. When asked what combination of risk and return they would require to undertake a new investment relative to the risk and return obtained on a previous investment, only 4 manufacturers replied that it would have to be more favorable, while 7 answered that it need only be as favorable as before, and 22 indicated that it need not be as favorable as before. Even in the case of an investment that would be much larger, most still replied that they would not necessarily require a more favorable risk and return package. These results, the differences for enterprises of different characteristics and their possible application to the testing undertaken in experimental economics are elaborated upon in a more detailed commentary which is available upon request.[10]

The impact of recent major increases in economic liberalization and integration and the likelihood of further integration impacts introduced new uncertainties and adversities into the economic horizon of Uruguay. It might be claimed that Uruguayan manufacturers are, in a sense, worse off than before—if not in monetary terms, in many cases, then worse off in that it now requires more effort and/or risk than before to obtain a given level of profits and a given rate of return. Thus, it might be maintained that the findings here should not give rise to any new doubts about the Endowment Effect (and only the possibility of a small theoretical qualification that has to do with the characteristics of particular economic agents). The concern, however, is not whether there is an Endowment Effect in static terms, but whether loss aversion is a significant characteristic of businessmen in the dynamics of a competitive environment, in which there is always the likelihood of new challenges, and in which the future is often marked by higher risks than the past. The findings of this study would seem to have important implications for public policy; some of the traditional assumptions that have been made in designing policies to promote exports, investment and increased efficiency in the use of existing plant and equipment need to be modified, and our thinking about optimal policy instruments to obtain a desired effect may need to be revised. It is necessary to take into account that the response to favorable and unfavorable changes may not be symmetrical, and that the degree of responsiveness to a given change may vary according to aspiration levels, which in turn may be differentially affected for different groups by the same circumstances and policies. Deregulation may affect the aspiration levels of the formerly protected very differently than those of the formerly constrained; for example, policies with the same opportunity cost to the Treasury may lead to very different results because one is relatively most attractive to ambitious but possibly understaffed entrepreneurs while the other appeals to a broader group, more subject to considerations of loss aversion. This has particular relevance for the discussion of item 6 below.

3. A widely acclaimed recent text by Milgrom and Roberts discusses the advantages and disadvantages of using prices, hierarchical instructions or coordination to resolve problems within the firm, and argues strongly for increased use of coordination.[11] The information of the interviews makes it clear that while coordination has only begun to take hold in Uruguayan firms, it is bringing about major improvements, not the least of which is in an aspect not even mentioned by Milgrom and Roberts—in the reduction of problem-solving difficulties due to differences in the way in which the various members of the decision making team perceive the same information. Increased coordination within firms has led to improvements in data perception, and this may be helping to overcome the lack of a sense of urgency that has characterized so many Uruguayan firms even as economic liberalization has increased and the timetable for greater economic integration has moved forward. To the degree that use of the price mechanism can be efficient within firms, the interviews have noted that increased competitive pressures have fostered greater use of subcontracting and reduced reliance on the almost automatic inclination to obtain what was necessary by making it in-house.

4. Uruguayan enterprises are reticent to mention internal problems when asked directly (though a minority do note financial, scale or training limitations), but more widespread internal problems are acknowledged implicitly in the discussion of how the firms deal with the problems arising from government or other external factors that affect them adversely. The leading response of enter-

prises in dealing with such problems is to take measures to improve operational efficiency; lobbying, though often mentioned, is a clear second, contrary to what might be expected from economists who stress rent-seeking behavior. There are no significant differences in this respect between the various groups of enterprises in the five category classifications referred to above.

5. Businessmen complain a great deal about the costs of inefficient government, but they do not make serious efforts to estimate most of those costs (nor do most endeavor to get their trade associations to do so), even though such information would be useful in devising an optimal approach to deal with the problem. Here, too, there is little difference between the various classifications of enterprises; enterprises from all groups are inclined to affirm: (a) that the costs of inefficient government, while bothersome, are not so major as to warrant making such estimations; (b) that the costs are declining sufficiently so that the expense to prepare such estimates would not be warranted; or (c) the major fallback, that the conservative nature of Uruguayans makes it difficult to bring about change. A substantial number also state that it is the task of the trade associations to eliminate the inefficiencies of government, but, unfortunately, the latter are not influential enough to be able to accomplish much in that respect.

6. A major conflict between the private sector and the government in 1992–1993 and again in 1995 centered on the growing appreciation of the Uruguayan peso, particularly with respect to the U.S. dollar. This made exports less profitable and caused many exporters to shift from one market to another, often from markets which they themselves regarded as having greater long-term potential to those with lesser long-term potential. It also led to a sharp increase of competition in the domestic market, over and above what would have been the case even with the steep decline in tariffs and other trade barriers. The industrial sector was hard hit, as was agriculture, but the government first denied, then minimized the overvaluation (insisting on comparing the value of the peso to a rather large basket of currencies), and has taken a strong position against any acceleration in the scheduled rate of devaluation, in particular, because of the threat of accelerated inflation that such an action would be likely to bring. The result was an impasse, with still more damaging consequences, as many companies concluded that the government was indifferent to their plight and turned from manufacturing to importing some or all of what they sold, sometimes even without seriously examining the means to improve their competitiveness. The interviews provide information that might have offered a means of resolving the conflict, and that still might do so. When asked how they attempt to raise productivity, industrialists speak of investment in improved equipment, of training and of various means of improving the operational efficiency of the equipment they possess. When asked what they are doing to alleviate the difficulties emanating from the government or other external sources, industrialists mention lobbying, to be sure, but first they refer to various means of improving operational efficiency.

With industrial productivity increasing more than 8 percent a year in Uruguay, most economists do not pursue this area much more. But there are too many cases in which major efforts by local firms have led to productivity increases of 50 to 100 percent in one to two years to overlook the potential of industrial extension services (with new equipment as well as old). And there are too many cases of apparently very successful emphases on industrial extension services abroad, especially in several of the Asian countries. The government has undertaken activities in this area, but it is not easy to understand why it has not attempted much more, either with direct services or tax deductions for services contracted privately, so as to further increase productivity and reduce the clamor for and possibly even the need for accelerated devaluation. The further mystery is why the private sector has not pushed harder for more of that support, not only for relatively advanced technology, where the government has greatly increased its efforts (notably with the technology laboratory, LATU), or for assisting micro or very small enterprise, where a limited amount also has been done, but for really substantial efforts to improve the best practice techniques of the entire industrial sector and, indeed, the entire productive apparatus of the economy. It is not only a lack of information, but also, and perhaps more importantly, lags in perceiving the true meaning of some readily available information, and all-to-casual reasoning with the data that probably explain the failure of Uruguay to move more energetically along these lines—the same factors that also help explain the lack of a sense of urgency on the part of so many in both the private and public sector. The interviews reveal that, as in the case of the previously noted lack of a sense of urgency about liberalization and integration, private sector perceptions and judgments are beginning to change.

V. PRINCIPAL HYPOTHESES TO BE TESTED IN THE NEXT STAGE

1. Competitive pressures, adversity or threats of adversity influence the degree to which profit maximization is an enterprise objective and are critical to fostering operational implementation of cost minimization/profit maximization among those enterprises which have such objectives. Attention should be given to the possibly differential impact of different types of competitive pressure and, in particular, to adversity associated with increased economic integration.

2. In the face of new competitive pressures and adversity, enterprises which indicate that they seek to maximize profits and that undertake to improve their competitive position do not initially pursue guidelines in the search process that are of a strictly maximizing character, nor do the rules of thumb they follow approximate maximization very closely. A learning process that leads to more maximizing guidelines evolves and continues as long as the pressures or adversities are of the same type, but the learning process tends to be interrupted and sometimes reversed if the types of competitive pressures or adversities change.

3. Enterprises that have maximization objectives and that tend to use maxi-

mization guidelines in many of their analyses generally employ heuristics or rules of thumb to select the alternatives that they then evaluate more carefully, and they rely primarily on such rules of thumb to determine the amount of information to obtain in evaluating those alternatives.

4. The increase in intrafirm coordination and in certain forms of interfirm coordination among enterprises experiencing substantially greater competitive pressure or adversity tends to offset some of the failure to optimize that might otherwise be expected from the use of not-strictly-maximizing, rule-of-thumb decision guidelines.

5. Reasoning by analogy from past experiences is a rule of thumb that is used both by firms that attempt to maximize profits and by those that have other objectives. Among firms with a maximizing objective, it is used relatively least by firms that achieve better-than-average profits. In both maximizing and non-maximizing enterprises, however, reasoning by analogy is employed relatively most with certain classes of decisions and rarely with other types of decisions.

6. Problems of imperfect data perception are of the same order of importance as problems of the lack of data in explaining disappointing adjustment to new economic horizons, such as major increases in economic integration.

7. The loss aversion or endowment effect so amply documented by psychologists and experimental economics is of little significance in the early stages of increased economic integration, and is virtually absent for entrepreneurially-led firms in those circumstances, except for investments of a very large magnitude relative to the current asset levels of the enterprises in question.

8. An understanding of the way in which businessmen respond to what they perceive as obstacles is as important as the identification of the obstacles themselves in determining the most effective means of alleviating adverse consequences and of designing government policies that effectively foster the expansion of those enterprises.

In view of indications in the interviews of difficulties in recalling data critical for a meaningful evaluation of various aspects of these preliminary findings/ hypotheses, it is proposed that the initial verification should be by a limited number of case studies in which data is collected at several points in time over the course of a period such as a year, with the data relating exclusively to the period covered. This could be supplemented, in a few cases, with direct observation of on-going decision making processes.

How much relevance does what has been presented in this volume have for economic and financial activities generally? How much, if at all, would public policy recommendations be influenced if a behavioral approach to economic and financial policies were employed, and how much would it matter at the level of enterprise policies?

Beginning at the enterprise level, the determination of what is optimal from the point of view of a firm depends on the responses of other enterprises— competitors, suppliers and customers. Some of these are likely to have objectives that differ from profit maximization, especially in the case of those not destined for survival. Moreover, the deviations from maximization objectives may vary somewhat from one enterprise or customer to another. All this would require an optimum response pattern for the initial firm that would differ from that which would hold if it could be assumed that all sought to maximize. Determination of the course of action becomes much more difficult; moreover, the nature of some strongly-felt, but imprecise objectives that would hold for unusual situations might not be recognized in advance.

Second, the realization of anything even approximating optimization is unlikely because of implementation considerations. Critical data may be missing or, if available, may be imperfectly perceived. Offsetting this, it has become more common for enterprise leaders within an organization to meet with each other before making decisions and to expose their perceptions of information to the reactions of others. This tends to reduce the worst cases of imperfect data perception. At the same time, it can lead to costly decisions to obtain additional information of a type already available rather than to efforts to obtain information of an independent type that might be important for a correct resolution of problems.

Third, there is a need to identify suitable routines or rules of thumb for decision making where optimization techniques are not feasible, and to try to discover the rules or routines that are being employed within the organization. (It is necessary to avoid sloughing off serious analysis by accepting affirmations of all-too-many people that they handle many problems "by the seat of their pants.") Allowance must then be made for the direction and, to the degree possible, the magnitude of the biases of those second-best techniques, the degree that those biases are reduced in the case of frequently repeated actions or decisions on which a reliable feedback of information is available—and, of particular significance, the impact on the type and magnitude of the biases, of different ways of "framing" the decision rules and the objectives sought.

Fourth, in assessing the *likely* actions of others, there is need for a great deal of specific knowledge about others—about any changes in their desire and ability to optimize and about the routines or rules of thumb that they use, together with their awareness of and ability to reduce the biases of those second best approaches.

Finally, while some individuals, enterprises and government institutions may demonstrate a capacity of unifying or clarifying objectives in improving their perception of information, in learning, in moving toward optimization or in doing so for certain types of problems or in certain types of situations, others may not. A model of single purpose, optimizing behavior may predict reasonably well in certain types of situations but much less so in others, and while we may recognize some kinds of problems that fall clearly into one extreme or the other, there is a lack of good indicators for many that fall in between.

Can we even speak of optimizing behavior at the societal level, however? It is nearly 50 years since Arrow explained the extreme difficulty and limited circumstances under which it would be possible to arrive at a social welfare function that optimizing at the societal level would require (Kenneth J. Arrow, *Social Choice and Individual Values* [New York: John Wiley & Sons, 1951]). There is thus even more need to consider the second-best, less-than-optimizing approaches to problem solving than discussed in this exposition if we are to deal adequately with decision making at the level of society as a whole. To achieve this, economists and financial analysts had better incorporate not-strictly-economic variables in their analyses, drawing on the findings of the behavioral social sciences. If we fail to do so, the effort to deal with economic and financial policy is likely to be left increasingly to others—others who have shown their interest in combining the disparate elements but who often do so without the methodological discipline of economics and finance. The author has been engaged in initial efforts to gauge the role that behavioral economics might play in contributing to the evaluation of specific policies of the past and in considering policies that call for resolution at present, but they are too preliminary for publication at this time.

NOTES

This appendix is based on a project carried out under a contract between Development Technologies, Inc. of Washington, D.C. and the North-South Center of the University of Miami during the period January through September 1994, and revised for the annual economics meetings (Jornadas de Economía) of the Central Bank of Uruguay in December 1995, after preliminary presentations in late 1994 in Montevideo, Uruguay, Asunción, Paraguay and Santiago, Chile (at the University of the Republic in Montevideo, CEPPRO and CEPES in Asunción, and CEPALC in Santiago). The project was executed in cooperation with the Department of Economics, School of Social Sciences, University of the Republic, Montevideo, Uruguay. All but two of the interviews for this study were carried out by Francisco de Leon, a research associate with the University of the Republic who recently completed an M.A. in economics after 20 years of professional experience as an accountant.

1. The seminal reference is Kahneman, Slovic and Tversky 1982.

2. Hugh Schwartz, *Entrepreneurial Response to Economic Liberalization and Integration: An Inquiry About Recent Events in Uruguay Aimed at Developing Better Hypotheses about Economic Behavior* (Working Paper #208, April 1994, The Helen Kellogg Institute for International Studies, University of Notre Dame). (This reference and the others in this appendix that are cited in full are not included in the main bibliography.)

3. Akerlof and Yellen 1985.

4. For a brief review and criticism of such surveys, see Hugh Schwartz, "In-Depth Questionnaires of Decision-making Processes as a Major Exercise Preceding the Use of Large Surveys," paper prepared for the IAREP/SABE Conference, Integrating Views on Economic Behavior, Erasmus University, Rotterdam, July 10–13, 1994, available on request.

5. Cyert and March 1992.

6. The concern is with the use of rules of thumb by those who truly meant to do as well as possible and with situations in which it seems difficult to bring the necessary discipline to bear on a continuing basis. It is akin to the case of the banker who does

not consistently judge loans as well as a model based on criteria he or she has developed. (See Paul Slovic, "Psychological Study of Human Judgment: Implications for Investment Decision Making," *Journal of Finance*, Vol. xxvii, No. 4 [1972].) This is important because while the pressure of adversity or increasing competition on the one hand and the combination of instruction in maximizing techniques and increased computer capabilities on the other seems to be increasing the tendency of businessmen to adopt maximizing objectives, the implementation of maximization continues to present a challenge, with major implications for policy at the enterprise and economy-wide level. Of the 20 enterprises in this study that indicated that they sought to maximize profits, fully half offered responses to some questions that would not appear to be fully maximizing. This is not to deny that their answers reflected rules of thumb likely to lead to relatively high levels of profits. Even in the case of the responses that were consistent with maximization, it is difficult to believe that all of the cost-benefit type guidelines were implemented in a manner that could be described as truly maximizing.

7. On the former, see Cunningham and White, "The Behavior of Industrial Buyers in Their Search for Supplies of Machine Tools" and Hey, "Search for Rules of Search," both in Earl 1988 (159–89).

8. See especially Kahneman, Knetsch, and Thaler in Thaler 1992, 63–78.

9. Joshua Ronen, "The Rise and Decay of Entrepreneurship: A Different Perspective," *The Journal of Behavioral Economics*, Vol. 18, No. 3 (Fall 1989): 167–84.

10. A summary of that commentary is as follows: (a) Firms in a favorable international position were more inclined than those in an intermediate or unfavorable position to accept a risk/rate of return package that was not necessarily as favorable as that which they had received previously, though more likely to require more favorable terms for a new investment that involved a much larger amount; (b) Firms with a maximizing objective were more likely than those with high profits or multiple objectives to accept a risk/rate of return combination that was not necessarily as favorable, and they were not as likely as firms in a favorable international position to insist upon a more favorable risk/return package for a new investment that involved a much larger amount; (c) Enterprises with higher-than-average profits were most likely to accept a risk/return combination that was not necessarily as favorable, and not as likely as those in the average profits group to insist upon a more favorable risk/return package for a new investment that was substantially larger; (d) Foreign firms were more likely to accept a risk/return package not necessarily as favorable, and no more likely than domestic firms to demand more favorable terms in the case of a substantially larger new investment; and (e) Larger firms were more likely to accept a risk/rate of return package not necessarily as favorable and no more likely to demand more favorable terms for a substantially larger new investment than medium size or small firms.

11. Milgrom and Roberts 1992.

Part IV

Where to Go from Here: Bibliography and Reader's Guide

The first three sections list important references for those with each of three different levels of background in economics or finance. The fifth section gives other sources that also are useful, most at an advanced level. Section D attempts to provide enough information on many of the publications to further orient readers. In some cases this involves commentary, and in the larger works, an indication of the contents, with many of the chapter titles from conference collections and anthologies of articles. An index of the Bibliography and Reader's Guide is available from the author.

A. A FEW RECOMMENDATIONS FOR THE GENERAL READER AND THE INTRODUCTORY STUDENT OF ECONOMICS OR FINANCE

Bazerman, Max (1998). *Judgment in Managerial Decision Making*. Fourth Edition. New York: John Wiley. See also Section D.

The Economist (1994). "Rational Economic Man: The Human Factor," December 4, 1994–January 6, 1995, pp. 90–92; "Finance: Mind over Matter," April 23, 1994. See also Section D.

Etzioni, Amitai (1988). *The Moral Dimension: Toward a New Economics*. New York: Free Press. See also Section D.

Frank, Robert H. (1985). *Choosing the Right Pond: Human Behavior and the Quest for Status*. New York and Oxford: Oxford University Press. See also Section D.

——— (1988). *Passions Within Reason: The Strategic Role of the Emotion*. New York: W. W. Norton. See also Section D.

——— and Philip J. Cook (1995). *The Winner-Take-All Society*. New York: Marita Kessler Books, Free Press. See also Section D.

Kahneman, Daniel and Amos Tversky. (1982). "The Psychology of Preferences." *Scientific American* Vol. 246, No. 1 (January): 160–73.

Lewis, Alan, Paul Webley and Adrian Furnham (1995). *The New Economic Mind: The Social Psychology of Economic Behavior.* London: Harvester, Wheatsheaf. See also Section D.

Simon, Herbert A. (1986). "The Failure of Arm Chair Economics." *Challenge* Vol. 29, No. 5 (November–December): 18–25.

Thaler, Richard H. (1992). *The Winner's Curse: Paradoxes and Anomalies of Economic Life.* New York: Free Press. Paperback Edition: 1994, Princeton: Princeton University Press. See also Section D.

B. READINGS PRIMARILY AT AN INTERMEDIATE LEVEL

Akerlof, George A. (1983). "Loyalty Filters." *American Economic Review* Vol. 73, No. 1 (March): 54–63.

Antonides, Gerrit (1991). *Psychology in Economics and Business: An Introduction to Economic Psychology.* Introduction by W. Fred van Raaij. Dordrecht, Boston and London: Kluwer Academic Publishers. See also Section D.

Bazerman, Max (1998). *Judgment in Managerial Decision Making.* Fourth Edition. New York: John Wiley. See also Section D.

Boulding, Kenneth (1969). "Economics as a Moral Science." *American Economic Review* Vol. 59, No. 1 (March): 1–12. See also Section D.

Coleman, James S. (1984). "Introducing Social into Economic Analysis." *American Economic Review* Vol. 74, No. 2 (May): 84–88.

Coughlin, Richard, ed. (1991). *Morality, Rationality and Efficiency.* Armonk, NY and London: M. E. Sharpe. See also Section D.

Cyert, Richard M. and James G. March (1963). *A Behavioral Theory of the Firm.* Englewood Cliffs, NJ: Prentice-Hall. Second Edition: 1992, Oxford: Blackwell. See also Section D.

Dreman, David (1982). *The New Contrarian Investment Strategy.* New York: Random House. See also Section D.

———— and Michael A. Berry (1995a). "Analyst Forecasting Errors and the Implications for Security Analysis." *Financial Analysts Journal* (May–June): 30–41.

———— (1995b). "Overreaction, Underreaction, and the Low P/E Effect." *Financial Analysts Journal* (July–August): 21–30.

Earl, Peter E. (1995). *Microeconomics for Business and Marketing: Lectures, Cases and Worked Essays.* Aldershot, England and Brookfield, VT: Edward Elgar. See also Section D.

Elster, Jon (1983). *Sour Grapes: Studies in the Subversion of Rationality.* Cambridge: Cambridge University Press.

———— (1984). *Ulysses and the Sirens: Studies in Rationality and Irrationality.* Second Edition. Cambridge: Cambridge University Press.

————, ed. (1986). *The Multiple Self.* Cambridge: Cambridge University Press.

Etzioni, Amitai (1988). *The Moral Dimension: Toward a New Economics.* New York: Free Press. See also Section D.

Etzioni, Amitai and Paul R. Lawrence, eds. (1991). *Socio-Economics: Toward a New Synthesis.* Armonk, NY and London: M. E. Sharpe. See also Section D.

Frank, Robert H. (1985). *Choosing the Right Pond: Human Behavior and the Quest for Status.* New York and Oxford: Oxford University Press. See also Section D.

———— (1988). *Passions Within Reason: The Strategic Role of the Emotion.* New York: W. W. Norton. See also Section D.

———— (1994). *Microeconomics and Behavior.* Second Edition. New York: McGraw-Hill. See also Section D.

Frey, Bruno S. (1992). *Economics as a Science of Human Behavior: Towards a New Social Science Paradigm.* Boston, Dordrecht and London: Kluwer Academic Publishers. See also Section D.

Gilad, Benjamin and Stanley Kaish, eds. (1986). *Handbook of Behavioral Economics.* 2 vols. Greenwich, CT: JAI Press. See also Section D.

Hogarth, Robin M. and Melvin W. Reder, eds. (1987). *Rational Choice: The Contrast Between Economists and Psychologists.* Chicago: University of Chicago Press. See also Section D.

Journal of Economic Perspectives. See Section D.

Journal of Economic Psychology. See Section D.

Journal of Socio-Economics, formerly *The Journal of Behavioral Economics.* See Section D.

Kahneman, Daniel, Paul Slovic and Amos Tversky, eds. (1982). *Judgment Under Uncertainty: Heuristics and Biases.* Cambridge: Cambridge University Press. See also Section D.

Katona, George (1975). *Psychological Economics.* Amsterdam: Elsevier. See also Section D.

———— (1980). *Essays on Behavioral Economics,* with a Contribution by James N. Morgan. Ann Arbor, MI: Institute for Social Research, University of Michigan. See also Section D.

Knetsch, Jack L. (1995). "Assumptions, Behavioral Findings and Policy Analysis." *Journal of Policy Analysis and Management* Vol. 14, No. 1 (Winter): 68–78. See also Section D.

Kunreuther, Howard (1976). "Limited Knowledge and Insurance Protection." *Public Policy* Vol. 4, No. 2 (Spring): 227–61.

———— and Paul Slovic, eds. May 1996. *Challenges in Risk Assessment and Risk Management.* Thousand Oaks, CA: Sage Periodicals Press, for *The Annals of the American Academy of Political and Social Science.*

McCloskey, Donald and Arjo Klamer (1995). "One Quarter of GDP Is Persuasion." *American Economic Review* Vol. 85, No. 2 (May): 191–95.

Maital, Shlomo and Sharone L. Maital, eds. (1993). *Economics and Psychology.* Aldershot, England and Brookfield, VT: Edward Elgar. See also Section D.

March, James G. (1978). "Bounded Rationality, Ambiguity, and the Engineering of Choice." *Bell Journal of Economics* Vol. 9, No. 2 (Autumn): 587–608.

———— and Herbert Simon with the collaboration of Harold Guetzkow (1993). *Organizations.* Second Edition. Cambridge, MA and Oxford: Blackwell Business. Especially Introduction to the Second Edition, 1–19.

Scitovsky, Tibor (1976). *The Joyless Economy: An Inquiry into Human Satisfaction and Consumer Dissatisfaction.* New York: Oxford University Press.

Shapira, Zur (1995). *Risk Taking: A Managerial Perspective.* New York: Russell Sage Foundation.

Simon, Herbert A. (1982). *Models of Bounded Rationality.* Vol. 2. *Behavioral Economics and Business Organizations.* Cambridge, MA: MIT Press. See also Section D.

—— (1984). "On the Behavioral and Rational Foundation of Economic Dynamics."
  Journal of Economic Behavior and Organization Vol. 5, No. 1 (March): 35–56.
—— and Associates (1992). "Decision Making and Problem Solving." Ch. 2. In Mary
  Zey, ed., *Decision Making: Alternatives to Rational Choice Models*. Newbury
  Park, CA: Sage Publications.
Thaler, Richard H. *The Winner's Curse: Paradoxes and Anomalies of Economic Life*.
  New York: Free Press. Paperback Edition: 1994, Princeton: Princeton University
  Press. See also Section D.

C. SUGGESTIONS FOR ADVANCED STUDENTS, PROFESSIONAL ECONOMISTS AND FINANCIAL ANALYSTS

Akerlof, George A. (1991). "Procrastination and Obedience." *American Economic Review* Vol. 81, No. 2 (May): 1–9.
—— and Janet L. Yellen (1985). "Can Small Deviations from Rationality Make Significant Differences to Economic Equilibria?" *American Economic Review* Vol.
  75, No. 4 (September): 708–20. See also Section D.
Albanese, Paul, ed. (1988). *The Psychological Foundations of Economic Behavior*. New
  York: Praeger.
Allais, Maurice (1953). "Le Comportement de l'Homme Rationnel devant le Risque:
  Critique des Postulats et Axiomes de l'Ecole Americaine." *Econometrica* Vol.
  21, No. 4 (October): 503–46. See also Section D.
Altman, Morris (1996). *Human Agency and Material Welfare. Revisions in Microecon-
  omics and Their Implications for Public Policy*. Boston, Dordrecht and London:
  Kluwer Academic Publishers. See also Section D.
Antonides, Gerrit (1991). *Psychology in Economics and Business: An Introduction to
  Economic Psychology*. Introduction by W. Fred van Raaij. Boston, Dordrecht and
  London: Kluwer Academic Publishers. See also Section D.
Arrow, Kenneth J. (1982). "Risk Perception in Psychology and Economics." *Economic
  Inquiry* Vol. 20, No. 1 (January): 1–9. See also Section D.
——, Enrico Colombatto, Mark Perlman and Christian Schmidt, eds. (1996). *The Ra-
  tional Foundations of Economic Behavior*. Hampshire, UK: Macmillan, Houd-
  mills, Basingstoke. See also Section D.
Bell, David, Howard Raiffa and Amos Tversky, eds. (1988). *Decision Making: Descrip-
  tive, Normative, and Prescriptive Interactions*. Cambridge: Cambridge University
  Press. See also Section D.
Button, Kenneth, ed. (1989). *The Collected Essays of Harvey Leibenstein. Vol 2, X-
  Efficiency and Micro-Micro Theory*. New York: New York University Press. See
  also Section D.
Camerer, Colin F. (1990). "Behavioral Game Theory." Ch. 13. In Robin M. Hogarth,
  ed., *Insights in Decision Making: A Tribute to Hillel J. Einhorn*. Chicago and
  London: University of Chicago Press.
—— (1997). "Progress in Behavioral Game Theory." *Journal of Economic Perspec-
  tives* Vol. 11, No. 4 (Fall): 167–88.
Choi, Young Back (1993). *Paradigms and Conventions. Uncertainty, Decision Making
  and Entrepreneurship*. Ann Arbor: University of Michigan Press.

Conlisk, John (1996). "Why Bounded Rationality?" *Journal of Economic Literature* Vol. 34 (June): 669–700. See also Section D.

Cyert, Richard M. and Praveen Kumar (1996). "Economizing by Firms Through Learning and Adaptation." *Journal of Economic Behavior and Organization* Vol. 29, No. 2 (March): 211–31.

Darity, William, Jr. and Arthur H. Goldsmith (1996). "Social Psychology, Unemployment and Macroeconomics." *Journal of Economic Perspectives* Vol. 10, No. 1 (Winter): 121–40. See also Section D.

DeBondt, Werner F. M. and Richard H. Thaler (June 1994). *Financial Decision Making in Markets and Firms: A Behavioral Perspective*. Working Paper No. 4777. Cambridge, MA: National Bureau of Economic Research. See also Section D.

Earl, Peter E., ed. (1988a). *Behavioral Economics*. 2 vols. Aldershot, England and Brookfield, VT: Edward Elgar. See also Section D.

——— (1988b). *Psychological Economics*. Boston, Dordrecht and Lancaster: Kluwer Publishers. See also Section D.

——— (1990). "Economics and Psychology: A Survey." *Economic Journal* Vol. 100, No. 3 (September): 719–55. See also Section D.

Egidi, Massimo and Robin Marris, eds. (1992). *Economics, Bounded Rationality and the Cognitive Revolution*. Aldershot, England and Brookfield, VT: Edward Elgar.

Eichner, Alfred S., ed. (1983). *Why Economics Is Not Yet a Science*. Armonk, NY: M. E. Sharpe.

Einhorn, Hillel J. and Robin M. Hogarth (1986). "Decision Making under Ambiguity." *Journal of Business* Vol. 59, No. 4 (October): 225–50.

Fama, Eugene F. and Kenneth R. French (1996). "Multifactor Explanations of Asset Pricing Anomalies." *Journal of Finance* Vol. 51, No. 1 (March): 55–84.

Frantz, Roger S., ed. (1988). *X-Efficiency: Theory, Evidence and Applications*. Boston and Dordrecht: Kluwer Academic Publishers. See also Section D.

———, Hardinder Singh and James Gerber, eds. (1991). *Behavioral Decision Making: Handbook of Behavioral Economics*. Greenwich, CT: JAI Press.

Frey, Bruno S. (1992). *Economics as a Science of Human Behavior: Towards a New Social Science Paradigm*. Boston, Dordrecht and London: Kluwer Academic Publishers. See also Section D.

——— and Reiner Eichenberger (1994). "Economic Incentives Transform Psychological Anomalies." *Journal of Economic Behavior and Organization* Vol. 23, No. 2 (March): 215–34.

Friedman, Milton (1953). "The Methodology of Positive Economics." In M. Friedman, *Essays in Positive Economics*. Chicago: University of Chicago Press.

Gregory, Robin, Sarah Lichtenstein and Paul Slovic (1993). "Valuing Environmental Resources: A Constructive Approach." *Journal of Risk and Uncertainty* Vol. 7, No. 2 (April): 177–97.

———, Donald MacGregor and Sarah Lichtenstein (1992). "Assessing the Quality of Expressed Preference Measures of Value." *Journal of Economic Behavior and Organization* Vol. 17, No. 2 (March): 277–92.

Grossbard-Shechtman, Shoshana (1993). *On the Economics of Marriage: A Theory of Marriage, Labor and Divorce*. Boulder, CO: Westview Press. See also Section D.

Grossman, Sanford J. and Joseph E. Stiglitz (1976). "Information and Competitive Price Systems." *American Economic Review* Vol. 66, No. 2 (May): 246–53.

Heath, Chip and Amos Tversky (1991). "Preference and Belief: Ambiguity and Competence in Choice Under Uncertainty." *Journal of Risk and Uncertainty* Vol. 4, No. 1 (January): 5–28.

Herrnstein, Richard J. and Drazen Prelec (1991). "Melioration: A Theory of Distributed Choice." *Journal of Economic Perspectives* Vol. 5, No. 3 (Summer): 137–56.

Hogarth, Robin M., ed. (1990). *Insights in Decision Making: A Tribute to Hillel J. Einhorn.* Chicago and London: University of Chicago Press. See also Section D.

―――― (1995). "Decision Making Under Ignorance: Arguing with Yourself." *Journal of Risk and Uncertainty* Vol. 10, No. 1 (February): 15–36.

―――― and Melvin W. Reder, eds. (1987). *Rational Choice. The Contrast Between Economists and Psychologists.* Chicago: University of Chicago Press. See also Section D.

Irwin, Julie R., Paul Slovic, Sarah Lichtenstein and Gary H. McClelland (1993). "Preference Reversals and the Measurement of Environmental Values." *Journal of Risk and Uncertainty* Vol. 6, No. 1 (February): 5–18. See also Section D.

Journal of Behavioral Decision Making

Journal of Economic Behavior and Organization. See Section D.

Journal of Economic Perspectives. See Section D.

Journal of Economic Psychology. See Section D.

Journal of Finance. See Section D.

Journal of Financial Economics

Journal of Risk and Uncertainty. See Section D.

Journal of Socio-Economics (formerly *Journal of Behavioral Economics*). See Section D.

Kagel, John H. and Alvin E. Roth, eds. (1995). *The Handbook of Experimental Economics.* Princeton: Princeton University Press. See also Section D.

Kahneman, Daniel and Amos Tversky (1979). "Prospect Theory: An Analysis of Decisions Under Risk." *Econometrica* Vol 47, No. 2 (March): 263–91. See also Section D.

―――― , Paul Slovic and Amos Tversky, eds. (1982). *Judgment Under Uncertainty: Heuristics and Biases.* Cambridge University Press. See also Section D.

Kemp, Simon, Stephen E. G. Lea and Sharon Fussell (1995). "Experiments on Rating the Utility of Consumer Goods." *Journal of Economic Psychology* Vol. 16, No. 4 (December): 543–61.

Kleindorfer, Paul R., Howard C. Kunreuther and Paul J. H. Schoemaker (1993). *Decision Sciences: An Integrative Perspective.* New York: Cambridge University Press. See Chapter 9 of this volume.

Knetsch, Jack L. (1995). "Assumptions, Behavioral Findings and Policy Analysis." *Journal of Policy Analysis and Management* Vol. 14, No. 1 (Winter): 68-78. See also Section D.

Kunreuther, Howard (1976). "Limited Knowledge and Insurance Protection." *Public Policy* Vol. 4, No. 2 (Spring): 227–61.

―――― (1996). "Mitigating Disaster Losses Through Insurance." *Journal of Risk and Uncertainty* Vol. 12, Nos. 2/3: 171–87.

―――― , Ralph Ginsberg, Louis Miller et al. (1978). *Disaster Insurance Protection. Public Policy Lessons.* New York: John Wiley and Sons.

Lakonishok, Josef, Andrei Shleifer and Robert W. Vishny (1994). "Contrarian Investment, Extrapolation and Risk." *Journal of Finance* Vol. 49, No. 5 (December): 1541–78.

Lea, Stephen E. G., Paul Webley and Brian M. Young, eds. (1992). *New Directions in Economic Psychology. Theory, Experiment and Application*. Aldershot, England and Brookfield, VT: Edward Elgar. See also Section D.

Lewin, Shira B. (1996). Economics and Psychology: Lessons for Our Own Day from the Early Twentieth Century." *Journal of Economic Literature* Vol. 34, No. 3 (September): 1293–1323. See also Section D.

Loewenstein, George and Jon Elster, eds. (1992). *Choice over Time*. New York: Russell Sage. See also Section D.

Lunt, Peter (1996). "Rethinking the Relationship Between Psychology and Economics." *Journal of Economic Psychology* Vol. 17, No. 2 (April): 275–87.

McCain, Roger A. (1992). *A Framework for Cognitive Economics*. New York: Praeger Publishers.

McGuire, C. B. and Roy Radner, eds. (1986). *Decision and Organization*. Second Edition. Minneapolis: University of Minnesota Press.

Machina, Mark J. (1987). "Choice Under Uncertainty: Problems Solved and Unsolved." *Journal of Economic Perspectives* Vol. 1, No. 1 (Summer): 121–54. See also Section D.

Maital, Shlomo, ed. (1988). *Applied Behavioral Economics*. 2 vols. Brighton, England: Wheatsheaf. See also Section D.

———— and Sharone L. Maital, eds. (1993). *Economics and Psychology*. Aldershot, England and Brookfield, VT: Edward Elgar. See also Section D.

———— (1994). "Is the Future What It Used to Be? A Behavioral Theory of the Decline of Saving in the West." *Journal of Socio-Economics* Vol. 23, Nos. 1/2 (Spring/Summer): 1–32.

Modigliani, Franco (1988). "MM—Past, Present, Future." *Journal of Economic Perspectives* Vol. 2, No. 4 (Fall): 149–58.

———— and Richard A. Cohn (1979). "Inflation, Rational Expectations and the Market." *Financial Analysts Journal* Vol. 35, No. 2 (March): 19–44.

Myagkov, Mikhail and Charles R. Plott (1997). "Exchange Economies and Loss Exposure: Experiments Exploring Prospect Theory and Competitive Equilibria in Market Environments." *American Economic Review* Vol. 87, No. 5 (December): 801–28.

Nelson, Richard R. and Sidney G. Winter (1982). *An Evolutionary Theory of Economic Change*. Cambridge, MA and London: Belknap Press of Harvard University Press. See also Section D.

Pingle, Mark and Richard H. Day (1996). "Models of Economizing Behavior: Experimental Evidence." *Journal of Economic Behavior and Organization* Vol. 29, No. 2 (March): 191–209.

Radner, Roy (1996). "Bounded Rationality, Indeterminacy, and the Theory of the Firm." *Economic Journal* Vol. 106, No. 438 (September): 1360–73.

Rangard, Rob (1995). "Reversals of Preference Between Compound and Simple Risks: The Role of Editing Heuristics." *Journal of Risk and Uncertainty* Vol. 11, No. 2 (September): 159–75.

Roth, Alvin E., ed. (1987). *Laboratory Experimentation in Economics. Six Points of View*. New York, Cambridge and Melbourne: Cambridge University Press, especially 99–130, Richard H. Thaler, "The Psychology of Choice and the Assumptions of Economics." See also Chapter 5 of this volume.

Russell, Thomas and Richard H. Thaler (1985). "The Relevance of Quasi Rationality in Competitive Markets." *American Economic Review* Vol. 75, No. 4 (December): 1071–82.

Samuelson, William and Richard Zeckhauser (1988). "Status Quo Bias in Decision Making." *Journal of Risk and Uncertainty* Vol. 1, No. 1 (March): 7–59.

Sen, Amartya K. (1977). "Rational Fools. A Critique of the Behavioral Foundations of Economic Theory." *Philosophy and Public Affairs* Vol. 6 (Summer): 317–44.

Shafir, Eldar, Peter Diamond and Amos Tversky (1997). "Money Illusion." *Quarterly Journal of Economics* Vol. 112, No. 2 (May): 342–74.

Shiller, Robert J. (1989). *Market Volatility*. Cambridge, MA: MIT Press.

Simon, Herbert A. (1982). *Models of Bounded Rationality*. Vol. 2. *Behavioral Economics and Business Organization*. Cambridge, MA: MIT Press. See also Section D.

——— (1984). "On the Behavioral and Rational Foundations of Economic Dynamics." *Journal of Economic Behavior and Organization* Vol. 5. No. 1 (March): 35–56.

——— (1997). *Models of Bounded Rationality*. Vol. 3. *Empirically Grounded Economic Reason*. Cambridge, MA: MIT Press. See also Section D.

Slovic, Paul (1995). "The Construction of Preference." *American Psychologist* Vol. 50, No. 5 (May): 364–71. See also Section D.

Soderlund, Magnus and Mats Vilgm (1993). "Stability and Changes in Decision Makers' Perceptions of the Forms of Environment: An Empirical Study of Causal Attribution by a Top Management Team." *Journal of Economic Psychology* Vol. 14, No. 1 (March): 121–45.

Stigler, George J. and Gary S. Becker (1977). "De Gustibus Non Est Disputandum." *American Economic Review* Vol. 67, No. 1 (March): 76–90.

Sugden, Robert (1991). "Rational Choice: A Survey of Contributions from Economics and Philosophy." *Economic Journal* Vol. 101, No. 407 (July): 751–85.

Thaler, Richard H. (1991). *Quasi Rational Economics*. New York: Russell Sage Foundation. See also Section D.

———, ed. (1993). *Advances in Behavioral Finance*. New York: Russell Sage Foundation. See also Section D.

Tomer, John F. (1987). *Organizational Capital: The Path to Higher Productivity and Well-being*. New York: Praeger. See also Section D.

Tversky, Amos and Daniel Kahneman (1992). "Advances in Prospect Theory: Cumulative Representation of Uncertainty." *Journal of Risk and Uncertainty* Vol. 5, No. 4 (October): 297–323. See also Section D.

———, Paul Slovic and Daniel Kahneman (1990) "The Causes of Preference Reversal." *American Economic Review* Vol. 80, No. 1 (March): 204–17. See also Section D.

——— and Shumuel Sattath (1988). "Contingent Weighting in Judgment and Choice." *Psychological Review* Vol. 95, No. 3: 371–84. See also Section D.

van Raaij, W. F., G. M. van Veldhoven and K.-E. Wärneryd, eds. (1988). *Handbook of Economic Psychology*. Dordrecht, Boston and London: Kluwer Academic Publishers. See also Section D.

Viscusi, W. Kip (1996). "Alternative Institutional Responses to Asbestos." *Journal of Risk and Uncertainty* Vol. 12, Nos. 2/3: 147–70.

Vriend, Nicholas J. (1996). "Rational Behavior and Economic Theory." *Journal of Economic Behavior and Organization* Vol. 29, No. 2 (March): 263–85.

Weiermair, Klaus and Mark Perlman, eds. (1990). *Studies in Economic Rationality. X-Efficiency Examined and Extolled. Essays Written in the Tradition of and to Honor Harvey Leibenstein.* Ann Arbor: University of Michigan Press.

Zeckhauser, Richard (1996). "The Economics of Catastrophe." *Journal of Risk and Uncertainty* Vol. 12, Nos. 2/3: 113–40.

D. AN ANNOTATED BIBLIOGRAPHY

Akerlof, George and Janet L. Yellen (1985). "Can Small Deviations from Rationality Make Significant Differences to Economic Equilibria?" *American Economic Review* Vol. 75, No. 4 (September): 708–20. If, as this article shows, small deviations from rationality can indeed make significant differences to the overall economic results, what then can be expected from the larger deviations that are likely given the now proven difficulties in achieving what has been characterized as substantive or ex post rationality? In addition, consideration should be given to what may happen in the presence of multiple objectives—that may condition what is understood by rationality, to begin with.

Allais, Maurice (1953). "Le Comportement de l'Homme Rationnel devant le Risque: Critique des Postulats et Axiomes de l'Ecole Americaine." *Econometrica* Vol. 21, No. 4 (October): 503–46. This is the first article to seriously question the axioms of modern microeconomic analysis—neglected for many years.

Altman, Morris (1996). *Human Agency and Material Welfare: Revisions in Microeconomics and Their Implications for Public Policy.* Boston, Dordrecht and London: Kluwer Academic Publishers. This work treats human effort as a variable input, affecting productivity not only by changes in static efficiency, but also by influencing the choice of technology. One of its messages is that wage increases need not lead to reductions in employment or profits; rather, they may foster additional cooperative effort or lead a firm to reduce its level of x-inefficiency (raising the marginal product of labor).

Antonides, Gerrit (1991). *Psychology in Economics and Business: An Introduction to Economic Psychology.* Introduction by W. Fred van Raaij. Dordrecht, Boston and London: Kluwer Academic Publishers. Now that so much of the work of psychologists related to cognitive decision making is making its way into the analysis of economics and business administration, it is reasonable to inquire if there might be more in psychology that those in economics and business administration might find of interest (not just a few other areas such as the theory of cognitive dissonance). *Psychology in Economics and Business* is the first textbook in economic psychology that targets students of economics and business administration, and even those well advanced in both fields will find that it provides a very useful overview.

The book contains two introductions to economic psychology, the preface by van Raaij, and Antonides's first chapter, "Economics and Psychology," followed by chapters on motivation and personality, perception, learning, attitudes, emotions, well-being, limited information processing and economic expectations. The first part of the volume attempts to organize economic psychological themes within a common paradigm, though economists may conclude that there is more than a single paradigm here. Applications are made to entrepreneurial behavior, price perception and inflation, economic socialization, demand theory, attitudes and brand images, consumer decision making, economic expectations, well-being, poverty and consumer satisfaction. The second part features chapters on cognitive consistency, and on rationality and choice under uncertainty, which summarize much of the cognitive psychology that has captured the interest of economists in the last decade or so.

The organization of the material and even some of the conclusions differ a bit from those of economists and specialists in the field of management, which encourages useful classroom discussion. A possible limitation of the publication is that since this text is for those outside of the field of psychology, it would have been useful to provide greater distinction between the findings of psychologists that clearly point in a single direction and those on which different psychologists differ so greatly that use of the findings as assumptions in behavioral models had best be accompanied by major caution signals.

————, W. Fred van Raaij and Shlomo Maital, eds. (1997). *Advances in Economic Psychology.* Chichester: John Wiley and Sons. Of special note are: "Decision Making and the Search for Regularities: What Can Be Learned from a Process Perspective" by Svenson; "Demystifying Rational Expectations Theory Through an Economic-Psychological Model" by Wärneryd; and "Social Comparison, Fairness, and Rationality" by Bazerman.

Arrow, Kenneth J. (1982). "Risk Perception in Psychology and Economics." *Economic Inquiry* Vol. 20, No. 1 (January): 1–9. This article marks the recognition, by an eminent neoclassical economist, of the importance of the 1970s research in cognitive psychology for economic analysis.

————, Enrico Colombatto, Mark Perlman and Christian Schmidt, eds. (1996). *The Rational Foundations of Economic Behavior.* Hampshire, UK: Macmillan, Houdmills, Basingstoke. This work presents a major reconsideration of economic rationality. See especially the preface by Arrow; the introduction by Colombatto and Perlman; the postface by Schmidt; ch. 8 by Tversky (together with the comment by Roth); ch. 9 by Kahneman (together with the comment by Plott); ch. 10 by Plott; and ch. 11 by Roth.

Baxter, J. L. (1993). *Behavioural Foundations of Economics.* New York: St. Martin's Press. Baxter provides an overview of the potential gains from introducing behavioral findings and institutional realities into economic analysis in a comprehensive manner. There is good coverage of the empirical work related to the analysis of consumer demand, but, unfortunately no material is presented on behavioral finance and relatively little coverage is given to the results of experimental economics, some of which would drive home many of the points made throughout the volume about the inability to achieve a truly maximizing approach. The book is aimed at beginning and middle-level students in economics.

Bazerman, Max (1998). *Judgment in Managerial Decision Making* Fourth Edition. New York: John Wiley. This lively and easily accessible business school text incorporates the lessons of decision theory into managerial problem solving. Chapter content: 2: Biases; 3: Judgment Under Uncertainty: 4: The Nonrational Escalation of Commitment; 5: Fairness in Decision Making; 6: Motivational Biases; 7: Making Rational Decisions in Two-Party Negotiations; 8: Negotiator Cognition; 9:

Decision Making with More Than Two Parties; 10: Improving Decision Making. The book contains a sizable bibliography, most entries from fields covered to a much more limited extent in the present volume.

Bell, David, Howard Raiffa and Amos Tversky, eds. (1988). *Decision Making: Descriptive, Normative, and Prescriptive Interactions.* Cambridge: Cambridge University Press. Of particular interest are the following chapters: "Introduction"; 1: "Descriptive, Normative, and Prescriptive Interactions in Decision Making" by Bell, Raiffa and Tversky; 3: "Rationality as Process and as Product of Thought" by Simon; 6: "Behavioral Decision Theory: Processes of Judgment and Choice" by Einhorn and Hogarth; 8: "Response Mode, Framing and Information-Processing Effects in Risk Assessment" by Slovic, Fischoff and Lichtenstein; 9: "Rational Choice and the Framing of Decisions" by Tversky and Kahneman; 22: "Behavior Under Uncertainty and Its Implications for Policy" by Arrow; 24: and "How Senior Managers Think" by Isenberg.

Boulding, Kenneth (1969). "Economics as a Moral Science." *American Economic Review* Vol. 59, No. 1 (March): 1–12. Boulding long maintained that economic analysis needed to be set forth in a broader framework and in the 1980s was quite sympathetic to the newly developing behavioral approach to economic analysis.

Button, Kenneth, ed. (1989). *The Collected Essays of Harvey Leibenstein.* Vol. 2, *X-Efficiency and Micro-Micro Theory.* New York: New York University Press. Leibenstein came increasingly to stress the contribution of basic psychological and physiological aspects of human nature in explaining what he referred to as the "inert areas" underlying x-inefficiency—the deviation from cost minimization that differs from, and may sometimes be greater than the misallocation of resources that has so preoccupied traditional economic analysis. Leibenstein's evolving concern with the writings of psychologists is perhaps best seen in a 1987 article published in the *Journal of Economic Behavior and Organization* entitled "Entrepreneurship, Entrepreneurial Training and X-Efficiency" (reprinted as ch. 14 of the Button volume).

Choi, Young Back (1993). *Paradigms and Conventions. Uncertainty, Decision Making and Entrepreneursip.* Ann Arbor: University of Michigan Press. Choi emphasizes "paradigm seeking" as an alternative to the fixed paradigm of neoclassical economic analysis, rational maximization. He is particularly concerned with problems of coordination and develops the concept of conventions to explain the market as a social learning process. Much of the exposition is in terms of propositions and corollaries. Applications are offered to status and envy.

Conlisk, John (1996). "Why Bounded Rationality." *Journal of Economic Literature* Vol. 34, No. 2 (June): 669–700. This is an important survey article (the contents of which are outlined in a long endnote to Part II).

Coughlin, Richard, ed. (1991). *Morality, Rationality and Efficiency.* Armonk, NY and London: M. E. Sharpe. One chapter in this work, "The Socio-Economics of Labor Productivity" by Doeringer, shows that labor efficiency in so-called superefficient firms "is rooted far more in social, organizational and psychological considerations than in technology or compensation incentives." He concludes that "[t]he theoretical foundations of effort management in the superefficient firm come from sociology and psychology, rather than from economics" (Coughlin 1991, 110). Doeringer draws on the other social sciences in an effort to move toward a maximization, or fuller realization, of more broadly defined objectives. Most of the rest of the chapters, all taken from the Second Annual International Conference on Socio-Economics, held in 1990, are more concerned with tradeoffs in objectives. This is nicely summarized in "The Moral Dimension in Policy Analysis" by Etzioni. Other chapters of particular interest are: 2: "Social Dilemmas, Economic Self-Interest, and Evolutionary Theory" by Dawes; 4: "Job Libido and the Culture of Unemployment: An Essay in Sociological Economics" by Neubourg; 7: "Competing Games: Profit Maximization versus Strategic Conquest" by Thurow; 12: "The 'Junk Bond King' of Wall Street: A Discourse on Business Ethics" by Wilson; 13: "The Effect of Ethical Climate on Managers' Decisions" by Gaertner; 17: "Employee Ownership in the United States: Intentions, Perceptions and Reality" by Rooney; 19: "An Exit-Voice Analysis of Supplier Relations" by Helper; and 21: "The Socio-Economics of Environmental Risk: Comparing Air Quality, Acid Rain, and Global Change" by Rycroft.

Cyert, Richard. M. and James G. March (1963). *A Behavioral Theory of the Firm.* Englewood-Cliffs, NJ: Prentice Hall. Also, Second Edition: 1992, Oxford: Blackwell. This work was the first major study in behavioral economics following the pioneering articles of Herbert Simon, Cyert and March's senior colleague at Carnegie Institute of Technology (now Carnegie Mellon University). Perhaps the most notable contribution was the extensive documentation of what the authors had characterized as far back as 1955 as "organizational slack" (essentially what Farrell in 1957 referred to as a lack of technical efficiency and what Leibenstein in 1966 termed a lack of x-efficiency). Often cited, and influential in management analyses, *A Behavioral Theory* had little impact on economists for many years. The 1992 edition eliminates much of the detail of the earlier empirical work, but contains a new Epilogue that provides an overview of subsequent developments in the economic theories of the firm and in behavioral studies of organizational decision making. Cyert and March's present-day emphasis seems closer to that of articles on business administration than to those of the most recent writings in behavioral economics. According to March's comment in a personal communication, many findings about business behavior that investigators had been uncovering are now part of mainstream economics analyses.

Darity, William, Jr. and Arthur H. Goldsmith (1996). "Social Psychology, Unemployment and Macroeconomics." *Journal of Economic Perspectives* Vol. 10, No. 1 (Winter): 121–40. This article integrates the research of labor economists and social psychologists in an attempt to gain a better understanding of the causes and consequences of macroeconomic performance. It maintains that the social psychological consequences of exposure to unemployment are likely to affect personal productivity, motivation, attitudes toward participation in the labor force, as well as relations with family and friends, all of which contribute to the persistence of some unemployment. Thus, the traditional macroeconomic assumption that an exogenous shock to an economy can be offset by an appropriate strictly economic policy stimulus that returns the economy to its original point is probably mistaken.

De Bondt, Werner F. M. and Richard H. Thaler (June 1994). *Financial Decision Making in Markets and Firms: A Behavioral Perspective.* Working Paper No. 4777. Cambridge, MA: National Bureau of Economic Research. This concise summary (33 pages, 9 of them bibliography) of recent work in behavioral finance is concerned with actual rather than optimizing, normative decision-making behavior. Basically, it is an application of the psychology of decision making to finance, perhaps the field in which this approach has been most nearly accepted.

Dreman, David (1982). *The New Contrarian Investment Strategy.* New York: Random House. This book discusses applications of the emerging work of psychologists in decision analysis to the field of investment by a professional investment manager. It follows earlier volumes on the same topic published by Dreman in 1977 and 1979.

Earl, Peter E., ed. (1988a). *Behavioral Economics.* 2 vols. Aldershot, England and Brookfield, VT: Edward Elgar. This broad collection of articles published between 1949 and 1986 reflects, in part, the work of Herbert Simon and the Carnegie School with their emphasis on such topics as bounded rationality, organizational slack and satisficing. Other articles deal with the behavioral decision theory that has been developed by cognitive psychologists and their colleagues in economics and business administration. Of special note is the attention to articles on industrial organization, microeconomic theory and business administration that reflected the growing concern for the inadequacy of the existing paradigm of economic analysis. These latter articles draw on U.S. journals and on British sources that are much less well known in the United States. Earl's introductions give more than customary weight to ideas and approaches that have perhaps been neglected. All 47 reprints are worth considering, but the most important for understanding and/or developing a behavioral approach are noted with an asterisk.

Volume I (listed in order of appearance): *Leibenstein, H. (1979). "A Branch of Economics Is Missing: Micro-Micro Theory." *Journal of Economic Literature* Vol. 17, No. 2 (June): 477–502; Cyert, R. M. and H. A. Simon (1983). "The Behavioral Approach: With Emphasis on Economics." *Behavioral Science* Vol. 28, No. 2 (April): 95–108; *Simon, H. A. (1959). "Theories of Decision-Making in Economics and Behavioral Sciences." *American Economic Review* Vol. 49, No. 1 (March): 253–83; *Winter, S. G. (1964). "Economic 'Natural Selection' and the Theory of the Firm." *Yale Economic Essays* Vol. 4, No. 1 (Spring): 25–72; Day, R. G. (1967). "Profits, Learning and the Convergence of Satisficing to Marginalism." *Quarterly Journal of Economics* Vol. 81, No. 2 (May): 302–11; Hey, J. D. (1982). "Search for Rules for Search." *Journal of Economic Behavior and Organization* Vol. 3, No. 1 (March): 65–81; *Hogarth, R. M. and S. Makridakis (1981). "Forecasting and Planning: An Evaluation." *Management Science* Vol. 27, No. 1: 15–36; *Kahneman, D. and A. Tversky (1979). "Prospect Theory: An Analysis of Decision Under Risk." *Econometrica* Vol. 47, No. 1 (March): 263–91; *Loasby, B. J. (1967). "Managerial Decision Processes." *Scottish Journal of Political Economy* Vol. 14, No. 3 (November): 243–55; Radner, R. (1975). "A Behavioral Model of Cost Reduction." *Bell Journal of Economics* Vol. 6, No. 1 (Spring): 196–215; *Nelson, R. R. and S. G. Winter (1980). "Firm and Industry Response to Changed Market Conditions: An Evolutionary Approach." *Economic Inquiry* Vol. 18, No. 2 (April): 179–202; and Loasby, B. J. (1967). "Management Economics and the Theory of the Firm." *Journal of Industrial Economics* Vol. 15, No. 3 (July): 165–76.

Volume II (listed in order of appearance): *Etzioni, A. (1985). "Opening the Preferences: A Socio-Economic Research Agenda." *Journal of Behavioral Economics* Vol. 14 (Winter): 183–205; Olshavsky, R. W. and D. H. Granbois (1979). "Consumer Decision Making—Fact or Fiction?" *Journal of Consumer Research*

Vol. 6, No. 2 (September): 93–100; *Thaler, R. (1980). "Toward a Positive Theory of Consumer Choice." *Journal of Economic Behavior and Organization* Vol.
1, No. 1 (March): 39–60; Earl, P. E. (1986). "A Behavioral Analysis of Demand
Elasticities." *Journal of Economic Studies* Vol. 13. No. 3: 20–37; Bruno, A. V.
and A. R. Wildt (1975). "Toward Understanding Attitude Structure: A Study of
the Complementarity of Multi-Attribute Attitude Models." *Journal of Consumer
Research* Vol. 2, No. 2 (September): 137–45; Pickering, J. F. (1981). "A Behavioral Model of the Demand for Consumer Durables." *Journal of Economic Psychology* Vol. 1, No. 1 (February): 59–77; Littlechild, S. C. (1982). "Controls on
Advertising: An Examination of Some Economic Arguments." *Journal of Advertising* (UK) Vol. 1, No. 1: 25–37; Dickinson, R., A. Herbst and J. O'Shaugh-
nessy (1986). "Marketing Concept and Customer Orientation." *European Journal of Marketing* Vol. 20, No. 10: 18–23; Mosley, P. (1976). "Towards a 'Satisficing' Theory of Economic Policy." *Economic Journal* Vol. 86, No. 341
(March): 59–72; Wärneryd, K.-E. (1982). "The Life and Work of George
Katona." *Journal of Economic Psychology* Vol. 2, No. 1 (February): 1–31; Gilad,
B., S. Kaish and P. D. Loeb (1984). "From Economic Behavior to Behavioral
Economics: The Behavioral Uprising in Economics." *Journal of Behavioral Ec-
onomics* Vol. 13, No. 1 (Summer): 1–22.

———, ed. (1988b). *Psychological Economics*. Boston, Dordrecht and Lancaster: Kluwer Publishers. This collection of essays, most of them by economists with little
previous contact with the findings of psychology, offers some valuable insights
and perspectives, though other references reflect research by more economists and
psychologists who have been working longer in the area. The volume includes
an introduction and fifteen chapters, including "Learning and Decision-Making
in Economics and Psychology: A Methodological Perspective" by Rutherford;
"Neoclassical Economics and the Psychology of Risk and Uncertainty" by Heij-
dra; "Prospects for Mathematical Psychological Economics" by Hey; "The Psychological Economics of Conspicuous Consumption" by Mason; "Toward a
Behavioral Analysis of Public Economics" by Brooks; "Economics and Psychology: A Resurrection Story by Coats" and "On Being a Psychological Economist and Winning the Games Economists Play" by Earl.

——— (1990). "Economics and Psychology: A Survey." *Economic Journal* Vol. 100,
No. 3 (September): 719–55. This article presents a wide-ranging overview of the
fields of psychology that might be of interest and use to the economist. It is
directed toward the professional economist or advanced student.

——— (1995). *Microeconomics for Business and Marketing. Lectures, Cases and
Worked Essays*. Aldershot, England and Brookfield, VT: Edward Elgar. This text
on intermediate microeconomic theory is so unusual, stimulating and helpful that
everyone teaching the subject should own a copy. Even those who teach the more
traditional and, in some cases, more rigorous courses that are based on certain
other texts might consider placing several copies of this one on reserve for supplementary reading and for required reading on some points. This is the only
intermediate micro text that integrates commentaries from behavioral economics
throughout the presentation. (For the first text to introduce behavioral economics
into intermediate microeconomic theory, see Frank, *Microeconomics and Behavior*, later in this section.)

The Economist (1994). "Rational Economic Man: The Human Factor," December 24,

1994–January 6, 1995, pp. 90–92; "Finance: Mind over Matter," April 23, 1994, pp. 73–75. These were the first substantial summaries of behavioral economics and finance to appear in a major popular publication aimed at the financial community.

Edwards, Ward (1954). "The Theory of Decision Making." *Psychological Bulletin* Vol. 51, No. 4 (July): 380–417. This article marks the beginning of the new interest of psychologists in decision making.

Egidi, Massimo and Robin Marris, eds. (1992). *Economics, Bounded Rationality and the Cognitive Revolution.* Aldershot, England and Brookfield, VT: Edward Elgar. In addition to a symposium on bounded rationality and four original papers, this volume reprints four papers by Simon, of which the most appropriate followups to this volume are: "Rational Choice and the Structure of the Environment" (1956) and "Scientific Discovery as Problem Solving" (1988).

Eichner, Alfred S., ed. (1983). *Why Economics Is Not Yet a Science.* Armonk, NY: M. E. Sharpe. See especially "A Behavioral Theory of Economists' Behavior" by Earl.

Etzioni, Amitai (1988). *The Moral Dimension. Toward a New Economics.* New York: Free Press. The book that launched the recent focus on socioeconomics, *The Moral Dimension* draws on a tremendous body of learning from many fields but emphasizes two points. First, it maintains that individual preferences do not emerge as economists assume. Rather, they are heavily influenced by the community and the institutional circumstances in which individuals find themselves. Second, while some decisions may involve careful calculation aimed at achieving optimization, as traditional economics assumes (they are logical/ empirical decisions in Etzioni's terminology), others are primarily of a moral character (normative/affective). Most decisions, he states, involve elements of both types, with moral and affective considerations the most important, and even determining the "limited zone" in which the logical/empirical factors enter. Moreover, *"normative-affective factors shape to a significant extent the information that is gathered, the way it is processed, the inferences that are drawn, the options that are being considered, and the options that are finally chosen"* (p. 94). The volume provides strong support for a behavioral approach to the analysis of economic problems but did not convince many traditional economists, perhaps because Etzioni is more concerned with normative policy than with a behavioral, multidisciplinary approach to the analysis of socioeconomic problems.

———— and Paul R. Lawrence, eds. (1991). *Socio-Economics. Toward a New Synthesis.* Armonk, NY and London, England: M. E. Sharpe. This volume contains selected papers from the First International Conference on Socio-Economics, held in 1989 at Harvard Business School, which led to the founding of the Society for the Advancement of Socio-Economics. The principal theme of this work is the need to take account of other than strictly maximizing motives. Among those papers that perhaps most contribute to a behavioral approach to economics are: " 'The Battle of Methods': Toward a Paradigm Shift" by Coughlin; "Rethinking Utility Theory: A Summary Statement" by Juster; "The 'Theory as Map' Analogy and Changes in Assumption Sets in Economics" by Goldfarb and Griffith; "Values and Principles: Some Limitations in Traditional Economic Analysis" by Prelec; "Human Values and Economic Behavior: A Model of Moral Economy" by

Wilson; "The Boundries of the Firm" by Bodaracco; and especially, "Stake-holders, Shareholders, Managers: Who Gains What from Corporate Performance" by Preston, Sapienza and Miller. This last-mentioned chapter, based on data collected over seven years from a group of leading U.S. corporations (approximately 100 each year), concludes that multiple objectives, including social and economic considerations, are simultaneously and successfully pursued within large, complex organizations that account for a major part of all economic activity.

Frank, Robert H. (1985). *Choosing the Right Pond: Human Behavior and the Quest for Status*. New York and Oxford: Oxford University Press. In an extension of the argument of Hirsch and others about "positional" goods, Frank maintains that where people stand on the totem pole (and their concerns about where they stand) shapes their behavior in systematic, observable and often unexpected ways. Among the chapters are: "How Much Is Local Status Worth?"; "Why Redistributive Taxation?"; "The Positional Treadmill, Why Do Ethical Systems Try to Limit the Role of Money?"; and "The Libertarian Welfare State." Like the preceding volume by Frank, this book is written primarily for a general audience, but most economists will also find it of interest.

———— (1988). *Passions Within Reason. The Strategic Role of the Emotion*. New York: W. W. Norton. This is a tremendously engaging little book. Frank sidesteps the issue of whether people pursue altruistic objectives independent of their economic and financial consequences and stresses that noble human tendencies might not only have survived the ruthless pressures of the material world but might have been nurtured by them. "In many situations, the conscious pursuit of self-interest is incompatible with its attainment," Frank declares in the Preface. Included are discussions of shirking, wage and price setting, foreign relations, taxes, the importance of stable environments and behaviorally traditional institutions. Apparent altruism may be the most effective means of gaining long-term commitment. Is material gain a proper motive for morality? In responding, Frank maintains that (1) people do not always behave as predicted by the self-interest model; (2) the reason for irrational behavior is not always that people miscalculate; (3) emotion is often an important motive for irrational behavior; and (4) being motivated by emotion is an advantage. Frank closes with what he characterizes as "A Friendly Amendment to the Self-Interest Model."

———— (1994). *Microeconomics and Behavior*. Second Edition. New York: McGraw-Hill. This is the first text in intermediate microeconomic theory to introduce the behavioral decision analysis of cognitive psychology into economic analysis, although largely in chapters labeled "Supplementary." The end of Chapter 6, "The Economics of Information and Choice Under Uncertainty," contains material on inconsistent choices and on the "Winner's Curse." Chapter 7, "Explaining Tastes: The Importance of Altruism and Other Nonegoistic Behavior," covers a topic that has long been of interest to behaviorally oriented economists and incorporates some of the argument of Frank's book, *Passions Within Reason* (1988). Chapter 8, "Cognitive Limitations and Consumer Behavior," summarizes important components of the work of Kahneman, Thaler and Tversky.

———— and Philip J. Cook (1995). *The Winner-Take-All Society*. New York: Marita Kessler Books, Free Press. This book uses the insights and tools of economic analysis and other social sciences to conclude that much of the rivalry for society's top prizes that has led to such an extraordinary gap between the earnings of the most successful in the various fields of activity and those even only slightly below them is both costly and unproductive. A lively presentation, this work is easily accessible to noneconomists, with recommendations for public policy.

Frantz, Roger S., ed. (1988). *X-Efficiency: Theory, Evidence and Applications.* Boston and Dordrecht: Kluwer Academic Publishers. This first book-length assessment of x-efficiency is particularly notable for its recompilation of a wide range of empirical material related to the topic. In addition, Chapter 4 contains material on the dual personality, selective rationality, heuristics and a brief summary of psychological studies on human cognition.

Frey, Bruno S. (1992). *Economics as a Science of Human Behavior. Towards a New Social Science Paradigm.* Boston, Dordrecht and London: Kluwer Academic Publishers. This book is one of the best references for the professional economist or the advanced student to begin an inquiry into the behavioral approach to economics or to orient those who have solid knowledge of only one or two of the relevant topics. After concise summaries of what is involved in the traditional approach to economics (primarily in Chapter 1), Frey outlines many of the underlying behavioral challenges to the discipline (notably in "Economics and Psychology," "Limits and Further Development of Homo Oeconomicus," "The Price System and Morals," and "Behavioral Anomalies and Economics"). More innovative, but perhaps in part for that reason more controversial, are Frey's applications to such topics as politics and conflict, the family, the environment and the arts, as well as his final offering, "An Ipsative Theory of Human Behavior." Frey has condensed a tremendous amount into little more than 200 pages of text. In addition to the suggested readings offered at the end of each chapter, there is a 30-page bibliography that includes articles from a wide range of journals in economics and psychology, as well as a few journals from other fields.

Gilad, Benjamin and Stanley Kaish, eds. (1986). *Handbook of Behavioral Economics.* 2 vols. Greenwich, CT: JAI Press. Based on a 1984 conference, these papers represent the results of the first effort to bring together a diverse group of economists who were attempting to infuse economics with a more behavioral focus. The Preface defines behavioral economics as research designed to achieve a more realistic picture of economic processes as well as a more accurate understanding of the equilibrium toward which those processes move.

The Introduction of Volume A, *Microeconomics*, sets out four tenets underlying a behavioral approach. Part I (Methods and Tools) includes an essay on past developments in economics, psychology and philosophy that have served as antecedents to the emerging interest in behavioral economics, and another on the application of laboratory methods to the testing of theories of resource allocation under uncertainty. Part II (Consumer Behavior) includes chapters by Van Raaij, Wärneryd and Morgan. Van Raaij takes note of Kevin Lancaster's view of commodities as bundles of attributes and maintains that rational selection would be long and complex. This leads to cognitive simplifications, which he elucidates. Wärneryd discusses learning processes that contribute to the simplification of cognitive processes, and Morgan questions the rationality assumption of economics. Part III (The Theory of the Firm) contains sections on entrepreneurial and managerial behavior, intrafirm considerations in productivity, extrafirm considerations in productivity and industrial organization.

The papers in Part III include "The Research Program of the Behavioral Theory of the Firm: Orthodox Critique and Evolutionary Perspective" by Winter and "Entrepreneurial Decision Making. Some Behavioral Considerations" by Gilad. Winter first notes and then refutes the orthodox critique of the behavioral theory of the firm. This critique is stated as follows: (1) events "inside" individual firms are not part of the subject matter of economics; (2) evidence obtained from individual firms by interviews or survey methods is of dubious validity; (3) even if behavioral research correctly describes patterns of enterprise behavior, it is only a transitory reflection of economic mechanisms in a particular context; and (4) behavioral research on individual firms is too expensive relative to the benefits it produces.

The section on intrafirm considerations in productivity contains papers by Harvey Leibenstein and John Tomer. They are followed by a discussion of marriage and productivity by Grossbard-Shechtman, and an analysis of the supply of effort by Filer.

In the section on industrial organization, Frantz's paper on X-efficiency summarizes Frantz 1988. Dickens's piece, "Safety Regulation and Irrational Behavior," offers a more comprehensive overview of the subject than his more famous article on the subject, co-authored with George Akerlof.

The papers that remain most relevant from Volume B are: "Behavioral Economics in the Theory of the Business Cycle" by Kaish; "Behavioral Insights for Public Policy: ExAnte/ExPost Considerations" by Kunreuther; "Aggregate Variables in Psychology and Economics: Dependence and the Stock Market" by Schachter; "What Do People Bring to the Stock Market (Besides Money)" by Maital et al.; and "Understanding (and Misunderstanding) Social Security: Behavioral Insights Into Public Policy" by Coughlin.

Grossbard-Shechtman, Shoshana (1993). *On the Economics of Marriage. A Theory of Marriage, Labor and Divorce*. Boulder, CO: Westview Press. Perhaps the most comprehensive analysis of marriage and the family by an economist, this study is in the tradition of Gary Becker ("people marry when a [conscious or unconscious] comparison of costs and benefits makes marriage look profitable" (p. 8). The author emphasizes, however, that "[b]enefits can be material, social or spiritual" and that "[c]osts are not simply financial or material" (p. 8). Although the book draws heavily on sociological and cultural findings (and the need to obtain more results of that type) and calls for a "social science of marriage" to explore the content of utility functions, it is not likely to disturb orthodox economists. This is because the study maintains that marriage markets consist of markets for spousal labor and that the individuals who participate in such markets undertake a kind of cost-benefit analysis and try to maximize their utility. Utility can include social and spiritual aspirations, it is insisted, and it is recognized that measurement is difficult—but the author nonetheless finds it useful to employ traditional optimization techniques. This may be in part because the main thrust is to contribute to the development of a theory of marriage. In addition, a number of empirical findings are presented, most notably with respect to the participation of married women in the labor force. Grossbard-Shechtman stresses a reliance on economics to harness the various social science elements, as reflected in her focus on labor supply, earnings and productivity, the use of demand and supply analysis for spousal labor, the use of a general as well as a partial equilibrium approach, and the use of wage and income as an explanatory variable.

Hogarth, Robin, ed. (1990). *Insights in Decision Making. A Tribute to Hillel J. Einhorn.* Chicago and London: University of Chicago Press. Major issues in decision making are presented, together with commentaries. Most of the contributors are psychologists who are also cited elsewhere in the present bibliography. Two- to three-page introductory comments precede each of the book's six sections.
—— and Melvin W. Reder, eds. (1987). *Rational Choice. The Contrast Between Economists and Psychologists.* Chicago: University of Chicago Press. This is a useful collection of papers and commentaries by leading economists and psychologists, including some who are not especially convinced of this approach such as Robert Lucas. The omitted reply of Nobel Prize Winner Gary Becker to a strong critique of his work by Herbert Simon was revised and can be found in Section 7 of the Introduction to Becker's 1996 volume, *Accounting for Tastes.*
Irwin, Julie R., Paul Slovic, Sarah Lichtenstein and Gary McClelland (1993). "Preference Reversals and the Measurement of Environmental Values." *Journal of Risk and Uncertainty* Vol. 6, No. 1 (February): 5–18. Irwin et al. cite the "compatibility effect" and the "prominence effect" as important causes of preference reversals and show that the combined effects of the two lead to predictable preference reversals in the context of certain environmental alternatives. The article is critical of contingent valuation as capturing attitudinal intentions rather than behavior and cites several references substantiating that position.
Journals: *The American Economic Review, The Economic Journal, Econometrica, Quarterly Journal of Economics, The Journal of Political Economy* and other long-time leading economics journals all now publish several articles each year that use or discuss behavioral approaches to economic and financial analysis. (The May 1997 issue of the *Quarterly Journal of Economics* is devoted entirely to articles in memory of Amos Tversky.) Beyond that, several journals have dedicated considerably more space to the field.

The first economics journal chronologically was the *Journal of Behavioral Economics,* now the *Journal of Socio-Economics.* Behavioral economics is concerned with the best way to analyze real-world economic problems and processes, and draws on the other social sciences, on philosophy (sometimes biology) and often on relatively more contact with individuals and enterprises through interviews and even direct observation. This multidisciplinary approach begins in response to a descriptive challenge, though many behaviorally oriented economists are concerned as much or even more, first, with developing hypotheses about the kind of behavior manifested by various groups, including of course, the most successful financially and economically—the survivors to which traditional economic analysis has long referred—and, second, with attempting to verify those hypotheses. Socioeconomics, on the other hand, might be characterized as having primarily normative concerns and as employing behavioral analyses to help advance those norms, particularly through public policy measures. The founder of the Society for the Advancement of Socio-economics, the sociologist Amitai Etzioni, views socioeconomics as an alternative to economics for analyzing problems that have an economic component but broader-than-economic consequences. Most behavioral economists also have various socioeconomic objectives but would distinguish these objectives from their concerns about the appropriate methodology for analyzing economic issues. By and large, those who have made the most important advances in behavioral economics seek principally to modify the methodology of economics rather than replace it with something different called socioeconomics. The *Journal of Behavioral Economics* published more articles that focused on the methodology of a behavioral approach and had a greater coverage of such topics as entrepreneurship (on the latter of which, see especially the Fall 1989 Special Issue on Entrepreneurship—Vol. 18, No. 3— and, in particular, "The Rise and Decay of Entrepreneurship: A Different Perspective" by Ronen), and preference formation (on which, see the Spring 1988 Special Issue—Vol. 17, No. 1—in particular the Introduction by Albanese and the articles by Frank, Lewis and Cullis).

The second journal is *The Journal of Economic Psychology*. Although the chief editor has always been a psychologist, economists have served on the editorial board and have contributed many important articles over the years. Its emphasis has tended to be on consumers, households and tax matters, but the focus has been broadening.

The Journal of Economic Behavior and Organization was perhaps the most important vehicle for the publication of behavioral economics in the 1980s and remains one of the most important at this time, particularly for theory and for work in experimental economics. Even so, it occasionally publishes more institutional material, as in the June 1987 issue (Vol. 8, No. 2), most of which was dedicated to Studies on Entrepreneurship. It featured articles by Etzioni, Leibenstein, and Hilke and Philip B. Nelson, along with comments by Ronen. Among the other special issues of particular interest to this volume have been the March 1994 issue (Vol. 23, No. 2), Papers on Psychological Aspects of Economics and the 1996 issue (Vol. 29), On the Economics of Limited Cognition.

The Journal of Risk and Uncertainty is another very important journal in behavioral economics, particularly for theory and sophisticated empirical analyses. Nonetheless, because it aims at an interdisciplinary audience, most articles begin and end with nonmathematical discussions that are accessible to those with intermediate-level training in economics. It has given considerable attention to issues such as liability and insurance (see, in particular, February 1993, Vol. 7, No. 1) and catastrophic risk (1996, Vol. 12, Nos. 2/3).

The Journal of Finance has published the largest number of articles in the emerging field of behavioral finance. *The Journal of Financial Economics* and *Financial Analysts Journal* are also important sources.

The Journal of Economic Perspectives has assumed a major role in presenting some of the most important findings of a behavioral approach in a manner that is accessible to those with an intermediate-level preparation in economics. The best example of this research has been the series of articles on anomalies written or co-authored by Richard Thaler (see Thaler, *The Winner's Curse* later in this section).

Many other specialized economics and business journals also publish some work in behavioral economics and finance. In addition, many journals in psychology publish material of interest to the behaviorally oriented economist or financial analyst. A journal dominated by psychologists, but multidisciplinary in nature is the *Journal of Behavioral Decision Making*.

Kagel, John H. and Alvin E. Roth, eds. (1995). *The Handbook of Experimental Economics*. Princeton, NJ: Princeton University Press. Kagel and Roth present a breathtaking overview of experimental economics, an area that has been responsible for generating much of the recent interest in behavioral economics. See especially, "Introduction to Experimental Economics" by Roth, especially Section F, Individual Choice Behavior, and "Individual Decision Making" by Camerer. The other chapters that also offer extremely important material for the behavioral field are "Public Goods: A Survey of Experimental Research" by Ledyard; "Coordination Problems" by Ochs; "Bargaining Experiments" by Roth; "Industrial Organization: A Survey of Laboratory Research" by Holt; "Experiments; Asset Markets: A Survey" by Sunder; and "Auctions: A Survey of Experimental Research" by Kagel.

Kahneman, Daniel and Amos Tversky (1979). "Prospect Theory: An Analysis of Decisions Under Risk." *Econometrica* Vol. 47, No. 2 (March): 263–91. This is the article most responsible for enlisting the interest of those who previously had dismissed the need to consider the findings of psychology in economic analysis. It provides a conceptual explanation for experiments, revealing that individuals assess their welfare in response to changes (reference points), and not to overall states of wealth, and that they are not consistent in their attitudes toward risk. They are risk averse in the domain of gains and risk taking in the domain of losses, which they view as loss averting more than risk taking.

———, Paul Slovic and Amos Tversky, eds. (1982). *Judgment Under Uncertainty: Heuristics and Biases*. Cambridge: Cambridge University Press. The volume, *Judgment Under Uncertainty*, together with the preceding article by Kahneman and Tversky, were the seminal publications of the recent work of psychologists on decision theory, permeating more than half a dozen fields, including even medicine. The chapters of the book are made up of articles published between 1968 and 1982, as well as pieces written especially for the volume. The back cover explains that "a great deal of research has been devoted to understanding and evaluating the ways in which people judge uncertain events. We now know that people's intuitive inferences, predictions, probability assessments, and diagnoses do not conform to the laws of probability theory and statistics. Instead, people replace the laws of chance by judgment strategies of heuristics. Although these are efficient and effective in many circumstances, all too often they lead to judgmental biases that are large, persistent, and serious in their implications for decision making. The blemished portrait of human capabilities that emerges from this work thus stands in sharp contrast to the highly favorable image of "rational man" that dominated the study of thinking and decision making in the two decades following World War II."

Of particular note for economists and those in business administration are the following chapters: 1. "Judgment Under Uncertainty: Heuristics and Biases" by Tversky and Kahneman; 2. "Belief in the Law of Small Numbers" by Tversky and Kahneman; 3. "Subjective Probability: A Judgment of Representativeness" by Kahneman and Tversky; 4. "On the Psychology of Prediction" by Kahneman and Tversky; 7. "Popular Induction: Information Is Not Necessarily Informative" by Nisbett, Borgida, Crandall and Reed; 19. "Learning from Experience and Suboptimal Rules in Decision Making" by Einhorn; 25. "Conservatism in Human Information Processing" by Edwards; 28. "The Robust Beauty of Improper Linear Models in Decision Making" by Dawes; 30. "Intuitive Prediction: Biases and Corrective Procedures" by Kahneman and Tversky; 33. "Facts versus Fears:

Understanding Perceived Risk" by Slovic, Fischhoff and Lichtenstein; 34. "On the Study of Statistical Institutions" by Kahneman and Tversky; and 35. "Variants of Uncertainty" by Kahneman and Tversky.

Katona, George (1975). *Psychological Economics*. Amsterdam: Elsevier. *Psychological Economics* represents the most complete statement of Katona's thought. Part I, "The Human Factor in Economic Affairs," covers such topics as cyclical fluctuations in consumer durable goods, inflation, saving, saturation versus rising levels of aspiration, the response to fiscal policy, GNP and quality of life, the affluent consumer, the relation of psychology and social psychology to economics, and learning. Part II, "The Influence of Attitudes and Expectations in the Short Run," discusses forecasting economic fluctuations, the psychology of inflation and the psychology of prosperity; the remaining four parts are entitled "Psychological Principles of Consumer Behavior," "Saving," "Business Behavior," and "Economy and Society."

——— (1980). *Essays on Behavioral Economics*. With a Contribution by James N. Morgan. Ann Arbor, MI: Institute for Social Research, University of Michigan. This is the final exposition of the psychologist who succeeded in getting economists to take consumer and business surveys seriously and whose work so improved expectations estimates over the extraordinarily mistaken ones that prevailed at the end of the Second World War.

Knetsch, Jack L. (1995). "Assumptions, Behavioral Findings and Policy Analysis." *Journal of Policy Analysis and Management* Vol. 14, No. 1 (Winter): 68–78. Knetsch summarizes the anomalies in economic behavior that investigators have uncovered and notes that these are not being reflected in the policy analyses of economists.

Kunkel, John H (1970). *Society and Economic Growth. A Behavioral Perspective of Social Change*. New York: Oxford University Press. The term *behavioral* here refers to the behavioralism of operant conditioning. Only a very small number of economists have considered this approach seriously. One of the first of these economists was David Alhadeff, whose *Microeconomics and Human Behavior* was published by the University of California at Berkeley in 1982. There has been some regeneration of this approach in the work of those who focus on "animal economics."

Kunreuther, Howard (1976). "Limited Knowledge and Insurance Protection." *Public Policy* Vol. 4, No. 2 (Spring): 227–61. This work makes use of cognitive psychology's contributions to help explain why people confronted with potential disasters tend to behave somewhat irrationally.

Kuran, Timur (1995). *Private Truths, Public Lies. The Social Consequences of Preference Falsification*. Cambridge, MA: Harvard University Press. Although aimed primarily at larger subjects than those dealt with here, this book is of special interest for providing a dramatic case against any simple-minded view of interpreting individual preferences.

Lea, Stephen E. G., Paul Webley and Brian M. Young, eds. (1992). *New Directions in Economic Psychology. Theory, Experiment and Application*. Aldershot, England and Brookfield, VT: Edward Elgar. This volume includes fifteen recent essays by economists and psychologists, the most important of which are "Economic Psychology: A New Sense of Direction" by Lea, Webley and Young; "Socio-Economics: Select Policy Implications" by Etzioni; "On the Complementarity of Economic Applications of Cognitive Dissonance Theory and Personal Construct Psychology'' by Earl; ''Moral Constraints on Strategic Behavior'' by Casson; ''Experiments in Economics—and Psychology'' by Hey; ''An Endowment Effect in Market Experiments'' by Tietz; ''When Is a Cobweb Model Stable?'' by Fischer; and ''Entrepreneurial Motivation and the Smaller Business'' by Gray.

Lewin, Shira B. (1996). ''Economics and Psychology: Lessons for Our Own Day From the Early Twentieth Century.'' *Journal of Economic Literature* Vol. 34, No. 3 (September): 1293–1323. Lewin reviews the initial efforts to include psychology in economic analysis and the reaction of the economics profession, with methodological commentary. The article notes the current revival of interest in using the findings of psychology as a basis for the behavioral assumptions of economics, but it calls for attention to the findings of other social sciences as well, notably sociology.

Lewis, Alan, Paul Webley and Adrian Furnham. *The New Economic Mind. The Social Psychology of Economic Behavior* (1995). London: Harvester, Wheatsheaf. This is an updated and accessible overview of what psychologists have been calling economic psychology. Part I (''Aperitif'') includes cognitive psychology as well as the sometimes overlapping fields of developmental psychology, social psychology and experimental psychology. (It excludes the behavioralism of Skinner et al., which some behavioral economists utilize.) *The New Economic Mind* contains a clear and concise explanation of what psychologists seek to achieve, linked to Herbert Simon's distinction between substantive and procedural rationality. The topics in the remainder of the volume are: Part II, ''Socialization and the Psychology of Money'' (ch. 2: ''Socialization and Economics: Children's Understanding of and Behavior in the Economic World''; ch. 3: ''The Psychology of Money''); Part III, ''Social Issues and Social Problems'' (ch. 4: ''Debt, Gambling, Addictive Spending [and Saving]''; ch. 5: ''Poverty: Aspects of the Psychological Literature''; ch. 6 ''Wealth''; ch. 7: ''Unemployment''); Part IV, ''Morals and the Market'' (ch. 8: ''Fairness, Ethics and the 'Greens' ''; ch. 9: ''Welfare and Tax Evasion''); Part V, ''Work Ethics and Economics in Transition'' (ch. 10: ''The Protestant Work Ethic''; ch. 11: ''Economies in Transition: The New Europe''); and Part VI, ''Conclusions'' (ch. 12: ''Digestif'').

Loewenstein, George and Jon Elster, eds. (1992). *Choice over Time.* New York: Russell Sage Foundation. This is the most important source for the consideration of intertemporal decisions. It contains a preface with an extended summary of the contents and fifteen chapters. 1. ''The Fall and Rise of Psychological Explanations in the Economics of Intertemporal Choice'' by Loewenstein; 2. ''Intertemporal Choice and Political Thought'' by Elster; 3. ''Hyperbolic Discounting'' by Ainslie and Haslam; 4. ''Irrationality, Impulsiveness and Selfishness as Discount Reversal Effects'' by Rachlin and Raineri; 5. ''Anomalies in Intertemporal Choice: Evidence and an Interpretation'' by Loewenstein and Prelec; 6. ''Delay of Gratification of Children'' by Mischel, Shoda and Rodriguez; 7. ''Self-Command. A New Discipline'' by Schelling; 8. ''Self Control'' by Ainslie and Haslam; 9. ''Utility from Memory and Adaptation'' by Elster and Loewenstein; 10. ''Melioration'' by Herrnstein and Prelec; 11. ''The Role of Moral Sentiments in the Theory of Intertemporal Choice'' by Frank; 12. ''Mental Accounting, Saving, and Self Control'' by Shefrin and Thaler; 13. ''A Theory of Addiction'' by Herrnstein and Prelec; 14. ''Rational Addiction and the Effect of Price on Consumption'' by Becker, Grossman and Murphy; and 15. "Frames of Reference and the Intertemporal Wage Profile'' by Frank.

McCain, Roger (1992). *A Framework for Cognitive Economics*. New York: Praeger. Useful, sometimes provocative discussions of cognitive approaches to economics, followed by theoretical constructs.

Machina, Mark J. (1987). "Choice Under Uncertainty: Problems Solved and Unsolved.'' *Journal of Economic Perspectives* Vol. 1, No. 1 (Summer): 121–54. Machina has written an important review article, though perhaps one that is not quite as accessible to those with only moderate preparation in or recall of economics as a publication in the *Journal of Economic Perspectives* might seem to imply.

Maital, Shlomo, ed. (1988). *Applied Behavioral Economics*. 2 vols. Brighton, England: Wheatsheaf Books. This important collection of articles has been largely ignored, in part perhaps because the equations in the Keynote Paper were deleted by mistake. Though unfortunate, that paper is valuable even as it stands. The remainder of the papers, which were prepared for the 1986 International Conference on Economics and Psychology, sponsored by the International Association for Research in Economic Psychology and the Society for the Advancement of Behavioral Economics, are particularly suitable for those initiating their work in behavioral economics because the participants were obliged to keep them quite short. The following is a list of 37 of the 49 papers:

Volume I: Keynote Paper: Richard Herrnstein, "A Behavioral Alternative to Utility Maximization.'' *Part One: The Role of Perception and Information in Consumption and Saving*: "Consumer Information in the Electronic Data Media'' by Olander; "Aggregate Saving and the Saving Behavior of Saver Groups in Sweden Accompanying a Tax Reform'' by Wahlun and Wärneryd; "Level of Own Contribution Towards a Public Service as an Indicator for Consumer Appraisal'' by Francken and Kuylen; "A Psychological Opponent Process Theory of Consumption'' by Saldanha and Lancry. *Part Two. Consumer Choice and Marketing: Quality, Novelty and Learning*: "A Model of Advertising and Learning'' by Kotowitz; "An Alternative to the Random Utility Approach in Modeling the Preference for Variety'' by Middelton. *Part Three: Managerial Decision Making in Centralized Economies*: "Managerial Director's Motivation to Undertake Risk Economic Actions in the Context of Economy'' by Sokolowska; "Justification of Decisions Made in Adverse Circumstances'' by Tyszka and Gasparski. *Part Four: Economic Psychology of the Family*: "Is Altruism the Dominant Motivation in the Family?'' by Phelps; "Virtue, Work and Marriage'' by Grossbard-Shechtman; "Gender Differences in Family Affects on Human Capital and Earnings: an Empirical Study of Siblings'' by Neumark. *Part Five: Behavioral Aspects of Fertility and Migration*: "The Changing Motivation for Having Children'' by Albanese; "Behavioral Variability in Migration'' by Stark and Yitchaki. *Part Six: Expectations*: "Expert and Amateur Expectations'' by Friedman and Shapira. *Part Eight: Values and Attitudes*: "Rationalization of Action Through Value Development'' by Sevon.

Volume II: *Part Nine. Entrepreneurship*: "Economic Perception and Judgment in Small and Medium Size Manufacturing Enterprises: Findings and Preliminary Hypotheses from In-Depth Interviews in Argentina, Mexico and the United States'' by Schwartz; "Innovation, Entrepreneurship, Efficiency and the Strategy-Manager Fit in Irish Agricultural Co-perationes'' by O'Higgins; "The Entrepreneurial Way with Information" by Gilad, Kaitsh and Ronen. *Part Ten. Economic Psychology of Hazards and Stress*: "Hypertension Labeling as a Stressful Event Leading to an Increase in Absenteeism: A Possible Explanation for an Empirically Measured Phenomen" by Westman and Gafni; "Incorporating Anxiety Induced by Environmental Episodes in Life Valuation" by Schechter; "The Joy of Thinking About Nuclear Energy. Individual Differences in Search and Desire for External Information and in Beliefs-Attitude-Intention Consistency" by Pieters. *Part Eleven. Tax Evasion*: "Social Comparison and Tax Evasion in a Shop Simulation" by Webley, Robben and Morris; "A Linear Structural Model for Tax Evasion Measurements" by Elfers and Hessing; "Research in Tax Resistance. An Integrative Theoretical Scheme for Tax Evasion Behavior" by Hessing, Elfers and Weigel. *Part Twelve. Time Preference*: "Time Preferences. The Expectation and Evaluation of Decision Consequences as a Function of Time" by Jungermann; "The Time-Shape of Transactions. Relational Exchange, Repetition and Honesty" by Winston. *Part Thirteen. Behavioral Labor Economics*: "The Industrial Relations Systems Model as an Analytical Tool" by Meltz; "Quality Circles and Corporate Identity—Towards Overcoming the Crisis of Taylorism" by Wiendieck; "Worker Participation: Paths to Higher Productivity and Well-Being" by Tomer. *Part Fourteen. Choice Under Uncertainty*: "A Pilot Experimental Investigation into Optimal Consumption Under Uncertainty" by Hey; "The St. Petersburg Paradox and the Expectation Heuristic" by Treisman; "Framing and Communication Effects on Group Members' Responses to Environmental and Social Uncertainty" by Messick, Allison and Samuelson. *Part Fifteen. Aspects of Distributive Justice*: "On the Behavioral Approach to Distributive Justice—a Theoretical and Experimental Investigation" by Guth. *Part Sixteen. Social Security and Income Inequality*: "Memory and Anticipation Processes and Their Significance for Social Security and Income Inequality" by van Praag. *Part Seventeen. Economic Man, Who He Is, What He Knows*: "Passions Within Reason: The Strategic Role of the Emotions" by Frank; "Economic Measurement, Public Policy and Human Cognition: An Analytical Framework" by Graziano; and "Choice in a Modern Economy: New Concepts of Democracy and Bureaucracy" by Raven.

————— (1994). *Executive Economics. Ten Essential Tools for Managers*. New York: Free Press. The essence of the lively economics course offered by the executive training program of MIT's Sloan School of Management by a leading behavioral economist, this is basically a volume on managerial economics. However, it includes a number of examples and some more extended material reflecting the findings of a behavioral approach to economics, most notably in the discussions of risk (ch. 9) and sunk costs (chs. 2 and 4).

————— and Sharone L. Maital, eds. (1993). *Economics and Psychology*. Aldershot, England and Brookfield, VT: Edward Elgar. This is an important collection of articles published between 1950 and 1992 in the journals of economists and psychologists. Part I provides an overview of economics and psychology, Part II deals with the economic socialization of children, Part III with the contest for self-command, Part IV with rational choice, Part V with endogenous preferences, Part VI with the economic psychology of demand and markets, Part VII with behavior toward risk, Part VIII with capital markets, and Part IX with applying economics to psychology. None of the articles in Parts II and IX is listed here because of the nature of this presentation, but attention should be called to the introduction prepared by the editors and to nineteen of the other twenty-one papers. Perhaps the most famous article is Herbert Simon (1955), "A Behavioral Model of Rational Choice," *Quarterly Journal of Economics* Vol. 69, No. 1 (February): 99–118. The others include: Sharone L. Maital and Shlomo Maital (1984). "Psychology and Economics," in Marc L. Bornstein, ed., *Crosscurrents in Contemporary Psychology*. Vol. 2: *Psychology and Its Allied Disciplines*. Hillsdale, NJ: Lawrence Erlbaum Associates, pp. 55–87; George Ainslie (1975). "Specious Reward: A Behavioral Theory of Impulsiveness and Impulse Control." *Psychological Bulletin* Vol. 82, No. 4 (July): 463–96; Thomas C. Schelling (1984). "Self Command in Practice, in Policy, and in a Theory of Rational Choice." *American Economic Review* Vol. 74, No. 2 (May): 1–11; Shlomo Maital (1986). "Prometheus Rebound: On Welfare-Improving Constraints." *Eastern Economic Journal* Vol. 1, No. 3 (July–September): 337–44; Gordon C. Winston (1980). "Addiction and Backsliding: A Theory of Compulsive Consumption." *Journal of Economic Behavior and Organization* Vol. 1, No. 4: 295–324; Hersh M. Shefrin and Richard H. Thaler (1988). "The Behavioral Life-Cycle Hypothesis." *Economic Inquiry* Vol. 26, No. 4 (October): 609–43; George Loewenstein and Drazen Prelec (1992). "Anomalies in Intertemporal Choice: Evidence and an Interpretation." *Quarterly Journal of Economics* Vol. 107, No. 2 (May): 573–97; James G. March (1978). "Bounded Rationality, Ambiguity, and the Engineering of Choice." *The Bell Journal of Economics* Vol. 9, No. 1 (Spring): 587–608; R. J. Herrnstein (1990). "Rational Choice Theory: Necessary But Not Sufficient." *American Psychologist* Vol. 45, No. 3 (March): 356–67; George A. Akerlof and William T. Dickens (1982). "The Economic Consequences of Cognitive Dissonance." *American Economic Review* Vol. 7, No. 3 (June): 307–19; Tibor Scitovsky (1986). "How to Bring Joy into Economics," in Scitovsky, ed., *Human Desire and Economic Satisfaction: Essays on the Frontier of Economics*. Brighton, UK: Wheatsheaf Books, pp. 182–203; H. Leibenstein (1950). "Bandwagon Snob, and Veblen Effects in the Theory of Consumers' Demand." *Quarterly Journal of Economics*. Vol. 64, No. 2 (May): 183–207; S. E. G. Lea (1978). "The Psychology and Economics of Demand." *Psychological Bulletin* Vol. 85, No. 3 (May): 441–66; George Katona (1968). "Behavioral and Ecological Economics: Consumer Behavior: Theory and Findings on Expectations and Aspirations." *American Economic Review* Vol. 58, No. 2 (May); 19–30; Amos Tversky and Daniel Kahneman (1974). "Judgment Under Uncertainty: Heuristics and Biases." *Science* Vol. 185, No. 4157 (September 27): 1124–31; Robin M. Hogarth and Howard Kunreuther (1989). "Risk, Ambiguity, and Insurance." *Journal of Risk and Uncertainty* Vol. 2, No. 1 (April): 5–35; Stanley Schachter, Donald C. Hood, William Gerin, Paul Andreassen and Michael Rennert (1985). "Some Causes and Consequences of Dependence and Independence in the Stock Market." *Journal of Economic Behavior and Organization* Vol. 6, No. 4 (December): 339–57; and Werner F. M. De Bondt and Richard Thaler (1985). "Does the Stock Market Overreact?" *Journal of Finance* Vol. 15, No. 3 (July): 793–808.

National Bureau of Economic Research Conference on Behavioral Finance (1994). Among the preliminary documents, those of special interest to this volume are: "Institutional Memory, Inertia and Impulsiveness" by Hirshleifer and Welch; "Cognitive Dissonance and Mutual Fund Investors" by Goetzmann and Peles;

"Expectations and the Cross-Section of Stock Returns" by La Porta; and "Market Underreaction to Open Market Share Repurchases" by Ikenberry, Lakonishok and Vermaelen.

Nelson, Richard R. and Sidney G. Winter (1982). *An Evolutionary Theory of Economic Change.* Cambridge, MA and London, England: Belknap Press of Harvard University Press. Few books that dissent from mainstream economics have been cited as often as *An Evolutionary Theory of Economic Change* and have had as strong an impact, even on neoclassical economics. Nelson and Winter lamented that most economists ignored the findings of psychologists showing that individual choice under uncertainty follows principles that are quite different from those of Bayes's theorem and the von Neumann-Morgenstern utility axioms, but that certainly has begun to change. In chapter 17, "Retrospect and Prospect," Nelson and Winter maintain that the insistence of orthodox microeconomic theory on strict maximization "makes it awkward to deal with the fact that, in coping with exogenous change and in trying out new techniques and policies, firms have but limited bases for judging what will work best; they may even have difficulty establishing the range of plausible alternatives to be considered" (p. 399).

Nelson and Winter consider three characteristics or concepts of an evolutionary theory of economic change: organizational routine, search and "selection environment." They replace the concept of a social optimum with "notions that society ought to be engaging in experimentation and that the information and feedback from that experimentation are of central concern in guiding the evolution of the economic system . . ." (p. 402). Their evolutionary theory sees business firms as complex organizations, and denies that prices and markets are "the only social mechanisms that actively transmit information . . ." (p. 403). They characterize institutional development as a groping, incremental and evolutionary process (p. 404). The authors criticize the "as if" reasoning of so many optimization analyses, insisting on the need to base our notions of enterprise behavior on empirical observations. "The more we can learn about the way in which firms actually behave, the more we will be able to understand the laws of evolutionary development governing larger systems that involve many interacting firms in particular selection environments" (p. 410).

Schwartz, Hugh H. (1987). "Perception, Judgment and Motivation in Manufacturing Enterprises: Findings and Preliminary Hypotheses from In-Depth Interviews." *Journal of Economic Behavior and Organization* Vol. 8, No. 4 (December): 543–65. The article attempts to extract behavioral hypotheses from in-depth interviews. The interviews were undertaken with 113 enterprises in Argentina, Mexico and the United States in 1976–77, with many enterprises interviewed a second time. Some firms were observed in actual decision-making situations in a smaller third round of sessions. The questionnaire reflected some of the findings of cognitive psychologists as of the mid-1970s, and Schwartz used their work published in the late 1970s and early 1980s to help interpret his results. A prepared questionnaire occupied much less of the interview time than followup questions that attempted to obtain relatively full descriptions of contemporary or recent decision processes. The study adopts the concept of the Just Noticeable Difference into economic reasoning. Somewhat similar are references several years later by Earl and others referred to as Threshold Analyses.

Shapira, Zur (1995). *Risk Taking. A Managerial Perspective.* New York: Russell Sage

Foundation. This concise presentation of the principles of risk taking and risk management is followed by the results of a survey of 700 managers in the United States and Israel. The most important conclusions are as follows: (1) in making decisions, managers pay more attention to the magnitude of possible outcomes than to the probabilities of those outcomes, the statistical concepts of which they have difficulty in grasping. Certain possible outcomes, particularly worst possible outcomes, are the real concern, and in any event the focus in the analysis of choices is on downside risk, not overall variance. (2) Managers think of risk as a dynamic process; they think of many events as unique and not subject to traditional measures of probability. Nonetheless, they tend to believe that they can influence risk and the probabilities of given outcomes over the course of that process. (3) Managers pay more attention to actual losses than to opportunity losses. (4) Managers think separately and sequentially about problems.

Simon, Herbert A. (1982). *Models of Bounded Rationality*: Vol. 2. *Behavioral Economics and Business Organizations*. Cambridge, MA: MIT Press. The seriously interested student should consider all of the articles in the volume, but can start with six, listed in the order in which they appear in the volume: "A Behavioral Model of Rational Choice" (1955). *Quarterly Journal of Economics* Vol. 69, No. 1 (February): 99–118; "Theories of Decision-Making in Economics and Behavioral Science" (1959). *American Economic Review* Vol. 49, No. 1 (March): 253–83; "Economics and Psychology" (1963). In S. Koch, ed., *Psychology: A Study of a Science* Vol. 6: pp. 685–723. New York: McGraw-Hill; "From Substantive to Procedural Rationality" (1976). In S. J. Latsis, ed., *Method and Appraisal in Economics*, pp. 129–48. Cambridge: Cambridge University Press; "Rationality as a Process and as a Product of Thought" (1978). *American Economic Review*, Vol. 68, No. 2 (June): 1–16; and "Rational Decision Making in Business Organizations." *American Economic Review* Vol. 69, No. 4 (December): 493–513.

——— (1997). *Models of Bounded Rationality*. Vol. 3. *Empirically Grounded Economic Reason*. Cambridge, MA: MIT Press. The articles relevant to this book are: "A Mechanism for Social Selection and Successful Altruism." *Science* Vol. 250 (December 21, 1990): 1665–68; "Organizations and Markets." *Journal of Economic Perspectives* Vol. 5, No. 2 (Spring 1991): 25–44; "Altruism and Economics." *Eastern Economic Journal* Vol. 18, No. 1 (1992): 73–83; "Altruism and Economics." *American Economic Review* Vol. 83, No. 2 (May 1993): 156–61; Preface to B. Gilad and S. Kaisch (eds.), *Handbook of Behavioral Economics*. Greenwich, CT: JAI Press, 1986; "Behavourial Economics." In J. Eatwell, M. Milgate and P. Newman (eds.), *The New Palgrave: A Dictionary of Economics*. London: Macmillan, 1987, Vol. 1: 221–25; "Bounded Rationality." In J. Eatwell et al., *The New Palgrave*, Vol. 1: 266–68; "Satisficing." In J. Eatwell et al., *The New Palgrave*, Vol. 4: 243–45; "Behavioral Research: Theory and Public Policy." In *The 1979 Founders Symposium, The Institute for Social Research: Honoring George Katona*. Social Research Center, The University of Michigan, 1980: 11–36; "On the Behavioral and Rational Foundations of Economic Dynamics." *Journal of Economic Behavior and Organization* Vol. 5, No. 1 (February 1984): 35–55; "Rationality in Psychology and Economics." *The Journal of Business* Vol. 59 (Supplement 1986): S209–24; "The Failure of Armchair Economics" (report of an interview). *Challenge* Vol. 29, No. 5 (November/December 1986): 18–25; "Why Economists Disagree." *Journal of Business Administration* Vol.

18, Nos. 1 & 2 (1988/1989): 1–19; "The State of Economic Science." In W. Sichel (ed.), *The State of Economic Science: Views of Six Nobel Laureates*. Kalamazoo, MI: W. E. Upjohn Institute for Employment Research, 1989.

Slovic, Paul (1995). "The Construction of Preference." *American Psychologists* Vol. 50, No. 5 (May): 364–71. This award address of the American Psychological Association by the co-author of the articles that documented preference reversal succinctly sums up the empirical evidence of nearly three decades and outlines the implications for decision-making theories.

Thaler, Richard H. (1991). *Quasi Rational Economics*. New York: Russell Sage Foundation. This book reprints sixteen articles authored or co-authored by perhaps the leading behavioral economist: "Toward a Positive Theory of Consumer Choice" (1980)—this may be one of the 25 most often cited articles in economics and is probably the most cited article in behavioral economics; "Mental Accounting and Consumer Choice" (1985); "Gambling with the House Money and Trying to Break Even: The Effects of Prior Outcomes on Risky Choice" (1990), with Johnson; "An Economic Theory of Self Control" (1981), with Shefrin; "The Behavioral Life-Cycle Hypothesis (1988), with Shefrin; "Some Empirical Evidence on Dynamic Inconsistency" (1981); "The Psychology of Choice and the Assumptions of Economics" (1987)—this is the article one might show first to a theoretically inclined neoclassical economist, to be followed by the article below co-authored with Russell; "Experimental Tests of the Endowment Effect and the Coase Theorem" (1990), with Kahneman and Knetsch; "The Psychology and Economics Conference Handbook" (1986); "Fairness as a Constraint on Profit Seeking: Entitlements in the Market" (1986), with Kahneman and Knetsch; "Fairness and the Assumptions of Economics" (1986), with Kahneman and Knetsch; "The Relevance of Quasi Rationality in Competitive Markets" (1988), with Russell; "Does the Stock Market Overreact?" (1985), with De Bondt— perhaps one of the dozen or so most cited articles in financial economics and one of the most influential in stimulating research in this area; "Further Evidence on Investor Overreaction and Stock Market Seasonality" (1987), with De Bondt; "Do Security Analysts Overreact?" (1990), with De Bondt; and "Investor Sentiment and the Closed-End Fund Puzzle" (1991), with Lee and Shleifer.

——— (1992). *The Winner's Curse: Paradoxes and Anomalies of Economic Life*. New York: Free Press. Paperback edition: 1994, Princeton University Press. Thaler provides more complete explanations of many of the anomalies referred to in the present book, along with some others as well. The chapters of *The Winner's Curse* were originally published as articles in the *Journal of Economic Perspectives*. Although training in economics will help the reader get the most out of them, the expositions are so clear and the writing so lively that they have been enjoyed by many who have never taken more than an introductory course in the subject.

——— (1993). *Advances in Behavioral Finance*. New York: Russell Sage Foundation. Although by no means all of the most renowned authorities have embraced a behavioral approach to finance, there has been more acceptance in this field and in organizational behavior than in the other areas of economics and business administration. Most of the empirical findings are so at odds with what standard neoclassical theory would have predicted that as a result, a particularly large number of finance specialists have raised serious questions about the adequacy of the existing paradigm. This volume includes 20 previously published articles and one piece prepared especially for the collection. Perhaps the most influential of the articles was "Noise" given as a presidential address to the American Finance Association in 1985 by the former academic and at that time Wall Street partner, Fisher Black. The full contents are as follows: *Part I. Noise:* 1. Noise (1986) by Black; 2. Noise Trader Risk in Financial Markets (1990) by De Long, Schleifer, Summers and Waldmann; 3. Investor Sentiment and the Closed-End Fund Puzzle (1991) by Lee, Schleifer and Thaler. *Part II. Volatility:* 4. Do Stock Prices Move Too Much to Be Justified by Subsequent Changes in Dividends? (1981) by Shiller; 5. What Moves Stock Prices? Moves in Stock Prices Reflect Something Other Than News About Fundamental Values (1989) by Cutler, Poterba and Summers; 6. Does the Stock Market Rationally Reflect Fundamental Values? (1986) by Summers; 7. Stock Prices and Social Dynamics (1984) by Shiller; 8. Stock Return Variances. The Arrival of Information and the Reaction of Traders (1986) by French and Roll. *Part III. Overreaction:* 9. Does the Stock Market Overreact? (1986) by De Bondt and Thaler; 10. Measuring Abnormal Performance. Do Stocks Overreact? (1991) by Chopra, Lakonishok and Ritter; 11. Stock Price Reactions to Earnings Announcements. A Summary of Recent Anomalous Evidence and Possible Explanations (1993) by V. L. Bernard; 12. Overreactions in the Options Market (1989) by Stein. *Part IV. International Markets:* 13. Forward Discount Bias. Is It an Exchange Risk Premium? (1989) by Froot and J. Frankel; 14. Investor Diversification and International Equity Markets (1991) by French and Poterba. *Part V. Corporate Finance:* 15. Explaining Investor Preference for Cash Dividends (1984) by Shefrin and Statman; 16. Equilibrium Short Horizons of Investors and Firms (1990) by Shleifer and Vishny; 17. The Hubris Hypothesis of Corporate Takeovers (1986) by Roll; 18. The Long-Run Performance of Initial Public Offerings (1991) by Ritter. *Part VI. Individual Behavior:* 19. Speculative Prices and Popular Models (1990) by Shiller; 20. The Disposition to Sell Winners Too Early and Ride Losers Too Long. Theory and Evidence (1986) by Shefrin and Statman; 21. The Failure of Competition in the Credit Card Market (1991) by Ausubel.

Thoumi, Franciso E. (1995). *Political Economy and Illegal Drugs in Colombia.* Boulder, CO and London: Lynne Rienner Publishers. Chapter 9, "The Demand for Psychoactive Drugs and Drug Addiction," contains a valuable discussion of economists' efforts to explain drug addiction, in particular through the "two-self" models. (See especially pp. 251–57.) This book, by perhaps the leading authority on the Colombian drug industry, is directed primarily at noneconomists but contains sections that probably will be best appreciated by the professional economist.

Tomer, John F. (1987). *Organizational Capital. The Path to Higher Productivity and Well-being.* New York: Praeger. In this interdisciplinary study drawing on organizational behavior as well as economics, Tomer states: "Investment in organizational capital refers to the using up of resources in order to bring about lasting improvement in productivity and/or worker well-being through changes in the functioning of the organization. Organizational capital formation could involve (1) changing the formal and informal social relationships and patterns of activity within the enterprise, (2) changing individual attributes important to organizational functioning, or (3) the accumulation of information useful in matching workers with organization situations. Organizational capital is human capital in which the attribute is embodied in either the organizational relationship, particular organization members, the organization's repositories of information, or some combination of the above in order to improve the functioning of the organization." (p. 2)

Tversky, Amos and Daniel Kahneman (1992). "Advances in Prospect Theory: Cumulative Representation of Uncertainty." *Journal of Risk and Uncertainty* Vol. 5, No. 4 (October): 297–323. This article is an updated synthesis of the influential work of Tversky and Kahneman on decision making under uncertainty. Section 3, Discussion, is so clear and succinct that even those with limited economics background or little familiarity with this area will be able to appreciate the exposition. (The original 1979 article is only for the professional economist or advanced student.)

————, Paul Slovic and Daniel Kahneman (1990). "The Causes of Preference Reversal." *American Economic Review* Vol. 80, No. 1 (March): 204–17. Three of the psychologists most identified with the discovery of preference reversals examine the possible causes and explain why the phenomenon is attributable primarily to procedure invariance rather than to a lack of transitivity or to violations of independence or the reductiuon axiom.

————, Paul Slovic and Shumuel Sattath (1988). "Contingent Weighting in Judgment and Choice." *Psychological Review* Vol. 95, No. 3 (July): 371–84. This important article in the preference reversal controversy explains differences in preferences inferred from direct choice, on the one hand, and a matching procedure, on the other.

Van Raaij, W. F., G. M. van Veldhoven and K.-E. Wärneryd eds. (1988). *Handbook of Economic Psychology*. Dordrecht, Boston and London: Kluwer Academic Publishers. Aimed primarily at advanced students of psychology and marketing, the volume is also of interest to economists. Economists might turn first to the general overview, Economic Psychology as a Field of Study by Karl-Erik Wärneryd, and to the short introductions to the four sections (Part I. "Theoretical Background"; Part II. "Household Economic Behavior"; Part III. "Business Behavior"; and Part IV. "The Societal Perspective"). Of the eighteen topic overviews, those likely to be of interest to the largest number of economists are Information Processing and Decision Making. Cognitive Aspects of Economic Behavior by van Raaij; Social Influences on Economic Behavior by Wärneryd; Behavioral Perspectives on the Theory of the Firm by March and Sevon; The Psychology of Innovative Entrepreneurship by Wärneryd; and Economic Agents' Expectations in a Psychological Perspective by Abeele.

Weiermair, Klaus and Mark Perlman, eds. (1990). *Studies in Economic Rationality. X-Efficiency Examined and Extolled. Essays Written in the Tradition of and to Honor Harvey Leibenstein*. Ann Arbor: University of Michigan Press. An overview by the editors is followed by Part 1. "Micro-Microtheory Revisited"; Part 2. "Motivational Foundations of Economic Behavior"; Part 3. "The Design and Structuring of Organizations"; Part 4. "Organizational Adaptation and Change"; Part 5. "Normative Implications of X-Efficiency in Business Strategy and Government Policies"; Part 6. "Measurement Problems"; and Part 7. "Summary and the Outlook for X-Efficiency Theory."

E. ADDITIONAL REFERENCES

Ainslie, George (1991). "Derivation of 'Rational' Economic Behavior from Hyperbolic Discount Curves." *American Economic Review* Vol. 81, No. 2 (May): 334–40.

Akerlof, George and Janet L. Yellen (1987). "Rational Models of Irrational Behavior." *American Economic Review* Vol. 77, No. 2 (May): 137–42.

Albanese, Paul J. (1987). "The Nature of Preferences: An Exploration of the Relationship Between Economics and Psychology." *Journal of Economic Psychology* Vol. 7, No. 4 (March): 3–18.

Alchian, Arman A. (1950). "Uncertainty, Evolution and Economic Theory." *Journal of Political Economy* Vol. 58, No. 1 (February): 211–21.

Altman, Morris (1993). "Human Agency as a Determinant of Material Welfare." *Journal of Socio-Economics* Vol. 2, No. 2 (Summer): 199–218.

Anderson, Barry F. and John W. Settle (1996). "The Influence of Portfolio Characteristics and Investment Period on Investment Choice." *Journal of Economic Psychology* Vol. 17, No. 3 (June): 343–58.

Anderson, Michael A. and Arthur H. Goldsmith (1994). "Rationality in the Mind's Eye: An Alternative Test of Rational Expectations Using Forecast and Evaluations Data." *Journal of Economic Psychology* Vol. 15, No. 3 (September): 379–403.

Antonides, Gerrit, W. Fred van Raaij and Shlomo Maital, eds. (1997). *Advances in Economic Psychology*. Chichester, UK: John Wiley and Sons. See also Section D.

Archibald, Robert B. (1994). "Intertemporal Trades and Problems of Self-Control." *Journal of Economic Behavior and Organization* Vol. 25, No. 1 (September): 73–91

Baxter, J. L. (1993). *Behavioral Foundations of Economics*. New York: St. Martin's Press. See also Section D.

Baumol, William J. and Maco Stewart (1971). "On the Behavioral Theory of the Firm." In Robin Marris and Adrian Wood, eds., *The Corporate Economy. Growth, Competition and Innovation Potential*. London and Basingstoke: Macmillan.

Becker, Gary S. (1996). *Accounting for Tastes*. Cambridge, MA: Harvard University Press.

Bernstein, Peter L. (1996). *Against the Gods. The Remarkable Story of Risk*. New York: John Wiley and Sons.

Billot, Antoine (1991). "Cognitive Rationality and Alternative Belief Measures." *Journal of Risk and Uncertainty* Vol. 4, No. 3 (July): 299–328.

Blinder, Alan. "On Sticky Prices: Academic Theories Meet the Real World." (1994). In N. Gregory Mankiw, ed., *Monetary Policy*. National Bureau of Economic Research. Chicago: University of Chicago Press, 117–50. (See also Oliver Jean Blanchard, "Comment," 150–54.)

Bohm, Peter and Hans Lind (1993). "Preference Reversals, Real-World Lotteries, and Lottery-Interested Subjects." *Journal of Economic Behavior and Organization* Vol. 22, No. 3 (December): 327–48.

Callahan, Charlene and Catherine S. Elliott (1996). "Listening: A Narrative Approach to Everyday Undertakings and Behavior." *Journal of Economic Psychology* Vol. 17, No. 1 (February): 79–114.

Conlisk, John (1988). "Optimization Cost." *Journal of Economic Behavior and Organization* Vol. 9, No. 3 (April): 213–28.

Cross, John (1983). *A Theory of Adaptive Economic Behavior*. Cambridge: Cambridge University Press.

Dawes, Robyn M. (1988). *Rational Choice in an Uncertain World*. San Diego and New York: Harcourt Brace Jovanovich.

Day, Richard H. and Vernon L. Smith, eds. (1993). *Experiments in Decision, Organization and Exchange*. Amsterdam: North-Holland.

Dietz, Thomas and Paul C. Stern (1995). "Toward a Theory of Choice: Socially Imbedded Preference Construction." *Journal of Socio-Economics* Vol. 24, No. 2 (Summer): 261–79.

Dixit, Avinash K. and Robert J. Pindyck (1994). *Investment Under Uncertainty*. Princeton: Princeton University Press.

Duesenberry, James (1949). *Income, Saving and the Theory of Consumer Behavior*. Cambridge, MA: Harvard University Press.

Edwards, Ward (1954). "The Theory of Decision Making." *Psychological Bulletin* Vol. 51, No. 4 (July): 380–417. See also Section D.

Einhorn, Hillel J. and Robin M. Hogarth (1986). "Decision Making Under Ambiguity." *Journal of Business* Vol. 59, No. 4 (October): 225–50.

Eliasson, Gunnar (1996). *Firm Objectives, Controls and Organization: The Use of Information and the Transfer of Knowledge within the Firm*. Dordrecht, Boston and London: Kluwer Academic Publishers, ch. III, "The Firm as an Experimental Machine—Its Decision Problem," 53–116.

Elliott, Catherine S. and Donald M. Hayward, (1998). "The Expanding Definition of Framing and Its Particular Impact on Economic Experimentation," Forthcoming, *Journal of Socio-Economics* Vol. 27, No. 2.

Ellsberg, Daniel (1961). "Risk, Ambiguity and the Savage Axioms." *Quarterly Journal of Economics* Vol. 75 (November): 643–69.

Elmslie, Bruce and Stanley Sedo (1996). "Discrimination, Social Psychology and Hysteresis in Labor Markets." *Journal of Economic Psychology* Vol. 17, No. 4 (August): 465–78.

Elster, Jon (1989). "Social Norms and Economic Theory." *Journal of Economic Perspectives* Vol. 3, No. 4 (Fall): 99–117.

Evans, Dorla (1997). "The Role of Markets in Reducing Expected Utility Violations," *Journal of Political Economy* Vol. 105, No. 3 (June): 622–36.

Fishburn, Peter C. (1989). "Nontransitive Preferences in Decision Theory." *Journal of Risk and Uncertainty* Vol. 4, No. 2 (April): 113–34.

Frank, Robert H. (1987). "If Homo Economicus Could Choose His Own Utility Function, Would He Want One with a Conscience?" *American Economic Review* Vol. 77, No. 4 (September): 593–604.

Frey, Bruno S. and Reiner Eichenberger (1994). "Economic Incentives Transform Psychological Anomalies." *Journal of Economic Behavior and Organization* Vol. 23, No. 2 (March): 215–34.

George, David (1984). "Meta-Preferences: Reconsidering Contemporary Notions of Free Choice." *International Journal of Social Economics* Vol. 11, Nos. 3/4: 92–107.

——— (1989). "Social Evolution and the Role of Knowledge." *Review of Social Economy* Vol. 47, No. 1 (Spring): 55–73.

——— (1993). "Does the Market Create Planned Preferences." *Review of Social Economy* Vol. 51, No. 3 (Fall): 323–46.

Gilad, Benjamin, Stanley Kaish and Peter D. Loeb (1987). "Cognitive Dissonance and Utility Maximization." *Journal of Economic Organization and Behavior* Vol. 8, No. 1: 61–73.

Goldsmith, Arthur H., Jonathan R. Veum and William Darity, Jr. (1996). "The Impact of Labor Force History on Self-Esteem and Its Compenent Parts, Anxiety,

Alienation and Depression." *Journal of Economic Psychology* Vol. 17, No. 2 (April): 183–220.

Gramm, Warren S. (1988) "Rise and Decline of the Maximization Principle." *Journal of Behavioral Economics* Vol. 17, No. 3 (Fall): 157–72.

Grether, David M. (1992). "Testing Bayes Rule and the Representativeness Heuristic: Some Experimental Evidence." *Journal of Economic Behavior and Organization* Vol. 17, No. 1 (January): 31–57.

Grossman, Sanford J. and Joseph E. Stiglitz (1980). "On the Impossibility of Informationally Efficient Markets." *American Economic Review* Vol. 70, No. 3 (June): 393–408.

Grunert, Klaus G. and Folke Olander, eds. (1989). *Understanding Economic Behavior.* Dordrecht: Kluwer Academic Publishers.

Gueegy, Uri and Jan Potters (1997). "An Experiment on Risk Taking and Evaluation Periods." *Quarterly Journal of Economics* Vol. 112, No. 2 (May): 631–45.

Hall, R. L. and Charles J. Hitch (1939). "Price Theory and Business Behavior." *Oxford Economic Papers* Vol. 2, No. 2 (May): 12–45.

Hausman, Daniel M. (1991). *The Inexact and Separate Science of Economics.* Cambridge: Cambridge University Press.

——— (1991). "On Dogmatism in Economics: The Case of Preference Reversals." *Journal of Socio-Economics* Vol. 20, No. 3 (Fall 1991): 205–25.

Herrnstein, Richard J. (1991), "Experiments on Stable Optimality in Individual Behavior." *American Economic Review* Vol. 81, No. 2 (May): 360–64.

Hey, John D. (1994). "Expectations Formation: Rational or Adaptive or . . . ?" *Journal of Economic Behavior and Organization* Vol. 25, No. 3 (December): 329–49.

Hirschman, Albert O. (1965). "Obstacles to Development: A Classification and a Quasi-Vanishing Act." *Economic Development and Cultural Change* Vol. 13, No. 4, Part I (July): 385–93.

——— (1981). *Essays in Trespassing. Economics to Politics and Beyond.* New York: Cambridge University Press.

——— (1982). *Shifting Involvements. Private Interest and Public Action.* Princeton: Princeton University Press.

——— (1984). "Against Parsimony: Three Easy Ways of Complicating Some Categories of Economic Discourse." *American Economic Review* Vol. 74, No. 2 (May): 89–96.

Hirshleifer, Jack and John G. Riley (1992). *The Analytics of Uncertainty and Information.* Cambridge: Cambridge University Press, ch. 1, sec. 6.

Janis, Irving and Leon Mann (1977). *Decision Making: A Psychological Analysis of Conflict, Choice and Commitment.* New York: Free Press.

Kahneman, Daniel, Peter P. Wakker and Rakesh Sarin (1997). "Back to Bentham? Explorations of Experienced Utility." *Quarterly Journal of Economics* Vol. 112, No. 2 (May): 375–405.

Kayaalp, Orhan (1989). "Reconciling Economic Postulates: Does 'Adaptive' Egoism Satisfice?" *Journal of Behavioral Economics* Vol. 18, No. 4 (Winter): 289–306.

Kirzner, Israel M. (1979). *Perception, Opportunity and Profit. Studies in the Theory of Entrepreneurship* Chicago and London: University of Chicago Press.

Koh, Winston T. H. (1994). "Making Decisions in Committees. A Human Fallibility Approach." *Journal of Economic Behavior and Organization* Vol. 23, No. 2 (March): 195–214.

Kuhn, Thomas (1970). *The Structure of Scientific Revolution.* 2nd ed. Chicago: University of Chicago Press.

Kunkel, John H. (1970). *Society and Economic Growth. A Behavioral Perspective of Social Change.* New York: Oxford University Press. See also Section D.

Kuran, Timur (1995). *Private Truths, Public Lies. The Social Consequences of Preference Falsification.* Cambridge, MA: Harvard University Press. See also Section D.

Kunreuther, Howard (1996). "Mitigating Disaster Losses Through Insurance." *Journal of Risk and Uncertainty* Vol. 12, Nos. 2/3: 171–87.

————, Ralph Ginsberg, Louis Miller et al. (1978). *Disaster Insurance Protection. Public Policy Lessons.* New York: John Wiley and Sons.

————, Jacquelin Meszaros, Robin Hogarth and Mark Spranca (1995). "Ambiguity and Underwriter Decision Processes." *Journal of Economic Behavior and Organization* Vol. 26, No. 3 (May): 337–52.

———— and Paul Slovic (1978). "Economic Psychology and Protective Behavior." *American Economic Review* Vol. 68, No. 2 (May): 64–69.

Langley, Pat and Herbert A. Simon (1981). "The Central Role of Learning in Cognition." Ch. 12 in J. R. Anderson, ed., *Cognitive Skills and their Acquisition.* Hillsdale, NJ: Lawrence Erlbaum Associates.

Larkin, Jill and Herbert A. Simon (1981). "Learning through Growth of Skill in Mental Modeling." *Proceedings of the Third Annual Conference of the Cognitive Science Society:* 106–11. Berkeley, CA.

Lee, Li Way (1987). "Cognitive and Market Failures; Some Complex Policy Implications." *Journal of Behavioral Economics* Vol. 16, No. 3 (Fall): 51–57.

———— (1988). "The Predator-Prey Theory of Addiction." *Journal of Behavioral Economics* Vol. 17, No. 4 (Winter): 249–62.

———— (1991) "Behavioral Theory of Oligopoly." *Journal of Socio-Economics* Vol. 20, No. 1 (Spring): 1–18.

Leibenstein, Harvey. (For most articles, see the listing above for Kenneth Button in Sections C and D.)

———— (1976). *Beyond Economic Man. A New Foundation for Microeconomics.* Cambridge, MA: Harvard University Press.

———— (1986). "On Relaxing the Maximization Postulate." With comments by John F. Tomer, Stanislaw Wellsiz, Marvin E. Rozen, T. Y. Shen, Dieter Bos, Eirik G. Furubotn, Joshua Ronen, and a "Final Comment" by Leibenstein. *Journal of Behavioral Economics* Vol. 15 (Winter): 3–63.

———— and Shlomo Maital (1994). "The Organizational Foundation of X-Efficiency. A Game-Theoretic Interpretation of Argyris' Model of Organizational Learning." *Journal of Economic Behavior and Organization* Vol. 23, No. 3 (May): 251–68.

Loomes, Graham and Robert Sugden (1982). "Regret Theory: An Alternative Theory of Rational Choice Under Uncertainty." *Economic Journal* Vol. 9, No. 4 (December): 805–24.

Luce, R. Duncan (1992). "Where Does Subjective Expected Utility Fail Descriptively?" *Journal of Risk and Uncertainty* Vol. 5, No. 1 (February): 5–28.

Lutz, Mark and Kenneth Lux (1988). *Humanistic Economics. The New Challenge.* New York: Bootstrap Press.

MacDonald, Don N. and William L. Huth (1989). "Individual Valuation, Market Valuation, and the Preference Reversal Phenomenon." *Journal of Behavioral Economics* Vol. 18, No. 2 (Summer): 99–114.

MacFadyen, Alan J. and Heather W., eds. (1986). *Economic Psychology. Intersections in Theory and Applications*. Amsterdam: North Holland.

Maital, Shlomo (1982). *Minds, Markets and Money*. New York: Basic Books.

———— (1994). *Executive Economics, Ten Essential Tools for Managers*. New York: Free Press. See also Section D.

March, James G. (1988). *Decisions and Organizations*. Oxford: Basil Blackwell.

————, with the assistance of Chip Heath (1994). *A Primer on Decision Making*. New York: Free Press.

———— and Zur Shapira (1987). "Managerial Perceptions on Risk Taking." *Management Science* Vol. 33, No. 4 (November): 1404–18.

Markowitz, Harry M. (1991). *Portfolio Selection. Efficient Diversification of Investments*. Second edition. Oxford: Basil Blackwell.

Mas-Colell, Andreu, Michael D. Whinston and Jerry Green (1995). *Microeconomic Theory*. New York: Oxford University Press.

Mayer, Thomas (1988). "Interpreting Federal Reserve Behavior." *Journal of Behavioral Economics* Vol. 17, No. 4 (Winter): 263–77.

Milgrom, Paul and John Roberts (1992). *Economics, Organization and Management*. Englewood Cliffs, NJ: Prentice-Hall.

Mirowski, Philip (1988). *Against Mechanism*. Totowa, NJ: Rowman and Littlefield.

Mui, Vai-Lam (1995). "The Economics of Envy." *Journal of Economic Behavior and Organization* Vol. 26, No. 3 (May): 311–36.

Naish, Howard F. (1993). "The Near Optimality of Adaptive Expectations." *Journal of Economic Behavior and Organization* Vol. 20, No. 1 (January): 3–22.

Olsen, Robert A. (1997). "Investment Risk: The Expert's Perspective." *Financial Analysts Journal* Vol. 10, No. 1 (March): 65–72.

———— (forthcoming). "Desirability Bias Among Professional Investment Managers: Some Evidence from Experts." *Journal of Behavioral Decision Making*.

Olson, Mancur (1982). *The Rise and Decline of Nations. Economic Growth, Stagnation, and Social Rigidities*. New Haven, CT: Yale University Press.

Parayre, Roch (1996). "The Strategic Implications of Sunk Costs: A Behavioral Perspective." *Journal of Economic Behavior and Organization* Vol. 28, No. 4 (December): 417–42.

Phelps, Charlotte (1995). "Wives, Motives and Fertility." *Journal of Economic Behavior and Organization* Vol. 27, No. 3 (September): 49–67.

Piore, Michael J. (1996), "Review of the Handbook of Economic Sociology." *Journal of Economic Literature* Vol. 34, No. 2 (June): 741–54.

Prelec, Drazen and R. S. Herrnstein (1991). "Preferences or Principles: Alternative Guidelines for Choice." In Richard J. Zeckhauser, ed., *Strategy and Choices*. Cambridge, MA: MIT Press.

Rabin, Mathew (1994). "Cognitive Dissonance and Social Change." *Journal of Economic Behavior and Organization* Vol. 23, No. 2 (March): 177–94.

Rawls, John (1971). *A Theory of Justice*. Cambridge, MA: Belknap Press of Harvard University Press.

Redman, Deborah A. (1991). *Economics and the Philosophy of Science*. New York, Oxford, Toronto and Melbourne: Oxford University Press.

Rodrik, Dani (1996). "Understanding Economic Policy Reform." *Journal of Economic Literature* Vol. 34, No. 1 (March): 9–41.

Ronen, Joshua, ed. (1983). *Entrepreneurship*. Lexington, MA: Lexington Books.

Russell, Thomas and Richard H. Thaler (1985). "The Relevance of Quasi Rationality in Competitive Markets." *American Economic Review* Vol. 75, No. 4 (December): 1071–82.

Schelling, Thomas (1960). *The Strategy of Conflict*. New York: Oxford University Press.

——— (1984). *Choice and Consequence. Perspectives of an Errant Economist*. Cambridge, MA: Harvard University Press.

——— (1984b). "Self-Command in Practice, in Policy and in a Theory of Rational Choice." *American Economic Review* Vol. 74, No. 2 (May): 1–11.

Schwartz, Hugh H. (1987). "Perception, Judgment and Motivation in Manufacturing Enterprises. Findings and Preliminary Hypotheses from In-Depth Interviews." *Journal of Economic Behavior and Organization* Vol. 8, No. 4 (December): 543–65. See also Section D.

Seeley, Eric (1992). "Human Needs and Consumer Economics: The Implications of Maslow's Theory of Motivation for Consumer Expenditure Patterns." *Journal of Socio-Economics* Vol. 21, No. 4 (Winter): 303–24.

Sen, Amartya K. (1973). "Behavior and the Concept of Preferences." *Economica* N.S. 40, No. 159 (August): 241–59.

——— (1977). "Rational Fools: A Critique of the Behavioral Foundations of Economic Theory." *Philosophy and Public Affairs* Vol. 6 (Summer): 317–44.

——— (1987). *On Ethics and Economics*. Oxford: Basil Blackwell.

Shen, T. Y. (1991). "Towards a General Theory of X-Efficiency." *Journal of Socio-Economics* Vol. 20, No. 4 (Winter): 277–95.

Shiller, Robert J. (1993). *Macro Markets. Creating Institutions for Managing Society's Largest Economic Risks*. Oxford: Clarendon Press.

Shoemaker, Paul J. H. (1993). "Determinants of Risk Taking: Behavioral and Economic Views." *Journal of Risk and Uncertainty* Vol. 6, No. 1 (February): 49–73.

Simon, Herbert A. (1957). *Models of Man*. New York: John Wiley and Sons.

——— (1975). *Learning with Understanding*. Columbus, OH: ERIC Science, Mathematics and Environmental Education Clearinghouse.

——— (1986). "Some Computer Models of Human Learning." Ch. 4. In M. Shafto, ed., *How We Know*. New York: Harper and Row.

——— (1987). "Satisficing." In John Eatwell, Murray Milgate and Peter Newman, eds., *The New Palgrave: A Dictionary of Economics*. London: Macmillan, pp. 243–45.

——— (1990). "A Mechanism for Social Science Selection and Successful Altruism." *Science* Vol. 250 (December 21): 1665–68.

——— (1991). "Organizations and Markets." *Journal of Economic Perspectives* Vol. 5, No. 2 (Spring): 25–44.

Sjostrand, Sven-Erik (1993). "Introduction: European Contributions to Studies in Socioeconomics." *Journal of Socio-Economics* Vol. 22, No. 4 (Winter): 307–10.

Slovic, Paul and Sarah Lichtenstein (1983). "Preference Reversals: A Broader Perspective." *American Economic Review* Vol. 73, No. 4 (September): 596–605.

Smelser, Neil J. and Richard Swedberg, eds., (1994). *The Handbook of Economic Sociology*. Princeton: Princeton University Press.

Smith, Vernon (1989). "Theory, Experiment and Economics." *Journal of Economic Perspectives* Vol. 3, No. 1 (Winter): 151–69.

——— (1991). "Rational Choice: The Contrast Between Economics and Psychology." *Journal of Political Economy* Vol. 90, No. 4 (August): 877–97.

―――― (1992). *Experimental Economics*. Aldershot, England and Brookfield, VT: Edward Elgar.

―――― (1994). "Economics in the Laboratory." *Journal of Economic Perspectives* Vol. 8, No. 1 (Winter): 113–31.

Stark, Oded (1995). *Altruism and Beyond. An Economic Analysis of Transfers and Exchanges Within Families and Groups*. Cambridge: Cambridge University Press.

Stern, Paul C. (1993). "The Socio-Economic Perspective and Its Institutional Prospects." *Journal of Socio-Economics* Vol. 22, No. 1 (Spring): 1–11.

Sugden, Robert (1991). "Rational Bargaining." Ch. 10. In Michael Bacharach and Susan Hurley, eds., *Foundations of Decision Theory Issues and Advances*. Oxford: Basil Blackwell.

Thaler, Richard H., Amos Tversky, Daniel Kahneman and Alan Schwartz (1997). "The Effect of Myopia and Loss Aversion on Risk Taking: An Experimental Test." *Quarterly Journal of Economics* Vol. 112, No. 2 (May): 647–61.

Thoumi, Francisco E. (1995). *Political Economy and Illegal Drugs in Colombia*. Boulder, CO and London: Lynne Rienner Publishers. See also Section D.

Tomer, John (1992). "Rational Organization Decision Making in the Human Firm: A Socio-Economic Model." *Journal of Socio-Economics* Vol. 21. No. 2 (Summer): 85–107.

Viscusi, W. Kip (1989). "Prospective Reference Theory: Toward an Explanation of the Paradox." *Journal of Risk and Uncertainty* Vol. 2, No. 3 (September): 235–64.

――――, Wesley A. Magat and Joel Huber (1987). "An Investigation of the Rationality of Consumer Valuations of Multiple Health Risks." *Rand Journal of Economics* Vol. 18, No. 4 (Winter): 465–79.

von Winterfeldt, Detlof and Ward Edwards (1986). *Decision Analysis and Behavioral Research*. New York: Cambridge University Press.

Wakker, Peter and Amos Tversky (1993). "An Axiomatization of Cumulative Prospect Theory." *Journal of Risk and Uncertainty* Vol. 7, No. 2 (October): 147–75.

Wärneryd, Karl-Erik (1997). "Demystifying Rational Expectations Theory Through an Economic-Psychological Model." In G. Antonides, W. F. van Raaij and S. Maital, eds., *Advances in Economic Psychology*. Chichester, UK: John Wiley and Sons, pp. 211–36,

Williamson, Oliver E. and Sidney G. Winter, eds. (1991). *The Nature of the Firm. Origins, Evolution, and Development*. New York and Oxford: Oxford University Press.

Winkler, Robert L. (1991). "Ambiguity, Probability, Preference and Decision Analysis." *Journal of Risk and Uncertainty* Vol. 4, No. 3 (July): 285–98.

Winston, Gordon (1980). "Addiction and Backsliding. A Theory of Compulsive Consumption." *Journal of Economic Behavior and Organization* Vol. 1, No. 4 (December): 295–324.

―――― (1989). "Imperfectly Rational Choice: Rationality as the Result of a Costly Activity." *Journal of Economic Behavior and Organization* Vol. 12, No. 1 (August): 67–86.

Winter, Sidney G. (1971). "Satisficing, Selection and the Innovating Remnant." *Quarterly Journal of Economics* Vol. 85, No. 2 (May): 237–82.

Yang, Bijou and David Lester (1995). "New Directions for Economics." *Journal of Socio-Economics* Vol. 4, No. 3 (Fall): 433–46.

Zey, Mary, ed. (1992). *Decision Making. Alternatives to Rational Choice Models.* Newbury Park, CA: Sage Publications.

Zhu, Xinming and Herbert A. Simon (1987). "Learning Mathematics from Examples and by Doing." *Cognition and Instruction* Vol. 4, No. 3: 137–66.

———, Yiflei Lee, Herbert A. Simon and Dan Zhu (1996). "Cue Recognition and Cue Elaboration in Learning from Examples." *Proceedings of the National Academy of Sciences* Vol. 93 (February): 1346–51.

Index

About the Author

HUGH SCHWARTZ is Visiting Professor in the Department of Economics at the Federal University of Paraná in Brazil. He has taught at the University of Kansas, Yale University, and Case Western Reserve University and served as a Senior Economist at the Inter-American Development Bank. He left the bank to devote more time to the interrelationship between psychology and economics, particularly with respect to entrepreneurial decision makers.

ISBN 0-275-96014-5

90000>

EAN

9 780275 960148

HARDCOVER BAR CODE